Reading Essentials
An Interactive Student Workbook

red.msscience.com

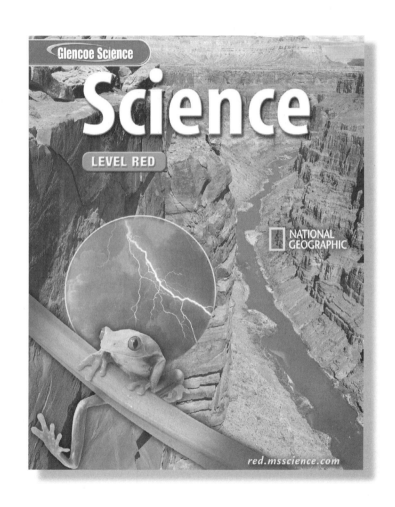

Glencoe Science

Science

LEVEL RED

NATIONAL GEOGRAPHIC

red.msscience.com

Glencoe

New York, New York   Columbus, Ohio   Chicago, Illinois   Peoria, Illinois   Woodland Hills, California

To the Student

In today's world, knowing science is important for thinking critically, solving problems, and making decisions. But understanding science sometimes can be a challenge.

Reading Essentials takes the stress out of reading, learning, and understanding science. This book covers important concepts in science, offers ideas for how to learn the information, and helps you review what you have learned.

In each chapter:

- **Before You Read** sparks your interest in what you'll learn and relates it to your world.
- **Read to Learn** describes important science concepts with words and graphics. Next to the text you can find a variety of study tips and ideas for organizing and learning information:
  - The **Study Coach** offers tips for getting the main ideas out of the text.
  - **Foldables™ Study Organizers** help you divide the information into smaller, easier-to-remember concepts.
  - **Reading Checks** ask questions about key concepts. The questions are placed so you know whether you understand the material.
  - **Think It Over** elements help you consider the material in-depth, giving you an opportunity to use your critical-thinking skills.
  - **Picture This** questions specifically relate to the art and graphics used with the text. You'll find questions to get you actively involved in illustrating the concepts you read about.
  - **Applying Math** reinforces the connection between math and science.
- Use **After You Read** to review key terms and answer questions about what you have learned. The **Mini Glossary** can assist you with science vocabulary. Review questions focus on the key concepts to help you evaluate your learning.

See for yourself. *Reading Essentials* makes science easy to understand and enjoyable.

Glencoe

The McGraw·Hill Companies

Send all inquiries to:
Glencoe/McGraw-Hill
8787 Orion Place
Columbus, OH 43240

ISBN 0-07-867214-7
Printed in the United States of America
1 2 3 4 5 6 7 8 9 10 024 09 08 07 06 05 04

Table of Contents

The Nature of Science

section ❶ What is science?

● Before You Read

Have you ever wondered how something works? On the lines below, describe a time that you wondered how something worked. Did you find out how it worked? Explain how.

_____

_____

● Read to Learn

Learning About the World

When you think of a scientist, do you think of someone in a laboratory with charts, graphs, and bubbling test tubes? Anyone who tries to learn about the natural world is a scientist—even you. **Science** is a way of learning more about the natural world. Scientists want to know why, how, or when something happened. Learning usually begins by keeping your eyes open and asking questions about what you see.

What kinds of questions can science answer?

Scientists ask many questions. How do things work? What are they made of? Why does something take place? Some questions cannot be answered by science. Science cannot help you find the meaning of a poem or decide what your favorite color is. Science cannot tell you what is right, wrong, good, or bad.

What are possible explanations?

Learning about your world begins with asking questions. Science tries to find answers to these questions. However, science can answer questions only with the information that exists at the time. Any answer found by science could be wrong or could change because people can never know everything about the world around them.

Copyright © Glencoe/McGraw-Hill, a division of The McGraw-Hill Companies, Inc.

What You'll Learn
- what science is and what science cannot answer
- what theories and laws are
- identify a system and its parts
- the three main branches of science

Study Coach

Outlining As you read the section, create an outline using each heading from the text. Under each heading, write the main points or ideas that you read.

FOLDABLES

Ⓐ Build Vocabulary
Make the following Foldable to help you define and learn the vocabulary terms in this section.

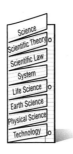

How does new information affect old explanations?

As time passes, people learn more about the world around them. As you can see in the diagram below, new information might make scientists look at old ideas and think of new explanations. Science finds only possible explanations. For example, people once thought Earth was the center of the solar system. Through the years, new information about the solar system showed this is not true.

Picture This

1. **Explain** Look at the diagram to the right. How can new information affect an old explanation for something?

_____

_____

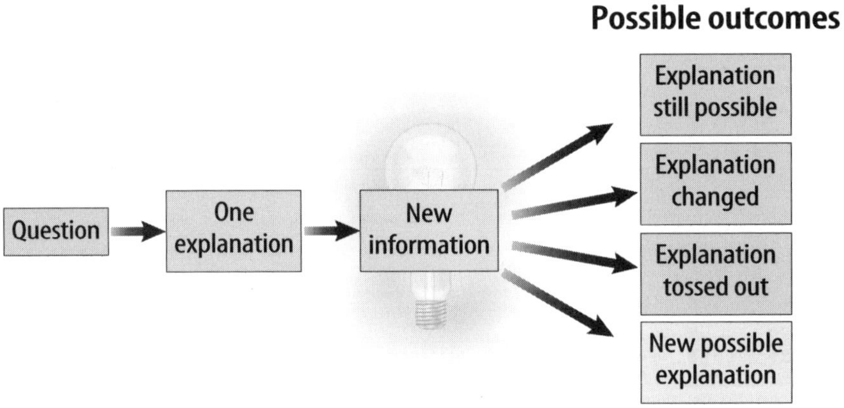

Possible outcomes

Question → One explanation → New information →

- Explanation still possible
- Explanation changed
- Explanation tossed out
- New possible explanation

What are scientific theories?

A <u>scientific theory</u> is an attempt to explain a pattern seen repeatedly in the natural world. Theories are not just guesses or opinions. Theories in science must have observations and results from many investigations to back them up. They are the best explanations that have been found so far. Theories can change. As new data are found, scientists decide how the new data fit the theory. Sometimes the new data do not support the theory. Then scientists can change the theory to fit the new data better.

What are scientific laws?

A <u>scientific law</u> is a rule that describes a pattern in nature. For an observation to become a scientific law, it must be observed happening over and over again. The law is what scientists use until someone makes observations that do not follow the law. A law helps you predict what will happen. If you hold an apple above the ground and drop it, it always will fall to Earth. The law tells you the apple will fall, but the law does not explain why the apple will fall. A law is different from a theory. It does not try to explain why something happens. It simply describes a pattern. ☑

☑ **Reading Check**

2. **Determine** Which describes a pattern in nature, a scientific theory or a scientific law?

_____

Copyright © Glencoe/McGraw-Hill, a division of The McGraw-Hill Companies, Inc.

Systems in Science

Scientists can study many different things in nature. Some scientists study how the human body works. Others might study how planets move around the Sun. Still others might study the energy in a lightning bolt. What do all of these things have in common? All of them are systems. A **system** is a group of structures, cycles, and processes that are related to each other and work together. Your stomach is a structure, or one part of, your digestive system. ☑

Where are systems found?

You can find systems in other places besides science. Your school is a system. It has structures like school buildings, furniture, students, teachers, and many other objects. Your school day also has cycles. Your daily class schedule and the school calendar are examples of cycles. Many processes are at work during the school day. Your teacher may have a process for test taking. Before a test, the teacher might ask you to put your books away and get out a pencil. When the test is over, the teacher might ask you to put down your pencil and pass the test to the front of the room.

In a system, structures, cycles, and processes work together, or interact. What you do and what time you do it depends on your daily schedule. A clock shows your teacher that it is time for your lunch break. So, you go to lunch.

How are parts of a system related to a whole system?

All systems are made up of other systems. For example, the human body is a system. Within the human body are many other systems. You are part of your school. Your school is probably part of a larger district, state, or national system. Scientists often solve problems by studying just one part of a system. A scientist might want to know how the construction of buildings affects the ecosystem. Because an ecosystem has many parts, the scientist might study one particular animal in the ecosystem. Another might study the effect on plant life.

The Branches of Science

Science is often divided into three main parts, or branches. These branches are life science, Earth science, and physical science. Each branch asks questions about different kinds of systems.

✔ **Reading Check**

3. List What are the three parts of a system?

_____

_____

_____

💡 **Think it Over**

4. Describe Buildings usually have a heating system. Write each of the following by the part of the system it best represents. *turning on and off, thermostat, spreading heat*

Structure:

_____

Process:

_____

Cycle:

_____

What is life science?

<u>Life science</u> is the study of living systems and the ways in which they interact. Life scientists try to answer questions like "How do whales know where they are swimming in the ocean?" and "How do vaccines prevent disease?" Life scientists can study living things, where they live, and how they act together.

People who work in the health field, like doctors and nurses, know a lot about life science. They work with systems of the human body. Some other people that use life science are biologists, zookeepers, farmers, and beekeepers.

What is Earth science?

<u>Earth science</u> is the study of Earth systems and systems in space. It includes the study of nonliving things such as rocks, soil, clouds, rivers, oceans, planets, stars, meteors, and black holes. Earth science also includes the weather and climate systems on Earth. Earth scientists ask questions like "How do you know how strong an earthquake is?" and "Is water found on other planets?" They make maps and study how Earth's crust formed. Geologists study rocks and Earth's features. Meteorologists study weather and climate. There are even volcanologists who study volcanoes. ☑

What is physical science?

<u>Physical science</u> is the study of matter and energy. Matter is anything that takes up space and has mass. Energy is the ability to cause matter to change. All systems—living and nonliving—are made of matter.

Chemistry and physics are the two areas of physical science. Chemistry is the study of matter and the way it interacts. Chemists ask questions like "What can I do to make aspirin work better?" and "How can I make plastic stronger?" Physics is the study of energy and its ability to change matter. Physicists ask questions like "How does light travel through glass?" and "How can humans use sunlight to power objects?"

How are science and technology related?

Learning the answers to scientific questions is important. However, these answers do not help people unless they can be used in some way. <u>**Technology**</u> is the practical use of science in our everyday lives. Engineers use science to create technology. The study of how to use the energy of sunlight is science. Using this knowledge to create solar panels is an example of technology.

☑ **Reading Check**

5. Apply What might an Earth scientist study that is not on Earth?

_____

_____

💡 **Think it Over**

6. Apply Which of the following is an example of technology? Circle the correct answer.
   a. finding out how light travels
   b. creating solar-powered cars
   c. deciding which rock is the hardest
   d. making strong plastic

● After You Read

Mini Glossary

Earth science: the study of Earth systems and systems in space

life science: the study of living systems and the ways in which they interact

physical science: the study of matter and energy

science: a way of learning more about the natural world

scientific law: a rule that describes a pattern in nature

scientific theory: an attempt to explain a pattern seen repeatedly in the natural world

system: a group of structures, cycles, and processes that are related to each other and work together

technology: is the practical use of science in our everyday lives

1. Review the terms and their definitions in the Mini Glossary. When you see lightning strike, you probably will hear thunder soon. Is this statement a scientific theory or a scientific law? Explain.

   _____

   _____

2. Fill in the graphic organizer below with explanations of science, each branch of science, and technology.

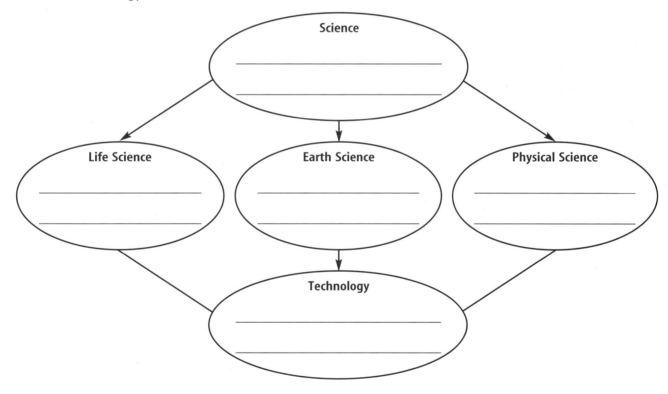

Science nline Visit **red.msscience.com** to access your textbook, interactive games, and projects to help you learn more about what science is.

End of Section

chapter 1

The Nature of Science

section 2 Science in Action

What You'll Learn

- skills that scientists use
- the meaning of hypothesis
- the difference between observation and inference

● Before You Read

Think of some skills that you have. You may be good at basketball. Of all the skills you have, which do you think is your best? How did you learn that skill?

_____

_____

Mark the Text

Highlighting As you read the text under each heading, highlight the science skills you see. When you finish reading the section, review the skills you have highlighted.

● Read to Learn

Science Skills

You already know that science is about asking questions. How does asking questions lead to learning? There is no single way to learn. A scientist doesn't just ask a question and then always follow the same steps to answer the question. Instead, scientists use many different skills. Some of these skills are thinking, observing, predicting, investigating, researching, modeling, measuring, analyzing, and inferring. Any of these skills might help answer a question. Some answers to scientific questions are also found with luck and using creativity.

What are some science methods?

Investigations often follow a pattern. Look at the diagram on the next page. Most investigations begin by observing, or seeing, something and then asking a question about what was seen. Scientists try to find out what is already known about a question. They talk with other scientists, and read books and magazines to learn all they can. Then, they try to find a possible explanation. To collect even more information, scientists usually make more observations. They might build a model, do experiments, or both.

FOLDABLES

B Organizing Information Make a Foldable like the one shown to describe science skills, drawing conclusions, and experiments.

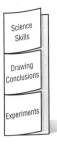

Science Skills

Drawing Conclusions

Experiments

A Scientific Method

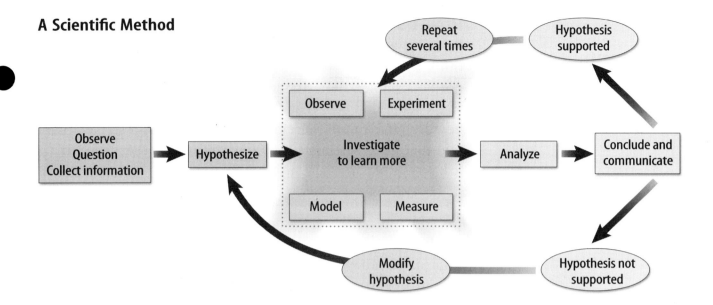

How do you question and observe?

You ask questions and make observations all the time. For example, Ms. Clark, a middle school science teacher, placed a sealed shoebox on the table at the front of the classroom. Everyone in the class began to ask questions about what was inside the box. Some students picked up the box. There was something loose inside it. Some students said it sounded like metal when it hit the sides of the box. It wasn't very heavy. Ms. Clark passed the box around. Each student made observations and wrote them in his or her journal. These students were using science skills without even knowing it.

How is guessing part of science?

Ms. Clark asked her students to guess what was in the box. One student thought it was a pair of scissors. Another student thought it was too heavy to be scissors. All agreed it was made of metal. The students then guessed that it was probably a stapler in the box. Ms. Clark told them that by guessing a stapler was in the box, they had made a hypothesis.

What is a hypothesis?

A <u>hypothesis</u> is a reasonable answer based on what you know and what you observe. The students observed that whatever was in the box was small, heavier than a pair of scissors, and made of metal. The students knew that a stapler is small, heavier than a pair of scissors, and made of metal. They used this information to make the hypothesis that there was a stapler in the box.

Picture This

1. Interpret a Diagram Why are there two arrows going in different directions at the right end of the diagram?

_____

_____

_____

Think it Over

2. Compare and Contrast How is a hypothesis different than a guess?

_____

_____

_____

How do you analyze a hypothesis?

Keeping an Open Mind Ms. Clark asked the students to think about the possibility that the object in the box might not be a stapler. One student said it had to be a stapler. Ms. Clark reminded him that they might be missing something because their minds were made up that it was a stapler. She said that good scientists keep open minds to every idea and to every explanation.

Finding New Information Ms. Clark asked them what would happen if they learned new information that does not fit with their hypothesis. They thought about what new information they could find to help prove their hypothesis true or not true.

The students decided they could get another shoebox and put a stapler in it. Then they could shake it to see whether it felt and sounded the same as the other box. By getting more information to find out if their hypothesis was correct, the students could analyze, or examine, their hypothesis.

How do you make a prediction?

Ms. Clark asked the students to predict what would happen if their hypothesis was correct. A prediction is what you think will happen. The students all agreed the second box should feel and sound like the mystery box.

How do you test a hypothesis?

Sometimes a hypothesis is tested by making observations. Sometimes building a model is the best way to test a hypothesis. To test their hypothesis, the students made a model. The new shoebox with the stapler inside of it was the model.

After making a model, you must test it to make sure it is the same as the original. So the students needed to test their model to see if it was the same as the original shoebox. When they picked up the model box, they found it was a little heavier than the first box. Also, when they shook the model box, it did not make the same sound as the first box.

The students decided to find the mass of each box. Then they would know how much more mass a stapler has compared to the object in the first box. The students used a balance to find that the box with the stapler had a mass of 410 g. The mystery box had a mass of 270 g.

 **Think it Over**

3. **Explain** What will the box sound and feel like if the students' hypothesis is correct?

_____

_____

_____

How do you organize your findings?

Ms. Clark suggested that the students organize the information they had before making any new conclusions. By organizing their observations, they had a summary to look at while making conclusions. The students put their information into a table like the one below.

Observation Chart		
Questions	Mystery Box	Our Box
Does it roll or slide?	It slides and appears to be flat.	It slides and appears to be flat.
Does it make any sounds?	It makes a metallic sound when it strikes the sides of the box.	The stapler makes a thudding sound when it strikes the sides of the box.
What is the mass of the box?		

Picture This

4. Complete a Table
Using information from the previous page, complete the last row of the table.

How do you draw conclusions?

When the students looked at the observations in their table, they decided that their hypothesis was not correct. Ms. Clark asked them if that meant that there was not a stapler in the mystery box. One student said that there could be a different kind of stapler in the mystery box. The students were inferring that the object in the mystery box was not like the stapler in their test box. To **infer** means to make a conclusion based on what you observe. ☑

Another student suggested that they were right back where they started with the mystery box. Ms. Clark pointed out that even though their observations did not support their hypothesis, they knew more information than when they started.

How do you continue to learn?

A student asked if she could open the box to see what was in it. Ms. Clark explained that scientists do not get to "open the box," to find answers to their questions. Some scientists spend their entire lives looking for the answer to one question. When your investigation does not support your first hypothesis, you try again. You gather new information, make new observations, and form a new hypothesis.

Reading Check

5. Determine What did the students in Ms. Clark's class infer?

_____

_____

_____

_____

_____

_____

_____

How do you communicate your findings?

Sometimes scientists try to continue or repeat the work of other scientists. It is important for scientists to explain the results of their investigations and how they did their investigations. Scientists write about their work in journals, books, and on the Internet. They also often go to meetings and give speeches about their work. An important part of doing science is showing methods and results to others.

Experiments

Different types of questions need different types of investigations. Ms. Clark's class needed to answer the question "What is inside the mystery box?" To answer the question, they built a model to learn more about the mystery box. Some scientific questions are answered by doing a type of investigation called a controlled experiment. A **controlled experiment** involves changing only one part in an experiment and observing what that change does to another part of the experiment.

What are variables?

A **variable** is a part of an experiment that can change. Imagine an experiment that tests three fertilizers to see which one makes plants grow tallest. This experiment has two variables. One variable is the fertilizer used. Since three different fertilizers are used, each one can have a different outcome in the experiment. The second variable is the height of the plants. The different fertilizers can affect the height of the plants.

Independent Variables The **independent variable** is a variable that is changed in an experiment. The fertilizer is changed by the scientist. So, the fertilizer is an independent variable. In an experiment, there should be only one independent variable.

Dependent Variables The **dependent variable** is a variable that depends on what happens in the experiment when the independent variable is used. The dependent variable is also the variable measured at the end of the experiment. The height of the plants is the dependent variable. The height of each plant may be different, depending on which fertilizer is used. The scientist will measure the height of each plant at the end of the experiment to see what fertilizer affects the height the most. ☑

☑ **Reading Check**

7. Explain what a dependent variable is in an experiment.

_____

_____

_____

Copyright © Glencoe/McGraw-Hill, a division of The McGraw-Hill Companies, Inc.

What are constants?

A <u>constant</u> is a part of an experiment that is not changed. There can be more than one constant. In the fertilizer experiment, the constants could be the type of plant, the amount of water or sunlight the plants get, or the kind of soil the plants are planted in. The scientist keeps all of these constants the same for all the types of fertilizer that are tested.

Laboratory Safety

In your science class, you will perform many kinds of investigations. Performing investigations involves more than just following steps. You must learn how to keep yourself and those around you safe. Always obey the safety symbol warnings shown below.

Safety Symbols

 Eye Safety

 Clothing Protection

 Disposal

 Biological

 Extreme Temperature

 Sharp Object

 Fume

 Irritant

 Toxic

 Animal Safety

 Flammable

 Electrical

 Chemical

 Open Flame

 Handwashing

How do you practice safety in the lab?

When scientists work in a lab, they take many safety precautions. You must also take safety precautions in the science lab. The most important safety advice is to think before you act. You should always check with your teacher during the planning stage of your investigation. Make sure you know where the safety equipment is in your lab or classroom. You also need to make sure you know how to use the safety equipment. Safety equipment includes eyewashes, thermal mitts, and the fire extinguisher. ☑

Picture This

8. **Recognize Cause and Effect** What is one kind of experiment in which you would need to wear eye goggles?

_____

_____

✔ Reading Check

9. **Describe** What is the most important safety advice in the lab?

_____

_____

💡 **Think it Over**

11. Infer If you are doing a science experiment in the lab or in the field, what is the one thing that you should always wear?

_____

What are some good safety habits?

Good safety habits include the following suggestions:

- Find and follow all safety symbols before you begin an investigation.

- Always wear an apron and goggles to protect yourself from chemicals, flames, and pointed objects.

- Keep goggles on until activity, cleanup, and handwashing are complete.

- Always slant test tubes away from yourself and others.

- Never eat, drink, or put on makeup in the lab.

- Report all accidents to your teacher.

- Always wash your hands after working in the lab.

How do you practice safety in the field?

Investigations are also done outside the lab. You can do investigations in streams, farm fields, and other places. Scientists call this working in the field. Scientists must follow safety regulations in the field as well as in the lab. Always wear eye goggles and other safety equipment that you need. Never reach into holes or under rocks. Always wash your hands after you have finished your work in the field or in the lab.

Why have safety rules?

Doing science in the lab or in the field can be much more interesting that just reading about it. But doing experiments can be dangerous and accidents can happen. If you follow safety rules closely, an accident is less likely to happen. Still, you cannot predict when something will go wrong.

Think of a person taking a trip in a car. Most of the time the person is not in a car accident. However, to be safe, drivers and passengers must wear their safety belts. Wearing safety gear in the lab is like wearing a safety belt in a car. It can keep you from being hurt in an accident. You should wear safety gear even if you are just watching an experiment. Always keep safety in mind when conducting an experiment.

● After You Read

Mini Glossary

constant: a part of an experiment that is not changed

controlled experiment: involves changing only one part of an experiment and observing what that change does to another part of the experiment

dependent variable: a variable that depends on what happens in the experiment when the independent variable is used

hypothesis: a reasonable answer based on what you know and what you observe

independent variable: a variable that is changed in an experiment

infer: to make a conclusion based on what you observe

variable: a part of an experiment that can change

1. Review the terms and their definitions in the Mini Glossary. In this section, what was an example of a controlled experiment?

_____

_____

2. In the flowchart below, complete the steps that a scientist might take when conducting a scientific investigation. Use these words or group of words to complete the chart:
   conclude and communicate
   hypothesize
   experiment, investigate, or model

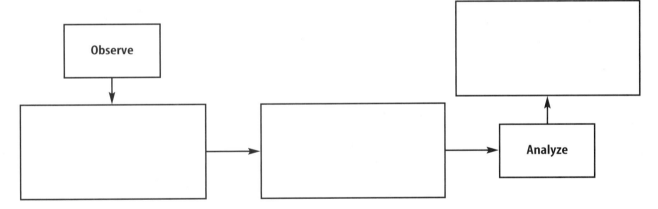

Observe →

Analyze

3. At the beginning of the section, you were asked to highlight science skills in the section. What is another method you could have used to learn about science skills?

_____

 **Science Online** Visit **red.msscience.com** to access your textbook, interactive games, and projects to help you learn more about action.

End of Section

The Nature of Science

section ❸ Models in Science

What You'll Learn

- to describe different types of models
- the uses of models

◀ **Study Coach**

Identifying the Main Point When you read a paragraph, look for the main idea and write it down on a piece of paper or in your notebook.

Picture This

1. **Label** the Sun in the model of the solar system.

⊜ Before You Read

Have you ever built a model? Why did you build the model? Tell about a model you built or want to build.

_____

_____

⊜ Read to Learn

Why are models necessary?

There are many ways to test a hypothesis. In the last section, Ms. Clark's class tested their hypothesis with a model of the mystery box. A **model** is something that represents an object, event, or idea in the natural world. Models can help you picture in your mind things that are hard to see or understand—like Ms. Clark's mystery box. Models can be of things that are too small or too big to see. They also can be of things that do not exist any more or of things that have not been made yet. Models also can show events that happen so slowly or quickly that you cannot see them. You may have seen models of cells, cars, or dinosaurs. The figure could be a model of the solar system. It could help you understand which planets are next to each other.

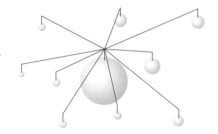

Types of Models

There are three main types of models—physical models, computer models, and idea models. Scientists can use one or more types of models to help them answer questions. Different models are used for different reasons.

What are physical models?

Models that you can see and touch are physical models. The figure on the previous page is a physical model. A globe of Earth is also a physical model. Models show how parts relate to each other. They also can show how things look when they change position or how things react when a force is put on them.

What are computer models?

Computer models are built using computer software. You can't touch them, but you can look at them on a computer screen. Computer models can show events that happen too quickly or too slowly to see. For example, a computer can show how large plates in Earth move. They also can be used to predict when earthquakes might happen.

Computers also can model movements and positions of things that might take hours or days to do by hand, or even using a calculator. They also can predict changes caused by different systems or forces. For example, computer models help predict the weather. They use the movement of air currents in the atmosphere to make these predictions.

What are idea models?

Some models are ideas that describe what someone thinks about something in the natural world. Idea models cannot be built like physical models because they are just ideas. A famous idea model is Albert Einstein's theory of relativity. One model for this theory is the mathematical equation $E = mc^2$. This explains that mass, m, can be changed into energy, E.

Making Models

Have you ever seen a sketch artist at work? The artist tries to draw a picture of someone from a description given by someone else. The more detailed the description is, the better the picture will be. Sometimes the artist uses descriptions from more than one person. If the descriptions have enough information, the sketch should look realistic. Scientific models are much the same way. The more information the scientist finds, the more accurate the model will be.

Copyright © Glencoe/McGraw-Hill, a division of The McGraw-Hill Companies, Inc.

FOLDABLES

C Organize Information
Use a half sheet of paper to help you organize information about models in science.

Models in Science

✔ **Reading Check**

2. **Determine** Which type of model can you see and touch: physical, computer, or idea model?

_____

_____

💡 **Think it Over**

3. **Apply** Suppose you want to make a model of a plant cell for your science project. What will help you make the most accurate model?

_____

_____

Using Models

When you think of a model, you might think of a model airplane or a model of a building. Not all models are for scientific uses. You may even use models and not know it. Drawings, maps, recipes, and globes are all models.

How are models used?

Communicate Some models communicate ideas. Have you ever drawn a map to show someone how to get to your home? If so, you used a model to communicate. It is sometimes easier to show ideas than to tell them.

Test Predictions Other models test predictions. Engineers often use models of airplanes or cars in wind tunnels to test predictions about how air affects them.

Save Lives, Money, and Time Models are often used because it is safer and less expensive than using the real thing. For example, crash test dummies are used instead of people in automobile crash tests. NASA has built a special airplane that models the conditions in space. It creates freefall for 20 to 25 seconds. Astronauts can practice freefall in the airplane instead of in space. Making many trips in the airplane is easier, safer, and less expensive than a trip into space.

Limitations of Models

The solar system is too big to see all at once. So, scientists have built models. The first solar system models had the planets and the Sun revolving around Earth. Later, as scientists learned new information, they changed their models.

A new model explained the solar system in a different way, but Earth was still the center. Still later, after more observations, scientists discovered that the Sun is the center of the solar system. A new model was made to show this. Even though the first solar system models were incorrect, the models gave scientists information to build upon. Models are not always perfect, but they are a tool that scientists can see and learn from. ✔

Think it Over

4. Describe What is another model, besides a map, you could use to communicate with?

_____

_____

_____

✔ Reading Check

5. Explain Why are models that have been proven to be wrong still helpful?

_____

_____

● After You Read

Mini Glossary

model: something that represents an object, event, or idea in the natural world

1. Review the term and its definition in the Mini Glossary. Which of the three types of models can you touch? Explain why you cannot touch the other types of models.

   _____

   _____

   _____

2. Complete the graphic organizer below to describe the three types of models and their uses.

Types of Models
Physical models are models you can see and touch.

Uses of Models
to save money, time, and lives

3. How do you think making a physical model can help you learn more about how models work?

   _____

   _____

   _____

Copyright © Glencoe/McGraw-Hill, a division of The McGraw-Hill Companies, Inc.

  Visit **red.msscience.com** to access your textbook, interactive games, and projects to help you learn more about models.

End of Section

The Nature of Science

section ❹ Evaluating Scientific Explanation

Copyright © Glencoe/McGraw-Hill, a division of The McGraw-Hill Companies, Inc.

What You'll Learn
- to evaluate scientific explanations
- how to evaluate promotional claims

◉ **Before You Read**

Have you ever played the game where you whisper a message into a person's ear, and then that person repeats the message to another person, and so on? What usually happens by the time the message gets to the last person?

_____

_____

Study Coach

Asking Questions As you read the section, write down any questions you might have about what you read.

◉ **Read to Learn**

Believe it or not?

Think of something someone told you that you didn't believe. Why didn't you believe it? You probably decided there was not enough proof. What you did was evaluate, or judge, the reliability of what you heard. You can evaluate the reliability of a statement by asking "How do you know?" If what you are told seems reliable, you can believe it.

What is critical thinking?

When you decide to believe information you read or hear, you use critical thinking. **Critical thinking** means using what you already know and new facts to decide if you agree with something. You can decide if information is true by breaking it down into two parts. Based on what you know, are the observations correct? Do the conclusions make sense?

⒟ Finding Main Ideas
Use a half sheet of paper to help you list the main ideas about how to evaluate scientific explanations.

> Evaluating Scientific Explanations

Evaluating the Data

Data are observations made in a scientific investigation. Data are gathered and recorded in tables, graphs, or drawings during a scientific investigation. Always look at the data when you evaluate a scientific explanation. Be careful about believing any explanation that is not supported by data.

Are the data specific?

The data given to back up a statement should be specific, or exact. Suppose a friend tells you that many people like pizza better than they like hamburgers. What do you need to know before you agree with your friend? You need some specific data. How many people were asked which food they like more? Specific data makes a statement more reliable and you are more likely to believe it.

How do you take good notes?

In this class you will keep a science journal. You will write down what you see and do in your investigations. Instead of writing "the stuff changed color," write "the clear liquid turned to a bright red when I added a drop of food coloring." It is important to record your observations when they happen. Important details can be forgotten when you wait. ✔

Evaluating Conclusions

When you think about a conclusion that someone has made, you can ask yourself two questions. First, does the conclusion make sense? Second, are there any other possible explanations? Suppose you hear that school will be starting two hours late because of bad weather. A friend decides that the bad weather is snow. You look outside. There is no snow on the roads. The conclusion does not make sense. Are there any other possible explanations? Maybe the roads are icy. The first conclusion is not reliable unless other possible explanations are proven to be wrong.

Evaluating Promotional Materials

Look at the newspaper advertisement. It seems unbelievable. You should hear some of the scientific data before you believe it. The purpose of an ad is to get you to buy something. Always keep this in mind when you read an ad. Before you believe ads like this one, evaluate the data and conclusions. Is the scientific evidence from a good, independent laboratory? An independent laboratory is not related to the company selling the product. Always evaluate data and ask questions before you spend your money.

1. **Explain** Why should you record your observations when they happen?

_____

_____

💡 **Think it Over**

2. **Describe** Think of an advertisement that you have seen that you did not believe. Explain why you did not believe the advertisement.

_____

_____

_____

_____

_____

● After You Read

Mini Glossary

critical thinking: using what you already know and new facts to decide if you should agree with something

data: observations made in a scientific investigation

1. Review the terms and their definitions in the Mini Glossary. Write one sentence using both terms.

_____

_____

2. Use the graphic organizer below to record some of the questions you should ask when you read the results of a scientific investigation.

Questions to ask when you evaluate a scientific investigation
Is the data specific?

3. How could you teach an elementary science class about how to use critical thinking?

_____

_____

_____

End of Section

Science●**nline** Visit **red.msscience.com** to access your textbook, interactive games, and projects to help you learn more about evaluating scientific explanations.

 **Measurement**

section ❶ Description and Measurement

Before You Read

Weight, height, and length are common measurements. List at least five things you can measure.

What You'll Learn
- how to estimate
- how to round a number
- the difference between precision and accuracy

Read to Learn

Measurement

A **measurement** is a way to describe objects and events with numbers. You use measurements to answer questions like how much, how long, or how far. You can measure how much sugar to use in a recipe, how long a snake is, and how far it is from home to school. You also can measure height, weight, time, temperature, volume, and speed. Every measurement has a number and a unit of measure. There are many different units of measure. Some are meter, liter, and gram.

How do measurements describe events?

Events like races can be described with measurements. In the 2000 summer Olympics, Marion Jones of the United States won the women's 100-m dash in a time of 10.75 s. In this example, measurements tell about the year of the race, its length, and the runner's time. The name of the event, the runner's name, and her country are not measurements.

Estimation

What happens if you want to know the size of something but it is too large to measure or you don't have a ruler? You can use **estimation** to make a rough guess about the size of an object. You can use the size of one object you know to help you estimate the size of another object. Estimation can help when you are in a hurry or don't need an exact measurement. You will get better at estimation with practice.

Study Coach

Make an Outline Make an outline of the main ideas in this section. Use the headings in the section as major headings. Be sure to include all words in bold.

FOLDABLES

Ⓐ Organize Make a Foldable, as shown below, and label the tabs Measurement, Estimation, Precision, and Accuracy.

Copyright © Glencoe/McGraw-Hill, a division of The McGraw-Hill Companies, Inc.

Picture This

1. Draw and Compare
You can show how the tree is about twice as tall as the person. Draw another person the same height that is standing on the shoulders of the person in the figure.

_____

_____

_____

☑ **Reading Check**

2. Identify What word tells you that a measurement is an estimate?

_____

_____

💡 **Think it Over**

3. Apply Give a time when estimating might be helpful.

_____

_____

_____

_____

How do you estimate measurements?

You can compare objects to estimate a measurement. For example, the tree in the figure is too tall to measure. You can estimate the height of the tree by comparing it to the height of the person. The tree is about twice the height of the person. If the person is about 1.5 m tall, the tree must be 2 × 1.5 m, or about 3 m tall.

Estimated measurements often use the word *about*. For example, a soccer ball weighs about 400 g. You can walk about 5 km in an hour. When you see or hear the word *about* with a measurement, the measurement is an estimation. ☑

When is estimation used?

Estimation is not only used when an exact measurement cannot be made. It is also used to check that an answer is reasonable. A reasonable answer makes sense. Suppose you calculate a friend's running speed as 47 m/s. Does it make sense that your friend can run that fast? Think about how far 47 m is. That's almost a 50-m dash. That means your friend could run a 50-m dash in about 1 s. Can your friend do that? No, he can't. So, 47 m/s is too fast and is not a reasonable answer. You need to check your work.

Precision

Precision describes how close measurements are to each other. Some measurements are more precise than others. Suppose you measure the distance from home to school four times. Each time you get 2.7 km. Your neighbor measures the same distance four times. He measures 2.9 km two times and 2.7 km two times. Your measurements are closer to each other than your neighbor's measurements. So, your measurements are more precise.

The timing for Olympic events has become very precise. Years ago, events were measured to tenths of a second. Now they are measured to hundredths of a second. The instruments we use to measure today are more precise than those used years ago.

Accuracy

Accuracy is the closeness of a measurement to the true value. Suppose you measured the length of your shoelace two times. One time you measured 12.5 cm and the other time you measured 12.3 cm. Your measurements are precise because they are close together. However, if the shoelace is actually 13.5 cm long, the measurements are not accurate.

What makes a good measurement?

A good measurement must be both precise and accurate. A precise measurement is not always a good measurement. A watch that has a second hand is more precise than a watch without one. But, the watch with the second hand could be set 1 hour earlier or later than the real time. In that case, the watch would not be accurate at all. Since the time on the watch is precise but not accurate, the time on the watch is not a good measurement.

How do you round a measurement?

Suppose you need to measure the length of the sidewalk outside your school. You could measure to the nearest millimeter. But, you probably only need to know the length to the nearest meter or tenth of a meter. Suppose you find that the length of the sidewalk is 135.481 m. How do you round this number to the nearest tenth of a meter? Follow these two steps:

1. Look at the digit to the right of the place being rounded to.
   • If the digit is 0, 1, 2, 3, or 4, the digit being rounded to stays the *same.*
   • If the digit is 5, 6, 7, 8, or 9, the digit being rounded to *increases by one.*

So, to round to the nearest tenth of a meter, look for the digit in the tenths place, 4. Find the digit to the right of 4. The 4 increases to 5 because the digit to the right of 4 is 8.

2. Look at the digit being rounded to. Then look at the digits to its right. If those digits are to the right of a decimal, they are removed. If they are to the left of a decimal, change them to zeros. For example, 432.9 rounded to the nearest hundred is 400. Since the 9 is to the right of the decimal, it is removed.

So, 135.481 rounded to the nearest tenth of a meter is 135.5 m.

Copyright © Glencoe/McGraw-Hill, a division of The McGraw-Hill Companies, Inc.

💡 Think it Over

4. Apply Give another example of a measurement that is precise but not accurate.

_____

_____

_____

_____

Applying Math

5. Rounding Values
What is 135.481 m rounded to the nearest ten meters?

_____

Some measurements are not precise.

If a measurement doesn't need to be precise, you can round your measurement. For example, suppose you want to divide a 2-L bottle of soda equally among seven people. When you use a calculator to divide 2 by 7, you get 0.285 714 28. You can round this number to 0.3. This is a little less than 0.333..., or $\frac{1}{3}$. You pour a little less than $\frac{1}{3}$ L of soda for each person.

What are significant digits?

Significant digits are the number of digits that show the precision of a number. For example, 18 cm has two significant digits: 1 and 8. There are four significant digits in 19.32 cm: 1, 9, 3, and 2. All non-zero digits are significant digits. Sometimes zeros are significant and sometimes they are not. Use these rules to decide if a zero is a significant digit.

	Rule	Example	Number of Significant Digits
Always significant	Final zeros after a decimal point	4.5300	5
	Zeros between other digits	502.0301	7
Not significant	Zeros at the beginning of a number	0.00059	2
May be significant	Zeros in whole numbers	16,500	3 or 5

How do you calculate with significant digits?

There are rules to follow when deciding the number of significant digits in the answer to a problem.

Multiplying or Dividing First, count the significant digits in each number in your problem. Then, multiply or divide. Your answer must have the same number of significant digits as the number with fewer significant digits in the problem. If it does not, you must round your answer.

$$6.14 \times 5.6 = \boxed{34}.384$$
3 digits   2 digits   round to 2 digits

Adding or Subtracting When you add or subtract, find the least precise number in the problem (the number with the fewest decimal places). Then add or subtract. Your answer can show only as many decimal places as the least precise number. If it does not, you must round your answer.

$$\begin{array}{r} 6.14 \text{ (hundredths)} \\ + \ 5.6 \ \text{ (tenths)} \\ \hline \overline{11.7}4 \text{ (round to the tenths)} \end{array}$$

6. Counting Significant Digits How many significant digits are in 28.070?

_____

7. Calculate What is 13.2 × 4.628, rounded to the nearest significant digit? Show your work.

_____

_____

_____

● After You Read

Mini Glossary

accuracy: the closeness of a measurement to the actual measurement or value

estimation: a method used to guess the size of an object

measurement: a way to describe objects and events with numbers

precision: describes how close measurements are to each other

1. Review the terms and their definitions in the Mini Glossary. How is precision different from accuracy?

   _____

   _____

2. Complete the chart that shows how to round a number.

   Look at digit to the _____ of the place being rounded to.

   If the digit is less than 5, the digit being rounded to

   _____ .

   If the digit is 5 or greater, the digit being

   rounded to _____ .

   If digit(s) to the right of the digit being rounded are to the *right* of a decimal,

   they are _____ . If they are to the *left* of a decimal,

   they are _____ .

3. You were asked to make an outline as you read this section. Did your outline help you learn about measurement? What did you do that seemed most helpful?

   _____

   _____

   _____

 Visit **red.msscience.com** to access your textbook, interactive games, and projects to help you learn more about description and measurement.

End of Section

chapter 2

Measurement

section 2 SI Units

What You'll Learn

- what the SI is and why it is used
- the SI units of length, volume, mass, temperature, time, and rate

Identify Definitions As you read, highlight the definition of each word that appears in bold.

Applying Math

1. **Converting Measurements** What do you multiply by to change a hectometer measurement into meters?

● Before You Read

Some people use metric units such as meters, grams, and liters. Others use units such as feet, pounds, and gallons. Explain why using different units might cause a problem.

_____

_____

● Read to Learn

The International System

Scientists created the International System of Units, or SI. The **SI** is a system of standard measurement that is used worldwide. Some of the units in the SI system are meter (m) for length, kilogram (kg) for mass, kelvin (K) for temperature, and second (s) for time.

Units in the SI system represent multiples of ten. You know the multiple of ten by looking at the prefix before the unit. For example, *kilo-* means 1,000. So, one *kilo*meter is equal to 1,000 meters.

To change a smaller unit to a larger SI unit, multiply by a power of 10 as shown in the table. To rewrite a *deci*meter measurement in meters multiply by 0.1.

$$10 \text{ dm} \times 0.1 = 1 \text{ m}$$

1 dm and 0.1 m describe the same length. So do 5 km and 5,000 m.

Prefix	Meaning	Multiply by:
giga-	one billion	1,000,000,000
mega-	one million	1,000,000
kilo-	one thousand	1,000
hecto-	one hundred	100
deka-	ten	10
[Unit]		1
deci-	one-tenth	0.1
centi-	one-hundredth	0.01
milli-	one-thousandth	0.001
micro-	one-millionth	0.0001
nano-	one-billionth	0.000 000 001

Length

Length is the distance between two points. Metric rulers and metersticks are used to measure length. A **meter** (m) is the SI unit of length. One meter is about as long as a baseball bat. A meter is used to measure distances such as the length and height of a building.

Some units are used to measure short distances. One millimeter (mm) is about the thickness of a dime. A millimeter is used to measure very small objects, such as the length of a word on this page. One centimeter (cm) is about the width of a large paper clip. A centimeter also can be used to measure small objects, such as the length of a pencil.

A kilometer is used to measure long distances, such as distances between cities. A kilometer (km) is a little over half of a mile.

Volume

Volume is the amount of space an object fills. To find the volume of a rectangular object like a brick, measure its length, width, and height. Then multiply them together.

$$\text{Volume} = \text{length} \times \text{width} \times \text{height}$$
$$V = l \times w \times h$$

The volume of a cube with side lengths of 10 cm is $10 \times 10 \times 10 = 1{,}000$ cubic centimeter (cm^3). You probably have seen water in 1-L bottles. A liter is a measurement of liquid volume. One liter is equal to 1,000 cm^3. So, a cube with side lengths of 10 cm has the same volume of a 1-L water bottle. A cube with side lengths of 1 cm has the volume of 1 cm^3. It can hold 1 mL (1 cm^3) of water.

How can you find the volume of ice cubes in water?

What happens when you add ice cubes to a glass of water? The height of the water increases, but the amount of water does not change. The ice cubes take up space because they have volume, too. So, the glass contains both the volume of the water and the volume of the ice.

Not all objects have a regular shape like a brick. A rock has an irregular shape. You cannot find the volume of a rock by multiplying its length, width, and height. When you want to measure the volume of an irregular object, you can find the volume by immersion.

B Compare and Contrast
Make the Foldable below to help you understand the different types of measurement using SI units. Take notes on each type of measurement as you read.

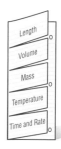

Length
Volume
Mass
Temperature
Time and Rate

Think it Over

2. **Infer** The volume formula can be used to find the volume of

   a. a tissue box.

   b. a lamp.

   c. a computer mouse.

Applying Math

3. **Calculating Volume**
Find the volume of a cube that measures 2 cm on each side. Show your work.

_____

_____

What is immersion?

Start with a known volume of water and place the object in it. Then find the volume of the water with the object in it. The difference between the two volumes is equal to the volume of the object.

For example, to find the volume of a rock, first find the volume of water in a container. Next, place the rock in the water, making sure the water covers all of the rock. Then find the volume of the water and rock together. Subtract the smaller volume from the larger one. The difference is the volume of the rock.

Mass

The **mass** of an object measures the amount of matter in the object. The **kilogram** (kg) is the SI unit for mass. One liter of water has the mass of about 1 kg. Smaller masses are measured in grams (g). The mass of a paper clip is about 1 g.

Mass versus Weight Why use the word *mass* instead of *weight*? Mass and weight are not the same. Mass depends only on the amount of matter in an object. Your mass on the moon would be the same as it is on Earth. **Weight** is a measure of the gravitational force, or pull, on the matter in an object. In other words, weight depends on gravity. You would weigh much less on the moon because the gravitational force on the moon is less than on Earth. ✓

How much would you weigh on other planets?

Keep in mind that weight is a measure of force. The SI unit for force is the newton (N). Suppose you weigh 332 N on Earth. That would be a mass of about 75 pounds, or 34 kg. Remember that the gravitational force is different on different planets. On Mars, you would weigh 126 N. On Jupiter, you would weigh much more—782 N. Your mass would still be the same on all the planets because the amount of matter in your body has not changed.

Time

Time tells how long it takes an event to happen. The SI unit for time is the second (s). Time is also measured in minutes (min) and hours (h). Time is usually measured with a clock or a stopwatch.

Reading Check

4. Determine What does weight depend on?

_____

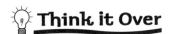

Think it Over

5. Infer Which has more gravity, Mars or Jupiter?

_____

Rate

A **rate** is the amount of change in one measurement that takes place in a given amount of time. To find a rate, a measurement is divided by an amount of time. Speed is a common rate that tells how fast an object is moving. Speed is the distance traveled in a given time. The formula for speed is distance (length) divided by time, such as 80 kilometers per hour (km/h). The unit that is changing does not have to be an SI unit. You can use rate to tell how many cars pass through an intersection in an hour (cars/h). ☑

Temperature

Temperature is how hot or cold an object is. The **kelvin** (K) is the SI unit for measuring temperature. The Fahrenheit (°F) and Celsius (°C) temperature scales are the scales used on most thermometers. Compare the scales in the figure. The kelvin scale starts at 0 K, absolute zero, the coldest possible temperature. One degree of change on the kelvin scale is the same as one degree of change on the Celsius scale.

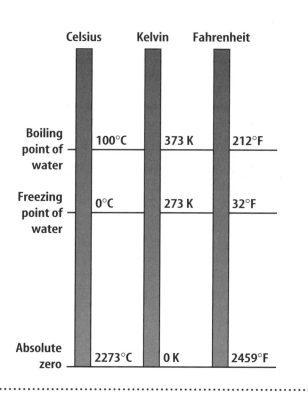

✔ **Reading Check**

6. Explain How do you calculate a rate?

_____

_____

_____

Picture This

7. Interpreting Graphs What is the boiling point of water on each of the temperature scales?

Celsius:

_____

Kelvin:

_____

Fahrenheit:

_____

● After You Read

Mini Glossary

kelvin: SI unit for measuring temperature (K)

kilogram: SI unit for measuring mass (kg)

mass: amount of matter in an object

meter: SI unit of length (m)

rate: the amount of change in one measurement that takes place in a given amount of time

SI: a system of standard measurement that is used worldwide

volume: amount of space that fills an object

weight: a measure of the gravitational force, or pull, on the matter in an object

1. Review the terms and their definitions in the Mini Glossary. What are four examples of rate?

   _____

   _____

2. Complete the table to identify common SI base units.

Quantity	SI Unit
Length	
Volume	cubic centimeter or _____
Mass	
Temperature	
Time	

3. Sometimes you need to find your own way to remember terms and main points. How could you remember what mass and volume mean?

   _____

   _____

   _____

End of Section

 **Science** nline Visit **red.msscience.com** to access your textbook, interactive games, and projects to help you learn more about SI units.

section ❸ Drawings, Tables, and Graphs

⬤ Before You Read

A common saying is "A picture is worth a thousand words." Use the lines below to explain what this means.

_____

_____

⬤ Read to Learn

Scientific Illustrations

Most science books include pictures. These pictures can be drawings or photographs. Drawings and photographs can often explain new information better than words can.

What does a drawing show?

Drawings are helpful because they can show details. Drawings can show things that you cannot see. The drawing below shows details of the water cycle that can't be shown in a photograph. You can also use drawings to help solve problems. For example, you could draw the outline of two continents to show how they might have fit together at one time.

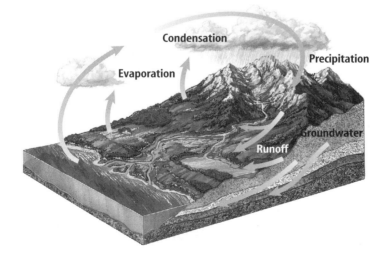

Condensation
Precipitation
Evaporation
Groundwater
Runoff

What You'll Learn
■ how pictures and tables give important information
■ how to use three types of graphs

▪ **Mark the Text**

Identify the Main Point
As you read, highlight two main points about pictures, tables, and each kind of graph.

Picture This
1. **Interpret a Drawing**
   What parts of the water cycle can be shown in a drawing but not in a photograph?

   _____

   _____

   _____

Applying Math

2. **Interpret Data** How many animal species were endangered in 1992?

   a. 192

   b. 284

   c. 321

   d. 389

3. **Describe** How many variables are shown on a line graph?

What does a photograph show?

A photograph shows an object at one moment in time. A video or movie is made of a series of photographs. A movie shows how an object moves. It can be slowed down or sped up to show interesting things about an object.

Tables and Graphs

Science books contain tables and graphs as well as drawings and photographs. Tables are a good way to organize information. A **table** lists information in columns and rows so that it is easy to read and understand. Columns are vertical, or go up and down. Rows are horizontal, or go across from left to right. This table shows the number of endangered animal species for each year from 1984 to 2002.

A **graph** is a drawing that shows data, or information. Sometimes it is easier to see the relationships when the data is shown in a graph. The three most common types of graphs are line graphs, bar graphs, and circle graphs.

Endangered Animal Species in the United States	
Year	Number of Endangered Animal Species
1984	192
1986	213
1988	245
1990	263
1992	284
1994	321
1996	324
1998	357
2000	379
2002	389

What does a line graph show?

A **line graph** shows changes in data over time. Things that change, like the number of endangered animals and the year, are called variables. A line graph shows the relationship between two variables. Both variables in a line graph must be numbers. ☑

In the line graph at the top of the next page, the horizontal axis, or *x*-axis, shows the year. The vertical axis, or *y*-axis, shows the number of endangered species. The line on the graph shows the relationship between the year and the number of endangered species. To find the number of endangered species in a given year, find that year on the *x*-axis. Find the point on the line that is above that year. See what number on the *y*-axis lines up with the point.

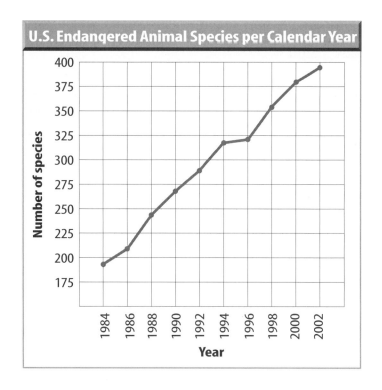

U.S. Endangered Animal Species per Calendar Year

Picture This

4. Interpret Data Look at the line graph. Between which two years did the number of endangered species increase the least? Circle your answer.

   a. 1986–1988

   b. 1992–1994

   c. 1994–1996

   d. 2000–2002

What does a bar graph show?

A **bar graph** uses rectangular blocks, or bars, to show the relationships among variables. One variable must be a number. This variable is divided into parts. The other variable can be a category, like kinds of animals, or it could be another number. In the bar graph on endangered species, the height of each bar shows the number of endangered species in each animal group. For example, there are about 30 species of endangered insects. Bar graphs make it easy to compare data.

Picture This

5. Describe Look at the bar graph. How many animal groups have fewer than 30 endangered species?

_____

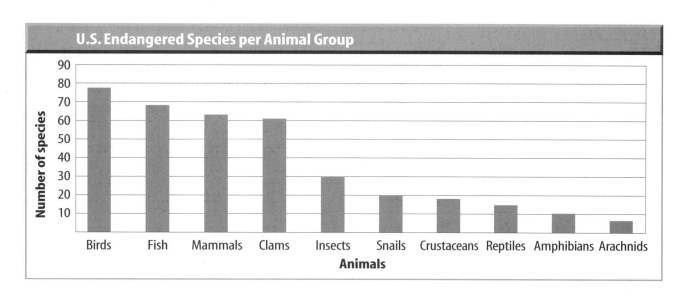

U.S. Endangered Species per Animal Group

What does a circle graph show?

A <u>circle graph</u> shows the parts of a whole. It is sometimes called a pie graph because it looks like a pie. The circle represents the whole pie. The slices are the parts of, or fractions of, the whole pie. Circle graphs help you compare the sizes of the parts. It is easy to see which parts are largest and which are smallest.

Look at the circle graph on endangered species. What is the largest piece of pie? Birds is the largest piece. This tells you that there are more endangered bird species than any other animal group. What is the smallest piece of pie? Arachnids is the smallest. There are fewer endangered arachnids than any other animal group.

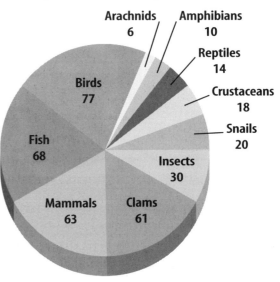

U.S. Endangered Species per Animal Group

Arachnids 6
Amphibians 10
Reptiles 14
Crustaceans 18
Snails 20
Insects 30
Clams 61
Mammals 63
Fish 68
Birds 77

Picture This

6. **Interpret Data** Use the circle graph. Which animal group has the second largest number of endangered species? How many endangered species does this group have?

_____

_____

Applying Math

7. **Find the Ratio** Look at the circle graph. Write a fraction to show the number of bird species compared to the total number of endangered animal species.

_____

How do you make a circle graph?

A circle has 360°. To make a circle graph, find what fraction of 360 each part is. First, find the total number of parts in the whole. The total number of endangered species is 367. Then, compare the number of each animal species with the total. Look at the part of the circle labeled Mammals. There are 63 endangered mammal species. Make a fraction to show 63 out of 367, which would be $\frac{63}{367}$.

Now find the part of 360° that are mammals. To find this, set up a proportion and solve for x. The answer is the size of the angle to draw in the circle graph.

$$\frac{63}{367} = \frac{x}{360°} \qquad x = 61.8°$$

The angle at the center of the circle for the part that represents mammals will have a measure of 61.8°. Use the same method to find the other angles to show data.

Why is the scale of a graph important?

The two graphs below do not look the same, but they both show the same data. Why do the graphs look different? The graphs look different because their scales are different. Look at the scale on the *y*-axis in each graph. Look at the lowest number. The first graph begins with 310 instead of 0. It appears as though there was a great increase in the number of endangered species from 1996 to 2002. The second graph does begin at 0. It shows that there was a slight increase in endangered species during these years.

A scale that does not start at 0 is called a broken scale. A broken scale makes it easier to see small changes in the data. However, you must read the graph carefully to see if there is a broken scale. When you see a bar graph or a line graph, look at the data carefully. If the graph seems odd, take a closer look at the scale. ☑

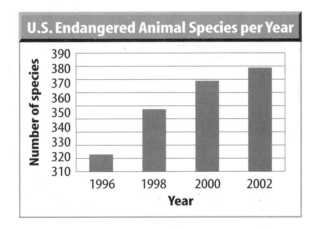

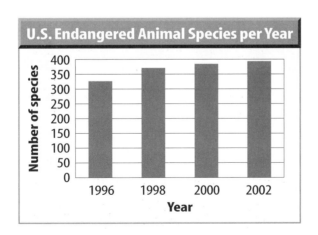

✔ Reading Check

8. Explain What is a broken scale?

_____

_____

_____

Picture This

9. Describe In your own words, tell when a broken scale in a bar graph or a line graph is useful.

_____

_____

_____

● After You Read

Mini Glossary

bar graph: a graph that uses bars to show the relationships between variables.

circle graph: a graph that shows the parts of a whole

graph: a kind of drawing that shows data, or information

line graph: a graph that shows changes in data over time

table: lists information in columns and rows so that it is easy to read and understand

1. Review the terms and definitions in the Mini Glossary. Write a sentence that tells how a graph helps you understand data.

_____

_____

2. Complete the chart below to describe when each graph is most useful.

Graph Type	When Useful
Line graph	
Bar graph	
Circle graph	compare parts to a whole

3. You were asked to highlight two main points about pictures, tables, and each kind of graph. How did you decide what to highlight?

_____

_____

_____

 Visit **red.msscience.com** to access your textbook, interactive games, and projects to help you learn more about drawings, tables, and graphs.

Copyright © Glencoe/McGraw-Hill, a division of The McGraw-Hill Companies, Inc.

Matter and Its Changes

section ❶ Physical Properties and Changes

● Before You Read

Describe an object in your classroom. What color is it? How is it shaped? What else can you say about the object?

_____

_____

Copyright © Glencoe/McGraw-Hill, a division of The McGraw-Hill Companies, Inc.

What You'll Learn
- to identify physical properties of matter
- what the states of matter are
- how to classify matter using physical properties

● Read to Learn

Using Your Senses

Most people make observations when they walk into a new room. Observing involves seeing, hearing, tasting, touching, and smelling. You use your senses to observe the physical properties of materials. **Physical properties** are characteristics of materials that can be observed or measured without changing the material. You can observe the color or smell of a material without changing the material.

You use your senses to observe materials in the laboratory. Remember never to smell, taste, or touch any materials in the lab without instructions. It may be unsafe. The figure shows which senses you should and should not use in the laboratory.

Watch

Listen

Do NOT touch

Do NOT smell

Do NOT taste

Mark the Text

Highlighting As you read this section, highlight different properties of matter. Then write an example of that property.

Picture This
1. **Conclude** Why do some symbols have a slash across them and some don't?

_____

_____

_____

_____

Physical Properties

There are many physical properties that can be observed easily. You can determine the color of an object by looking at it. You can also determine its shape. Other properties can be measured. You can measure the length or the mass of an object. Its volume or density also can be measured.

What is matter?

Imagine you are shopping for groceries. Everything in the grocery store is matter. **Matter** is anything that has mass and takes up space. The cans of vegetables and the potatoes and pineapples are all matter.

What can you observe about matter?

Suppose you need laundry soap. Laundry soap comes in bottles and boxes of different colors. Color is a physical property that is easy to observe. The bottles and boxes are also different shapes.

Most bottles are made of plastic. Plastic changes shape when it is molded into a bottle, but it is still plastic. The plastic went through a physical change. In a **physical change,** the physical properties of a substance change but the identity of the substance does not change. The laundry soap bottles are all made of plastic, regardless of the physical differences in color or shape.

What physical properties can be measured?

Some physical properties can be identified by measuring. Other physical properties can be identified by using your senses.

Length Length is one physical property that can be measured. A ruler, a meterstick, or a tape measure is used to find length. Objects can be classified by their lengths. Suppose you bought a cake mix. The directions might say to bake the cake in an 8-in-square cake pan. A 9 × 13 in cake pan has longer sides, but it is still a cake pan. The figure shows a beaker and a meterstick, which can be used to measure physical properties.

Mass Think about the laundry soap. A company may sell a small box and a large box of laundry soap. Both boxes contain laundry soap, but one will feel heavier than the other. This is because it has more mass. Mass is a physical property that describes the amount of matter in an object. Your senses can tell you which box has more mass.

Volume Volume measures the amount of space an object takes up. Liquids are usually measured by volume. The juice bottles on your grocery list are probably measured by volume.

Density Another measurable physical property is density. <u>Density</u> is the amount of mass a material has in a given volume. You notice density when you try to lift two things that have the same volume but different masses. You can find density by dividing the mass of an object by its volume.

$$\text{density} = \text{mass/volume}, \text{ or } D = m/V$$

Suppose you want to find the density of a piece of nickel. It has a mass of 39.2 g and a volume of 4 cm^3. Multiply 39.2 by 4. The density of the piece of nickel is 9.8 g/cm^3.

Can two objects be the same size but have different masses?

Two balls that are the same size may not have the same mass. A bowling ball is more dense than a kickball. Think about the bags of groceries you bought at the store. They all have different densities. How is a bag that is filled with canned goods different from a bag that contains only paper napkins? The bags are the same size but the bag with canned goods has more mass. The bag with the canned goods is more dense than the one with the napkins. The table below lists the densities of some elements.

Material	Density (g/cm³)	Material	Density (g/cm³)
Air	0.001293	Lead	11.3
Aluminum	2.7	Magnesium	1.7
Carbon dioxide	0.001977	Mercury	13.6
Copper	8.9	Milk	1.03
Gold	19.3	Platinum	21.4
Hydrogen	0.00009	Uranium	18.7
Iron	7.8	Water	1.00

Does density of a material change?

The density of a material does not change as long as temperature and pressure stay the same. But if the temperature or pressure are changed, the density of the material will change.

Applying Math

5. **Calculate** Use a calculator to find the density of 15.6 grams of lead with a volume of 2 cm^3. The units will be g/cm^3.

_____

Picture This

6. **Identify** Which material in the table has the greatest density? What is its density? Which material has the least density? What is its density?

_____

_____

_____

_____

7. Explain Why did the identity of the water not change when it formed ice?

_____

_____

8. Determine What two things does the state of matter of a substance depend on?

_____

_____

FOLDABLES™

Ⓐ Compare Make the following Foldable to compare and contrast the characteristics of solids, liquids, and gases.

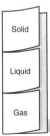

Change of State Water at room temperature has a density of 1.00 g/cm^3. Water kept in the freezer at 0°C is in the form of ice. The density of ice is 0.9168 g/cm^3. Has the identity of water changed? No, but the water has changed to a different state.

States of Matter

How does water change when it goes from 20°C to 0°C? It changes from a liquid to a solid. It changes state or form. The four **states of matter** are solid, liquid, gas, and plasma (PLAZ muh). A substance's state of matter depends on its temperature and pressure. The solid, liquid, and gas states are common. But the plasma state is unusual. The plasma state happens at very high temperatures. Plasma is found in fluorescent (floo RE sunt) lightbulbs, the atmosphere, and in lightning strikes. ✔

The state of matter of a material is another physical property. You could classify the items on your grocery list according to their states of matter.

How is energy related to states of matter?

Matter is made up of moving particles. The state of matter of a substance is determined by how much energy the particles have.

Solid The particles of a solid vibrate, or move back and forth, in a fixed place. They are packed close together and stay this way. This is why a solid has a definite shape and volume.

Liquid Particles in a liquid move much faster. They have enough energy to slide past one another. This is why a liquid takes the shape of its container.

Gas The particles of a gas move very quickly. They have enough energy to move freely away from other particles. The particles of a gas take up as much space as possible. They will spread out to fill any container.

Does temperature affect the movement of particles?

Particles of matter move faster at higher temperatures. What would happen if you added food coloring to a beaker of cold water and a beaker of hot water? The color would spread faster in the beaker of hot water.

Does matter change states?

Have you ever watched ice cubes melt? You watched matter change states. Water changed from a solid to a liquid. What happens when you put water in a freezer? It changes to a solid. The water itself does not change identity. Its state is all that changes.

What are melting and boiling points?

At what temperature will liquid water change to a gas? At what temperature will ice change into liquid water?

Melting Point <u>Melting point</u> is the temperature at which a solid becomes a liquid. Melting points are different for different substances. But the melting point of a pure substance never changes, no matter how much of the substance there is. This means that a small sliver of ice and a huge chunk of ice both will melt at 0°C. Lead always melts at 327.5°C. When a substance melts, it changes from a solid to a liquid. This is a physical change. The melting point is a physical property.

Boiling Point The <u>boiling point</u> is the temperature at which a liquid becomes a gas. Each pure substance has a certain boiling point at atmospheric pressure. Atmospheric pressure is the pressure caused by the weight of Earth's atmosphere. The boiling point of water is 100°C at atmospheric pressure. The boiling point of nitrogen is −195.8°C. The boiling point does not depend on the amount of a substance. The boiling point is a physical property. The table shows the melting and boiling points of some substances. ☑

Substance	Melting Point (°C)	Boiling Point (°C)
Hydrogen	−259.31	−252.89
Nitrogen	−209.97	−195.8
Oxygen	−218.79	−182.97
Ethyl alcohol	−114	78
Mercury	−39	357
Water	0	100
Sulfur	119	444.6
Lead	327.5	1750
Silver	960.8	2193
Gold	1063	2660
Copper	1083	2567

☑ **Reading Check**

9. **Determine** What happens to water at 100°C?

_____

_____

Picture This

10. **Use a Table** In what state is gold at a temperature of 800°C? Circle your answer.

   a. solid
   b. liquid
   c. gas
   d. plasma

How can melting and boiling points be used?

The boiling point and melting point can help you identify a substance. If you see a clear liquid boil at 56.1°C, you know it is not water. Water boils at 100°C. You can classify substances based on boiling and melting points.

Metallic Properties

You have learned how you can classify substances as solids, liquids, or gases. You also learned to classify things by color, shape, length, mass, volume, or density. Other physical properties let you classify substances as metals.

What do metals look like?

What is the first thing you notice about a metal? You may notice that it looks shiny. This is because of the way metal reflects light. The shine of a metal is called luster. New handlebars on a bike have a metallic luster. Silver forks, knives, and spoons also have a metallic luster.

How are metals used?

Metals can be used in many ways because of some of their physical properties. Many metals can be hammered, pressed, or rolled into thin sheets. This property of metals is called malleability (mal lee uh BIH luh tee). Artists use malleable metals like copper to make sculptures. The Statue of Liberty is made of copper. Many metals can be drawn into wires. This property is called ductility (duk TIH luh tee). Wires in buildings and most electrical equipment are made from copper. Silver and platinum are also ductile.

Do you have any magnets on your refrigerator at home? Your refrigerator door is made of metal. Magnets are attracted to some metals. This is another physical property of metals. Some metals have groups of atoms that can be affected by the force of a magnet. The metals are attracted to the magnet because of that force. Magnets are often used to find metallic objects.

Using Physical Properties

You have learned that many physical properties can be used to identify substances. Properties like color, shape, length, mass, volume, ability to attract a magnet, density, melting point, boiling point, malleability, and ductility can help you separate and classify substances.

💡 Think it Over

11. **Classify** Which of the following is made of metal? Circle your answer.

   a. eraser
   b. popsicle stick
   c. soda bottle
   d. tea kettle

FOLDABLES

B Classify Make the following Foldable. Find objects and record your observations of physical properties on the Foldable.

Object Observed	Physical Properties

How are physical properties used to identify things?

You can describe salt as a white solid. You can measure the mass, volume, and density of a sample of salt. You could also find out if it is attracted to a magnet. These are examples of how physical properties can be used to identify a substance.

Identifying a Dog Suppose you volunteer to help your friend choose a family pet. You spot a cute dog at the local animal shelter. The sign on its cage says the dog is male and one to two years old. It also says the dog's breed is unknown. What kind of information do you and your friend need to figure out the dog's breed?

First, you need to know all of the physical properties of the dog. What does the dog look like? Second, you need to know the descriptions of different breeds of dogs. Then you can match up the description of the dog with the correct breed. The dog you found is brown, black, and white. He is medium-sized. He also has long ears and short legs. What breed is the dog? ☑

How can you narrow your options?

To find out, you may need to find out more about different breeds of dogs. Sometimes the easiest way to identify something is to find out what it cannot be. This is called the process of elimination. You can eliminate small dog and large dog breeds. You can also eliminate breeds that have short ears. You might want to look at photos of different dog breeds. Then you could see which one looks most like your dog.

Dichotomous Key The figure below shows a dichotomous (di KAH tuh mus) key. The questions in the key help you eliminate dog breeds. Scientists use methods like these to figure out the identities of living and nonliving things.

What Kind of Dog?	
1. A. Small dog B. Medium-size dog	Jack Russell Terrier go to #2
2. A. Short ears that stick up B. Ears hang down	Boxer go to #3
3. A. Long ears, short legs, saggy skin B. Longer legs, medium-length ears	Bassett Hound Beagle

Copyright © Glencoe/McGraw-Hill, a division of The McGraw-Hill Companies, Inc.

✔ **Reading Check**

12. **Explain** What are two things you need to know to figure out the dog's breed?

_____

_____

_____

_____

💡 **Think it Over**

13. **Infer** What breed of dog might the dog at the animal shelter be?

_____

● After You Read

Mini Glossary

boiling point: the temperature at which a liquid becomes a gas

density: the amount of mass a material has in a given volume

matter: anything that has mass and takes up space

melting point: the temperature at which a solid becomes a liquid

physical change: a change where the physical properties of a substance change but the substance does not change

physical property: a characteristic of a material that you can observe or measure without changing the material

states of matter: solid, liquid, gas, and plasma

1. Read the key terms and definitions in the Mini Glossary. Write a sentence using the terms *melting point* and *physical property* on the lines below.

_____

_____

2. In the diagram fill in nine other physical properties of matter that can be used to identify a substance.

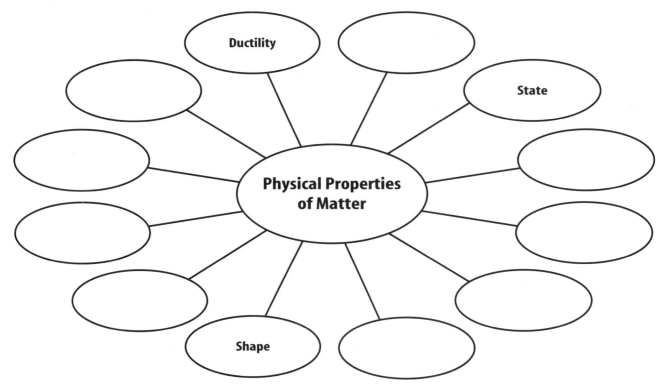

Science Online Visit **red.msscience.com** to access your textbook, interactive games, and projects to help you learn more about physical properties and changes.

End of Section

 **Matter and Its Changes**

section ❷ Chemical Properties and Changes

● Before You Read

How does cake batter change when it is baked in an oven?

_____

_____

What You'll Learn
■ to identify chemical properties and chemical changes
■ to classify matter by chemical properties
■ the law of conservation of mass

● Read to Learn

Ability to Change

Imagine you are at a campfire. What is needed for a campfire? You will need at least several large pieces of firewood and some small pieces of kindling. What happens to these things during the fire? After the campfire, all that is left is a pile of ash. Where did the wood go? What property of the wood is responsible for this change?

All of the properties you learned about in the first section were physical properties. You could see them easily. You also could use them to classify objects. Even when those properties changed, the identity of the object stayed the same. Why is the campfire different? Some properties tell you that the identity of the wood has changed. A **chemical property** is any characteristic that lets a substance change into a new substance.

Common Chemical Properties

Some changes are called chemical changes. A **chemical change** is a change in the identity of a substance because of the chemical properties of that substance. A new substance or substances are formed by a chemical change. You do not have to be in a laboratory to observe chemical changes. The campfire produced chemical changes. The oxygen in the air reacted with the wood. The reaction formed a new substance called ash.

Mark the Text

Underline As you read, underline each chemical property you read about.

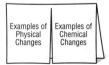 **FOLDABLES**

❸ Organize Information
Use the following Foldable to list examples of physical changes and chemical changes.

Examples of Physical Changes | Examples of Chemical Changes

Do all things burn?

Wood can burn. This chemical property is called flammability. Some products have warning labels to tell you they are flammable. These products should be kept away from heat or flames. What happens if you throw a stone onto the campfire? It will not burn. It has the property of being incombustible, or unable to burn. ☑

What are some common chemical reactions?

What happens to an unpainted iron gate? Over time it will rust. This is a chemical reaction.

Chemical Reactions with Metals Oxygen in the air reacts with the iron. This causes corrosion. The corrosion makes a new substance called iron oxide. The common name for iron oxide is rust. Other chemical reactions occur when metals react to other elements. Tarnish is a grayish-brown film that appears on silver. Silver reacts with sulfur in the air to form tarnish. The ability to react with oxygen or sulfur is a chemical property.

Chemical Reactions with Food Have you ever peeled a banana and then left part of it on the table? It probably turned brown. The same thing happens to sliced apples or avocadoes. The brown coloring is from a chemical reaction. The fruit reacts with the oxygen in the air. Although nothing is wrong with brown bananas, apples, or avocadoes, they do not look tasty. ☑

Can heat and light cause chemical reactions?

Vitamins often come in dark brown bottles. Do you know why? Many vitamins will change when they are exposed to light. This is a chemical property. The dark bottles protect the vitamins from going through a chemical change with light.

Some substances are sensitive to heat. They will go through a chemical change only when they are heated or cooled. One example is limestone. Some limestone has been around for hundreds of years without changing. But if limestone is heated, it goes through a chemical change. It produces carbon dioxide and lime. Lime is a chemical used in many industrial processes. This chemical property is the ability to change when heated. ☑

Another chemical property is the ability to change because of electrical contact. Electricity can cause a change in some compounds. It can also cause compounds to decompose, or break down. Water can be broken down with electricity.

☑ Reading Check

1. **Identify** Name a chemical property of wood.

_____

_____

☑ Reading Check

2. **Communicate** Why does a banana turn brown without its peel?

_____

_____

☑ Reading Check

3. **Determine** What chemical property allows limestone to turn into carbon dioxide and lime?

_____

Something New

The important difference between a physical change and a chemical change is that in a chemical change new substances are made. You enjoy many things because of chemical changes. What about that perfect, browned marshmallow roasted over a campfire? The fire caused a chemical change. The chemical change caused the marshmallow to look and taste different.

Sugar is normally white and made of crystals. When you heat it over a flame, it turns to a dark-brown caramel. A different substance is formed. Eggs, sugar, flour, and other ingredients change chemically when you bake them. If they did not, you could not eat a birthday cake. Cake begins as liquid and ends as solid. The baked cake has different properties than the batter.

What are the signs of a new substance?

Do you know you have a new substance just because it looks different? You could put salad in a blender and make it look different. But this would not be a chemical change. You would still have lettuce, carrots, and the other things that were in the salad.

You can look for signs to tell you if a new substance is made because of a chemical change. When a cake bakes, gas bubbles form. The bubbles grow within the ingredients. Bubbles are often a sign that a chemical change has happened. If you look closely at a piece of cake, you can see the airholes left from the bubbles. Other signs of change are the production of heat, light, smoke, and sound and a change in color.

Can you reverse a chemical change?

Physical changes usually can be reversed easily. Melted butter can become solid again if you put it in the refrigerator. Modeling clay can be smashed to fit back into its container. But chemical changes cannot be reversed by doing something physical. For example, you cannot glue the ashes from a fire together to make wood. You also cannot see the egg or the flour in a baked cake.

How can you classify matter according to chemical properties?

It is sometimes easier to classify by physical properties than it is to classify by chemical properties. You can see the physical properties of a substance easily. You cannot see chemical properties without changing the substance.

Think it Over

4. Determine Which of the signs of a chemical change would you see or hear at a campfire?

_____

_____

_____

Think it Over

5. Conclude What type of change does modeling clay go through in a person's hand?

_____

_____

_____

_____

_____

_____

Think it Over

7. **Think Critically** Why is it important to keep chemical properties in mind when arranging products in a grocery store?

_____

_____

_____

FOLDABLES

D **Summarize** Make the following Foldable. Use it to summarize the law of conservation of mass in your own words. Be sure to include examples.

Law of Conservation
of Mass

Comparing Properties Once you know chemical properties, you can classify and identify matter using those properties. Suppose you try to burn what looks like a piece of wood. It does not burn. You can decide that it is not wood. The table below compares the two kinds of properties.

Comparing Properties	
Physical Properties	color, shape, length, mass, volume, density, state, ability to attract a magnet, melting point, boiling point, malleability, ductility
Chemical Properties	flammability; ability to react with: oxygen, electricity, light, water, heat, vinegar, etc.

In a grocery store, the products sometimes are separated because of chemical properties. The produce section is away from big windows where light and heat come in. The fruit and vegetables would ripen too quickly near a window. You also will not find lighter fluid near the bakery where there could be heat and flames.

Architects and product designers also think about chemical properties when they design buildings and merchandise. For example, children's sleepwear and bedding cannot be made of flammable fabric. Architects choose building materials like titanium that do not react with oxygen like other metals.

The Law of Conservation of Mass

Think back to the campfire. After the campfire, all that was left was a small pile of ash. Many kilograms of wood were turned into only a few kilograms of ash. Could this be a solution to the problems with landfills and garbage dumps? Why not burn all the trash? Can the amount of trash be reduced without making unwanted materials?

Can mass be destroyed?

Before you celebrate finding the solution to problems of landfills and garbage dumps, think about it. Did mass really disappear during the fire? It seems that way. There is less ash than there was wood. The **law of conservation of mass** states that the mass of what you end with is always the same as the mass of what you start with.

Has this law been proven to be true?

This law was first studied about 200 years ago. Many experiments have been done since then. They all prove the law to be true. One experiment done by French scientist Antoine Lavoisier was like a small campfire. He determined that a fire does not make mass disappear. But where did the mass go? The ashes are not heavy enough to equal the mass of the pieces of firewood.

Where did the mass go?

The campfire example shows that the law of conservation of mass is true. You just have to look carefully. When flammable materials burn, they combine with oxygen. They produce smoke, gases, and ash. The smoke and gases escape into the air. The mass of the smoke, gases, and ashes is the same as the mass of the original firewood. ☑

How can you show the law of conservation of mass?

Mass is not destroyed or created during a chemical change. The law of conservation of mass is shown in the figure below. In the first picture, there is one substance in the flask. There is another substance in the test tube inside the flask. The total mass is 16.150 g. The substances mix when the flask is turned upside down. (The flask is sealed so nothing escapes.) When the flask is placed on the scale again, the total mass is still 16.150 g. Instead of disappearing or appearing, particles in substances rearrange. They make different combinations of substances which have different properties.

✔ **Reading Check**

8. **Explain** What did the firewood change into?

_____

_____

Picture This

9. **Classify** What kind of change took place in the bottle, a chemical change or a physical change?

_____

Conservation of Mass

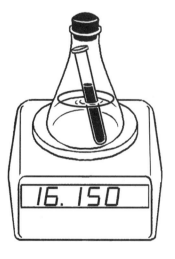
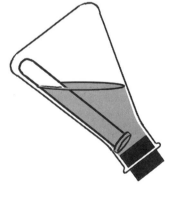

● After You Read

Mini Glossary

chemical change: a change in the identity of a substance because of the chemical properties of that substance

chemical property: any characteristic that lets a substance go through a change that turns it into a new substance

law of conservation of mass: states that the mass of what you end with is always the same as the mass of what you start with

1. Review the terms and their definitions in the Mini Glossary. How is the law of conservation of mass related to chemical changes?

_____

_____

2. Fill in the table about chemical properties.

Chemical Property	Example
	wood burning
ability to react with oxygen or sulfur	
	limestone producing carbon dioxide and lime
ability to react with electricity	

3. You were asked to underline different chemical properties. How did this help you understand and learn about chemical properties?

_____ _____

_____

_____

 **Science Online** Visit **red.msscience.com** to access your textbook, interactive games, and projects to help you learn more about chemical properties and changes.

Atoms, Elements, and the Periodic Table

section ❶ Structure of Matter

● Before You Read

Take a deep breath. What fills your lungs? Can you see it or hold it in your hand?

_____

● Read to Learn

What is matter?

Is a glass with some water in it half empty or half full? Neither is correct. The glass is completely full. It is half full of water and half full of air. What is air? Air is a mixture of several gases, including nitrogen and oxygen. Nitrogen and oxygen are kinds of matter. **Matter** is anything that has mass and takes up space. So, even though you cannot see it or hold it, air is matter. Water also is matter. Most of the things you can see, taste, smell, and touch are made of matter.

What isn't matter?

You could not read the words on this page without light. Light has no mass and does not take up space. So, light is not matter. Is heat matter? Heat has no mass and does not take up space. So, heat is not matter. Your thoughts, feelings, and ideas are not matter, either. ☑

What makes up matter?

Could you cut a piece of wood small enough so it no longer looks like wood? What is the smallest piece of wood you can cut? People have asked questions like these for hundreds of years. They wondered what matter is made of.

What You'll Learn

- what matter is
- what makes up matter
- the parts of an atom
- different atom models

◀ **Study Coach**

Make Flash Cards As you read, make flash cards to help you learn new science words. On one side of the card, write the word. On the other side of the card, write the definition. Review these cards as you study.

☑ **Reading Check**

1. **List** three things that are not matter.

_____

_____

_____

What was Democritus's idea of matter?

A Greek philosopher named Democritus lived from about 460 B.C. to 370 B.C. He thought the universe was made of empty space and tiny bits of stuff that he called atoms. The word *atom* comes from a Greek word that means "cannot be divided." Democritus believed atoms could not be divided into smaller pieces. Today, we define an **atom** as a particle that makes up most types of matter. The table below shows what Democritus thought about atoms. ☑

✔ **Reading Check**

2. Summarize What is an atom?

_____

_____

Democritus's Ideas About Atoms
1. All matter is made of atoms.
2. There are empty spaces between atoms.
3. Atoms are complete solids.
4. Atoms do not have anything inside them.
5. Atoms are different in size, shape, and weight.

Democritus also thought that different types of atoms existed for every type of matter. He thought the different atoms explained the different characteristics of each type of matter. Democritus's ideas about atoms were a first step toward understanding matter. In the early 1800s, scientists started building on the concept of atoms to form the current atomic theory of matter.

Can matter be made or destroyed?

For many years, people thought matter disappeared when it burned or rusted. Seeing objects grow, like trees, also made them think that matter could be made. A French chemist named Lavoisier (la VWAH see ay) lived about 2,000 years after Democritus. Lavoisier studied wood fires very carefully. Lavoisier showed that wood and the oxygen it combines with during a fire have the same mass as the ash, gases, and water vapor that are produced by the fire. So, matter is not destroyed when wood burns. It just changes into a different form.

Applying Math

3. Apply Suppose you increase the mass of wood you are burning in a fireplace. What will happen to the total mass of ash, gases, and water vapor?

_____

_____

$$\frac{\text{total mass of}}{\text{wood} + \text{oxygen}} = \frac{\text{total mass of}}{\text{ash} + \text{gases} + \text{water vapor}}$$

From Lavoisier's work came the law of conservation of matter. The **law of conservation of matter** states that matter is not created or destroyed—matter only changes form.

Models of the Atom

Models often are used for things that are too small or too large to be observed. Models also are used for things that are difficult to understand.

Smaller Models One way to make a model is to make a smaller version of something that is large. If you want to design a new sailboat, would you build a full-sized sailboat and hope it would float? It would be safer and cheaper to build and test a smaller version first. Then, if it didn't float, you could change your design and just build another model, not another full-sized sailboat. You could keep trying until the model worked.

Larger Models Scientists sometimes make models that are larger than the actual objects. Atoms are too small to see. So, scientists use large models of atoms to explain data or facts that are found during experiments. This means these models are also theories.

What was Dalton's model of an atom?

John Dalton was an English chemist. In the early 1800s, he made an atomic model that explained the results of the experiments of Lavoisier and others.

Dalton's atomic model was a set of ideas instead of an object. He believed matter was made of atoms that were too small to see. He also thought that each type of matter was made of only one kind of atom. For example, gold rings were made of gold atoms. Iron atoms made up an iron bar. Dalton also thought gold atoms are different from iron atoms. The different types of atoms explain why gold and iron are different. Other scientists made experiments and gathered data based on Dalton's model. Dalton's model became known as the atomic theory of matter. ☑

How small is an atom?

Atoms are so small it would take about 1 million of them lined up in a row to be about as thick as one human hair. Or, imagine you are holding an orange. If you want to see the atoms on the orange's skin, the orange would need to be as big as Earth. Then, imagine the Earth-sized orange covered with billions of marbles. Each marble would represent an atom on the skin of the orange.

FOLDABLES

A Compare and Contrast
Use two half-sheets of notebook paper to compare the past atomic model and the present atomic model.

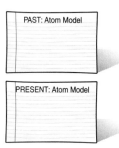

✓ Reading Check

4. **Explain** Dalton's atomic model was not an object. What was it?

_____

What is an electron?

An English scientist named J.J. Thomson discovered the electron in the early 1900s. He experimented using a glass tube with a metal plate at each end, like the one in the figure below. Thomson connected the metal plates to electricity. One plate, called the anode, had a positive charge. The other plate, called the cathode, had a negative charge.

Picture This

5. **Highlight** Highlight the area in the figure to show where the positive charge was in Thomson's experiment.

_____

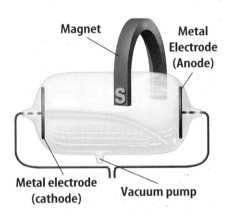

Magnet   Metal Electrode (Anode)

S

Metal electrode (cathode)   Vacuum pump

During his experiments, Thomson watched rays travel from the cathode to the anode. Then, he used a magnet to bend the rays. Since the rays could be bent, they were made of particles that had mass and charge. He knew that like charges repel each other and opposite charges attract each other. Since the rays were traveling to the positive plate (the anode), Thomson decided the rays must be made of particles with negative charges. These invisible particles with negative charges are **electrons**. Thomson showed that atoms can be divided into smaller particles.

Think it Over

6. **Explain** Why was Thomson's discovery important?

_____

_____

_____

What was Thomson's model of the atom?

Matter that has an equal amount of positive and negative charge is neutral. Most matter is neutral. So, Thomson thought an atom was made of a ball of positive charge with negatively charged electrons in it. ☑

Thomson's model of an atom was like a ball of chocolate chip cookie dough. The dough was positively charged. The chocolate chips were the negatively charged electrons.

What was Rutherford's model of the atom?

Scientists still had questions about how the atom was arranged and about particles with positive charge. Around the year 1910, an English scientist named Ernest Rutherford and his team of scientists tried to answer these questions.

✔ Reading Check

7. **Locate Information** What did Thompson think an atom was made of?

_____

_____

_____

Copyright © Glencoe/McGraw-Hill, a division of The McGraw-Hill Companies, Inc.

Rutherford's experiment Rutherford's team shot tiny, high-energy, positively charged particles, or alpha particles, at a very thin piece of gold foil. Rutherford thought that the alpha particles would pass easily through the foil. Most of the alpha particles did pass straight through. But, other alpha particles changed direction. A few of them even bounced back.

Since most particles passed straight through the gold, Rutherford thought that the gold atoms must be made of mostly empty space. But, because a few particles bounced off something, the gold atoms must have some positively charged object within the empty space. He called this positively charged object the nucleus. The **nucleus** (NEW klee us) is the positively charged, central part of an atom. Rutherford named the positively charged particles in the nucleus of an atom **protons.** He also suggested that negatively charged electrons were scattered in the empty space around the nucleus. Rutherford's model is shown in the figure below.

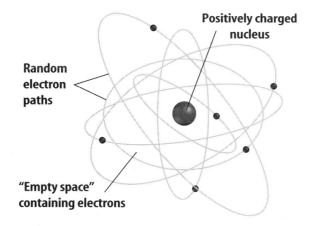

Random electron paths

Positively charged nucleus

"Empty space" containing electrons

How was the neutron discovered?

Rutherford was puzzled by one observation in his experiment with alpha particles. The nucleus of an atom seemed to be heavier after the experiment. He did not know where this extra mass came from. James Chadwick, one of Rutherford's students, answered the question: The nuclei were not getting heavier. But, the atoms had given off new particles. He found that the path of the new particles was not affected by an electric field. This meant the new particles were neutral—had no charge. Chadwick called these new particles neutrons. A **neutron** (NEW trahn) is a neutral particle in the nucleus of an atom. His proton-neutron model of the nucleus of an atom is still accepted today. ☑

Picture This

8. Draw Conclusions In Rutherford's model, what is an atom *mostly* made of?

_____

_____

✔ **Reading Check**

9. Identify What type of charge do neutrons have?

_____

_____

Improving the Atomic Model

A scientist named Niels Bohr found that electrons are arranged in energy levels in an atom. The figure shows his model. The lowest energy level is closest to the nucleus. It can have only two electrons. Higher energy levels are farther from the nucleus. They can have more than two electrons. To explain these energy levels, some scientists thought that electrons might orbit, or travel, around the atom's nucleus. The electrons were thought to travel in paths that are specific distances from the nucleus. This is similar to how the planets travel around the Sun.

Bohr's Model of an Atom

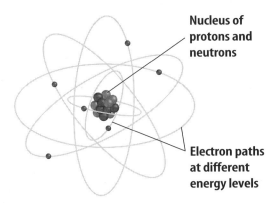

Nucleus of protons and neutrons

Electron paths at different energy levels

What is the modern atomic model?

Today, scientists realize that electrons have characteristics similar to both waves and particles. So, electrons do not orbit the nucleus of an atom in paths. Instead, electrons move in a cloud around the nucleus, as shown in the figure. The dark area shows where the electron is most likely to be in the electron cloud.

Modern Model of an Atom

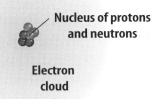

Nucleus of protons and neutrons

Electron cloud

Copyright © Glencoe/McGraw-Hill, a division of The McGraw-Hill Companies, Inc.

Picture This

10. **Compare and Contrast** How is Bohr's atomic model different from the modern atomic model?

Bohr's model:

_____

_____

Modern model:

_____

_____

● After You Read

Mini Glossary

atom: a small particle that makes up most types of matter

electron: an invisible particle with a negative charge around the nucleus of an atom

law of conservation of matter: matter is not created or destroyed—matter only changes form

matter: anything that has mass and takes up space

neutron: (NEW trahn) a neutral particle in the nucleus of an atom

nucleus: (NEW klee us) the positively charged, central part of an atom

proton: positively charged particle in the nucleus of an atom

1. Review the terms and their definitions in the Mini Glossary. Write a sentence to explain the law of conservation of matter.

_____

_____

2. Fill in each blank in the concept map.

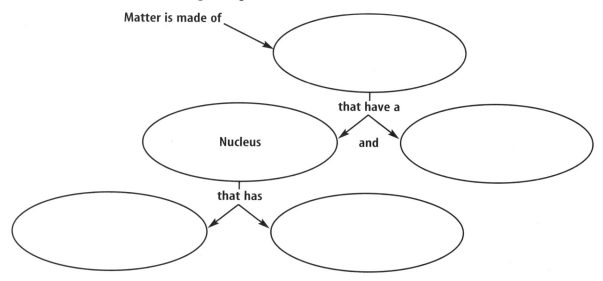

Matter is made of

that have a

Nucleus and

that has

3. How could you explain the modern atomic model to another student?

_____

_____

_____

 **Science Online** Visit **red.msscience.com** to access your textbook, interactive games, and projects to help you learn more about the structure of matter.

 End of Section

 **chapter 4**

Atoms, Elements, and the Periodic Table

section ❷ The Simplest Matter

What You'll Learn

- about elements in the periodic table
- what atomic mass and atomic number are
- what an isotope is
- about metals, metalloids, and nonmetals

◀ **Mark the Text**

Highlighting As you read, highlight the main ideas under each heading. After you finish reading, review the main ideas of the lesson.

Applying Math

1. **Calculate** About how many elements are synthetic elements?

● Before You Read

Have you ever taken something apart to see what it was made of? Describe a time when you did this.

_____

_____

● Read to Learn

The Elements

An **element** is matter made of only one kind of atom. For example, gold is made of only gold atoms. At least 115 elements are known. About 90 elements are found naturally on Earth, for example, oxygen, nitrogen, and gold. Some elements are not found in nature. These are called synthetic elements. Synthetic elements are used in smoke detectors and heart pacemaker batteries.

The Periodic Table

How would you find a certain book in a library? If you look at the books on the shelves as you walk past, you probably won't find the book you want. Libraries organize the books to help you quickly find the ones you want.

Scientists organize information about the elements, too. They created a chart called the periodic table of the elements. Each element in the chart has a chemical symbol. The symbols have one to three letters. The symbol for oxygen is O. The symbol for aluminum is Al. Scientists all over the world use these chemical symbols.

How are elements listed in the periodic table?

The periodic table has rows and columns that show how the elements relate to one another. The elements are grouped by their properties. The rows go from left to right and are called periods. The elements in a period have the same number of energy levels. The columns go up and down and are called groups. The elements in a group have similar properties related to their structures. They also tend to form similar bonds. The figure may help you remember the difference between periods and groups in the periodic table.

G
R
PERIOD
U
P

Picture This

2. Locate To help you remember the location of periods and groups in a periodic table, draw an arrow pointing left and right through PERIOD. Then draw an arrow pointing up and down through GROUP.

Identifying Characteristics

Each element is different and has unique properties. These differences can be described by looking at the relationships between the atomic particles, or parts of the atoms, in each element. Numbers in the periodic table describe these relationships.

What is the atomic number of an element?

The figure shows the periodic table block for chlorine. The symbol for chlorine is Cl. The number at the top, 17, is the atomic number for chlorine. The <u>atomic number</u> is the number of protons in the nucleus of each atom of an element. So, every chlorine atom has 17 protons in its nucleus. Each element in the periodic table has a different atomic number. This means that each element has a different number of protons in its nucleus. ✓

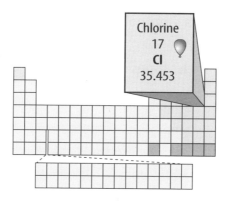

Chlorine
17
Cl
35.453

Picture This

3. Locate Circle the atomic number for chlorine in the periodic table block.

✔ Reading Check

4. Define What does the atomic number of an atom represent?

_____

_____

_____

What is an isotope?

The atomic number, or number of protons in the nucleus, is always the same for an element. But the number of neutrons in the nucleus is not always the same. For example, some chlorine atoms have 18 neutrons and some have 20 neutrons. Chlorine-35 is a chlorine atom that has 18 neutrons. Chlorine-37 has 20 neutrons. These two chlorine atoms are isotopes. <u>Isotopes</u> (I suh tohps) are atoms of the same element that have different numbers of neutrons.

Picture This

5. Read a Table How many neutrons does chlorine-37 have?

_____

What is a mass number?

You can refer to a certain isotope by using its mass number. An atom's **mass number** is the number of protons plus the number of neutrons in its nucleus. Look at the table below. Chlorine-35 has a mass number of 35 because the number of protons (17) plus the number of neutrons (18) equals 35. The isotope is named chlorine-35 because its mass number is 35.

Isotope	Number of protons		Number of neutrons	Mass number
Chlorine-35:	17	+	18	35
Chlorine-37:	17	+	20	37

Every particle in the nucleus adds to the mass of an atom. So, if an atom has more neutrons, its mass is greater. If it has fewer neutrons, its mass is less. The mass of chlorine-37 is greater than the mass of chlorine-35.

Hydrogen is the first element in the periodic table. Hydrogen has three isotopes with mass numbers of 1, 2, and 3, shown below. Every hydrogen atom always has one proton. Each isotope has a different number of neutrons.

Picture This

6. Understanding Figures What is the mass number of the hydrogen isotope deuterium?

Isotopes of Hydrogen

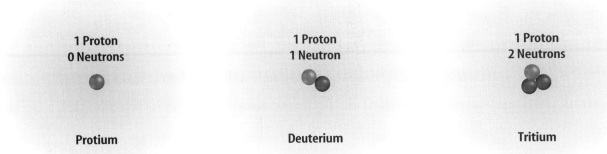

1 Proton 0 Neutrons	1 Proton 1 Neutron	1 Proton 2 Neutrons
Protium	Deuterium	Tritium

What is atomic mass?

The number below an element's chemical symbol is the atomic mass. **Atomic mass** is the average mass of all the isotopes of an element. The atomic mass takes into account how often the isotopes are found. For chlorine, the atomic mass is 35.45 u. The letter _u_ stands for "atomic mass unit," the unit of measure for atomic mass.

Classification of Elements

The elements are divided into three classes or categories—metals, metalloids (ME tuh loydz), and nonmetals. The elements in each category have similar properties.

What are some properties of metals?

<u>Metals</u> are elements that have a shiny or metallic appearance and are good conductors of heat and electricity. All metals, except mercury, are solids at room temperature. Metals also are malleable (MAL yuh bul). Malleable means they can be bent and pounded into shapes. Metals are ductile. Ductile means they can be stretched into wires without breaking. Gold, silver, iron, copper, and lead are examples of metals. Most of the elements in the periodic table are metals. ☑

What are some properties of nonmetals?

<u>Nonmetals</u> are elements that usually look dull and are poor conductors of heat and electricity. They are brittle, which means they cannot change shape easily without breaking. You cannot stretch or bend brittle materials. Many nonmetals are gases at room temperature.

Nonmetals are important to life. Look at the figure. More than 97 percent of your body is made up of different nonmetals. Examples of nonmetals include chlorine, oxygen, hydrogen, nitrogen, and carbon. Most of the elements on the right side of the periodic table are nonmetals.

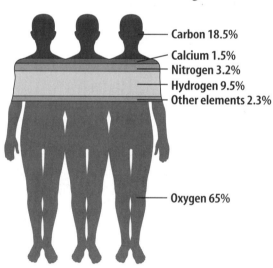

Carbon 18.5%
Calcium 1.5%
Nitrogen 3.2%
Hydrogen 9.5%
Other elements 2.3%
Oxygen 65%

What are some properties of metalloids?

<u>Metalloids</u> are elements that have properties of both metals and nonmetals. All metalloids are solids at room temperature. Some metalloids are shiny. Many metalloids can conduct heat and electricity, but not as well as metals can. On the periodic table, metalloids are found between metals and nonmetals. Silicon is an example of a metalloid. It is used in electronic circuits in computers and televisions.

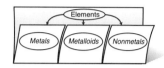

FOLDABLES™

B Compare and Contrast
Make the Foldable below to help you understand how metals, metalloids, and nonmetals are alike and different.

☑ **Reading Check**

7. Conclude Most of the elements in the periodic table are metals. Is this sentence true or false? Circle your answer.
True   False

Picture This
8. Compare Which nonmetal is found the most in your body?

_____

● After You Read

Mini Glossary

atomic mass: the average mass of all the isotopes of an element

atomic number: the number of protons in the nucleus of each atom of an element

element: matter made of only one kind of atom

isotope: (I suh tohps) atoms of the same element that have a different number of neutrons

mass number: the number of protons plus the number of neutrons in the nucleus of each atom of an element

metalloids: elements that have properties of both metals and nonmetals

metals: elements that have a shiny, or metallic, appearance and are good conductors of heat and electricity

nonmetals: elements that usually looks dull and are poor conductors of heat and electricity

1. Review the terms and their definitions in the Mini Glossary. Which two terms describe numbers that appear in an element's square on the periodic table?

   _____

2. Complete the table to identify properties of metals, metalloids, and nonmetals.

Properties	Metals	Metalloids	Nonmetals
Appearance—how they look			
Ability to conduct heat and electricity			
Ability to bend and stretch			

3. You were asked to highlight the main ideas under each heading. How did you decide what the main ideas were?

   _____

   _____

End of Section

 Science ⊕nline Visit **red.msscience.com** to access your textbook, interactive games, and projects to help you learn more about elements and the periodic table.

Copyright © Glencoe/McGraw-Hill, a division of The McGraw-Hill Companies, Inc.

Atoms, Elements, and the Periodic Table

section ❸ Compounds and Mixtures

● Before You Read

If you mix together salt and water, what happens to the salt? What happens to the water?

_____

_____

_____

What You'll Learn

■ what a compound is
■ how different types of mixtures are similar and different

● Read to Learn

Substances

Scientists classify matter depending on what it is made of and how it behaves. Matter that has the same composition and properties throughout is a **substance.** Elements such as gold and aluminum are substances. Substances also can be two or more elements combined, like brass. Brass is made of copper and zinc.

What is a compound?

A **compound** is a substance whose smallest unit is made up of atoms of more than one element bonded together. Water is a compound. It is made up of hydrogen and oxygen. Hydrogen and oxygen are both colorless gases. But, when they are combined, they make water. Water is sometimes written as H_2O. H stands for hydrogen and O stands for oxygen. Many compounds have properties that are different from those of its elements. For example, water is different from the gases hydrogen and oxygen. It also is different from hydrogen peroxide (H_2O_2), another compound made from hydrogen and oxygen.

◀ **Study Coach**

Create a Quiz As you read this section, write a quiz question for each paragraph. After you finish reading the section, answer your quiz questions.

FOLDABLES

❻ Identify Make the following Foldables from quarter-sheets of notebook paper to help you identify the differences between H_2O, C_2O, and CO.

What is a chemical formula?

Compounds have chemical formulas. A chemical formula shows the elements that make up a compound. It also shows how many atoms of each element are in the compound. For example, H_2O is the chemical formula of water. The small number to the right of an element tells how many atoms are in one unit, or molecule, of that compound. When no number is written, the molecule has one atom of that element. So, a molecule of water is made up of two atoms of hydrogen and one atom of oxygen.

H_2O_2 is the chemical formula for hydrogen peroxide. It has two hydrogen atoms and two oxygen atoms. So, the elements hydrogen and oxygen form two compounds—water and hydrogen peroxide. Look at the figures below to see the differences in their structure. The properties of water are very different from the properties of hydrogen peroxide.

Picture This

1. Circle the chemical formula in each figure.

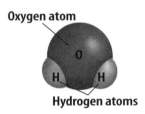

Oxygen atom

Hydrogen atoms

H_2O Water

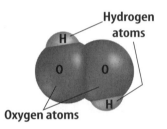

Hydrogen atoms

Oxygen atoms

H_2O_2 Hydrogen Peroxide

Think it Over

2. Identify What is the chemical formula for carbon dioxide?

Are compounds always the same?

A given compound always is made of the same elements and in the same proportion, or ratio. For example, one unit of water is always made of two hydrogen atoms and one oxygen atom. You can write the number of molecules of water that you have by putting a number in front of the formula. So, 6 H_2O means you have six molecules of water.

Mixtures

A mixture is made when two or more substances come together but do not combine to make a new substance. The substances can be elements, compounds, or elements and compounds. The proportions of the substances in a mixture can be changed without changing the identity of the mixture, unlike in a compound. Sand and water form a mixture. If you add more sand to the mixture, you still have a mixture of sand and water.

Air Another example of a mixture is air. Air is made of nitrogen, oxygen, and many other gases. There can be different amounts of these gases in the mixture. But you still have a mixture of air.

You see mixtures every day. A salad of lettuce, tomatoes, and cucumbers is a mixture. The mixture may have more tomatoes than cucumbers, but it is still a salad.

How can mixtures be separated?

You can separate many mixtures. A mixture of solids can be separated by using different screens or filters. For example, you could separate a mixture of pebbles and sand by pouring the mixture through a screen. The screen can catch the pebbles, but let the sand go through.

You also can use a liquid to separate some mixtures of solids. If you add water to a mixture of sugar and sand, only the sugar will dissolve in the water. Then, you can pour the mixture through a filter that catches the sand. Next, you can separate the sugar from the water by heating it. As shown in the figure, even your blood is a mixture that can be separated.

What are homogeneous and heterogeneous mixtures?

Homogeneous Mixtures Homogeneous means "the same throughout." So, homogeneous mixtures are those that look the same throughout. You cannot see the different parts of the mixture. Since you can't see the different parts, you might not know it is a mixture. Homogeneous mixtures can be solids, liquids, or gases. Brass, sugar water, and air are mixtures.

Heterogeneous Mixtures Heterogeneous means "completely different." Heterogeneous mixtures have larger parts that are different from each other. You can see the different parts of a heterogeneous mixture. Vegetable soup is a heterogeneous mixture. ☑

FOLDABLES™

D **Contrast** Make the following 2-tab Foldable to help you learn the differences between homogeneous mixtures and heterogeneous mixtures.

✔ Reading Check

3. **Explain** How is a heterogeneous mixture different from a homogeneous mixture?

_____

_____

_____

● After You Read

Mini Glossary

compound: a substance whose smallest unit is made up of atoms of more than one element bonded together

mixture: made when two or more substances come together but do not combine to make a new substance

substance: matter that has the same composition and properties throughout

1. Review the terms and definitions in the Mini Glossary. In your own words, describe the difference between a compound and a mixture.

_____

_____

_____

2. Complete the chart below to compare the substances discussed in this section.

Substance	Definition	Examples
Element		
Compound		
Mixture		

Copyright © Glencoe/McGraw-Hill, a division of The McGraw-Hill Companies, Inc.

End of Section

Science Online Visit **red.msscience.com** to access your textbook, interactive games, and projects to help you learn more about compounds and mixtures.

 **Motion, Forces, and Simple Machines**

section ❶ Motion

◉ Before You Read

You move all the time. How fast do you think you can walk? How fast can you run? How fast can you ride a bike?

_____

_____

◉ Read to Learn

Speed

Suppose you are riding a bike in a very hilly area. How can you tell how fast the bike is moving? You need to know two things. You need to know the distance, or how far, the bicycle has traveled. You also need to know how much time it took to travel that far.

What is average speed?

Suppose you ride the bike for one mile. You might speed up or slow down. How do you describe how fast you are going? One way is to find your average speed. **Average speed** is the distance traveled divided by the time it takes to travel the distance. Here is the equation for speed:

$$\text{average speed (in m/s)} = \frac{\text{distance traveled (in m)}}{\text{travel time (in s)}}$$

$$s = \frac{d}{t}$$

Units of speed are always a distance unit divided by a time unit. In the example above, the distance is in meters. The time is in seconds. So, the speed unit is meters per second.

What You'll Learn
- to describe speed and acceleration
- how acceleration is related to change in speed
- to calculate distance, speed, and acceleration

▸ **Mark the Text**

Highlight Definitions
Highlight the definitions and equations as you read this section. When you finish reading, review the equations to make sure you understand how to use them.

FOLDABLES

ⓐ **Compare and Contrast**
Make the following three-tab Foldable to understand how speed, velocity, and acceleration are similar and different.

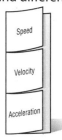

How do you find average speed?

Suppose that it takes you 30 minutes to ride your bike to your friend's house. Your friend lives 9 km away. Find the average speed for your trip to your friend's house.

You know: • the distance, d, is 9 km
• the time, t, is 30 min or 0.5 h

You want to find: • the speed, s, in km/h

Use the equation for average speed.

$$s = \frac{d}{t}$$

$$s = \frac{9 \text{ km}}{0.5 \text{ h}} = 18 \text{ km/h}$$

Check your answer. Multiply the speed by the time. You should get the distance.

$$18 \text{ km/h} \times 0.5 \text{ h} = 9 \text{ km} \checkmark$$

What is instantaneous speed?

Average speed doesn't give the details of the motion. Suppose you and your family traveled 640 km in 8 h. Your average speed is 80 km/h. But you may not have driven 80 km/h for 8 hours straight. You might have stopped to eat.

Sometimes, it is helpful to know how fast you are going at a certain time. For example, suppose the speed limit is 100 km/h. Drivers need to make sure they aren't speeding. They need to know their instantaneous speed. **Instantaneous speed** is the speed of an object at any instant of time. The speedometer in a car shows instantaneous speed. ✔

What is constant speed?

When an object's instantaneous speed doesn't change, it is moving with constant speed. At constant speed, an object's instantaneous speed and average speed are the same. In space, objects such as spacecraft may travel at constant speed.

How do you calculate distance?

In the example at the top of the page, how did you check your answer? You multiplied the speed by the time. You can use the same equation to find the distance that an object travels when it moves at constant speed. When both sides of the average speed equation are multiplied by time, you get the distance equation.

distance traveled (m) = **average speed** (m/s) × **time** (s)

$$d = st$$

💡 Think it Over

1. **Explain** When you go on a long car trip, why might the average speed be different than the speed you saw on the speedometer?

_____

_____

_____

✔ Reading Check

2. **Define** What is instantaneous speed?

_____

_____

_____

Velocity

Suppose you are walking on a street heading north. How would you describe your movement? To completely describe your movement, you would have to tell the speed you are moving and the direction of your motion. **Velocity** is the speed of an object and the direction of its motion.

Velocity changes when speed changes, direction of motion changes, or both change. Suppose you turn onto another street heading east, but keep walking at the same speed. Has your velocity changed? Yes, you are still walking at the same speed, but your direction of motion changed. This is a change in velocity.

Acceleration

At the top of a skateboard halfpipe, your speed and velocity are zero. When you skate down, you speed up, going faster and faster. How can you describe how your speed is changing? What if you change direction? How can you describe how your velocity is changing? You can describe the change with acceleration. **Acceleration** is the change in velocity divided by the time needed for the change to happen.

The figure below shows examples of acceleration. In these examples, speed changes but the direction of motion stays the same. The direction of acceleration depends on whether the object is speeding up or slowing down. On the left, the marble rolls straight downhill. Its motion and acceleration are in the same direction. In the middle, the marble rolls in a straight line on a level surface with constant velocity. The acceleration is zero. On the right, the marble rolls straight uphill. Its motion and acceleration are in opposite directions because the marble is slowing down.

Copyright © Glencoe/McGraw-Hill, a division of The McGraw-Hill Companies, Inc.

Think it Over

3. Summarize What is the difference between speed and velocity?

_____

_____

Picture This

4. Explain Look at the picture of the marble rolling on a level ramp in the middle of the diagram. Why is the acceleration zero for this marble?

_____

_____

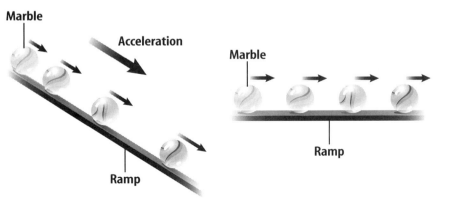

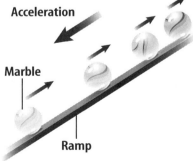

How do you calculate acceleration?

You can use a formula to calculate acceleration for an object that changes speed but not direction.

acceleration (in m/s^2)

$$= \frac{\textbf{final speed } (\text{in m/s}) - \textbf{initial speed } (\text{in m/s})}{\textbf{time } (\text{in s})}$$

$$a = \frac{(s_f - s_i)}{t}$$

The SI units for acceleration are m/s^2. This means meters/(seconds $\times$ seconds).

Suppose you are sledding down a snow-covered hill at 8 m/s. Then you hit a drop. Your speed increases to 18 m/s in 5 s. You can use the equation above to find your acceleration.

$$a = \frac{(s_f - s_i)}{t} = \frac{18 \text{ m/s} - 8 \text{ m/s}}{5 \text{ s}} = \frac{10 \text{ m/s}}{5 \text{ s}} = 2 \text{ m/s}^2$$

How do you graph speed?

Imagine you are inline skating down a hill, across a level valley, and then up another hill. If you graphed your speed over time, it would look like the graph below.

As you start downhill, your speed will increase with time (Part A). The line on the graph slopes upward because you are accelerating in the same direction as you are moving. When you travel across the level valley, you move at a constant speed (Part B). When your acceleration is zero, the line on the graph is flat, or horizontal. When you start to go up the hill, your speed decreases (Part C). The line on the graph slopes downward because you are accelerating in the opposite direction of your motion. ☑

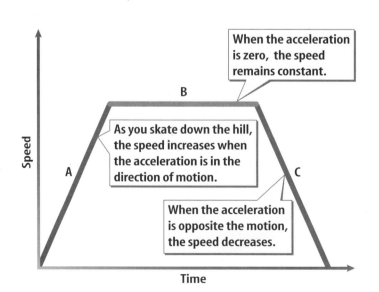

When the acceleration is zero, the speed remains constant.

As you skate down the hill, the speed increases when the acceleration is in the direction of motion.

When the acceleration is opposite the motion, the speed decreases.

Copyright © Glencoe/McGraw-Hill, a division of The McGraw-Hill Companies, Inc.

Applying Math

5. Evaluate What would the acceleration be if it took 10 seconds to go from 8 m/s to 18 m/s?

_____

Picture This

6. Interpret Graphs
What does a graph of speed over time look like when acceleration is going in the same direction as motion?

_____

_____

● After You Read

Mini Glossary

acceleration: change in velocity divided by the time needed for the change to happen

average speed: equals the distance traveled divided by the time it takes to travel the distance

instantaneous speed: the speed of an object at any instant of time

velocity: the speed of an object and the direction of its motion

1. Review the terms and their definitions in the Mini Glossary. Which term helps you know whether you are speeding in a car?

   _____

   _____

2. Fill in the graphic organizer with the equations.

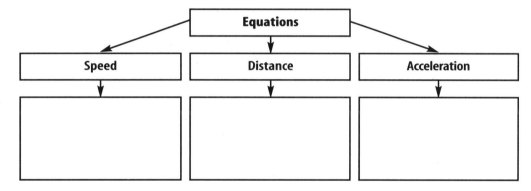

3. At the beginning of the section, you were asked to highlight important definitions and equations in this section. How did this help you learn about the topics of the lesson?

   _____

   _____

   _____

 Visit **red.msscience.com** to access your textbook, interactive games, and projects to help you learn more about motion.

End of Section

chapter 5

Motion, Forces, and Simple Machines

section 2 Newton's Laws of Motion

What You'll Learn

- how forces affect motion
- how to calculate acceleration
- Newton's second and third laws of motion

◄ Study Coach

Outline As you read each section, create an outline of the section. Use the headings in the text in your outline.

FOLDABLES

B Organize Information
Make the following Foldable out of two sheets of notebook paper to organize information about Newton's laws of motion.

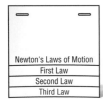

● Before You Read

You see objects move all the time. What do you think makes them move?

_____

_____

● Read to Learn

Force

What causes objects to move? Why does a chair in the lunchroom move when you pull on it? Forces cause things to move. A **force** is a push or a pull. Force is measured in the SI units newtons (N). One newton is about the amount of force it takes to lift a quarter-pound hamburger.

How are force and acceleration related?

Force causes an object's motion to change. When force is put on, or applied to an object, the object accelerates. When you throw a ball, your hand applies a force to the ball. The force causes the ball to speed up, or accelerate.

A force also can change the direction of an object's motion. After you throw a ball, its path curves downward until the ball hits the ground, as shown in the figure. The path curves and the ball hits the ground because of gravity. The force of gravity actually causes the ball to accelerate.

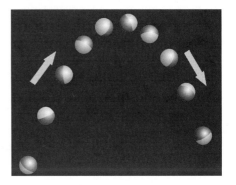

Acceleration is related to a change in velocity. The force of gravity causes the ball to change its velocity. This is acceleration. If an object accelerates, a force must have been applied to it.

What are balanced and unbalanced forces?

Suppose you and your friend both push on a wooden box. When more than one force acts on an object, the forces combine. Combined forces make a net force. The combined forces may be balanced or unbalanced. ☑

Balanced Forces Look at the first figure below. What happens if you and your friend push with the same force on the box in opposite directions? The box does not move. The forces are balanced—their effects cancel each other out and they do not cause change in an object's motion. With balanced forces, the net force is zero.

Unbalanced Forces How would things change if you pushed harder on the box than your friend? Look at the second figure. You and your friend are still pushing on the box in opposite directions. But the forces are unbalanced because you are pushing harder. The forces do not cancel each other out. To find the net force of two unbalanced forces, find the difference between the two forces. The motion is in the direction of the stronger force.

Look at the third figure. You and your friend both push in the same direction. When the combined forces are in the same direction, the net force equals the combined forces added together.

☑ Reading Check

1. Summarize What is a net force?

_____

_____

_____

Picture This

2. Explain Why is the net force on the box zero?

_____

_____

_____

Newton's Laws of Motion

Sir Isaac Newton was 23 years old in 1665. His college closed for a while because of the plague that was spreading through Europe. When he was home, he observed nature and did simple experiments. He made many discoveries. He figured out how to explain the effects of gravity. He also explained how and why objects move. **Newton's laws of motion** are a set of ideas that explain the motion of objects.

Newton's First Law

When you give a book on a table a push, it slides then stops. You might think that to keep an object moving, a net force must always be pushing on it. But Newton discovered that this isn't true.

Newton and some other scientists realized that an object can be moving even if no net force is acting on it. Newton's first law of motion says that an object will not change its motion unless an unbalanced force acts on it. Think of a book sitting on a desk. It will keep sitting on the desk until something pushes or pulls it.

What if an object is already moving, like the book on a table that you gave a push? Newton's first law says that the motion of the book won't change unless an unbalanced force acts on it. Once the book is moving, a force has to act on it to make it speed up, slow down, or change directions. So a moving object moves in a straight line with constant speed until an unbalanced force acts on it.

What is friction?

What causes the book to stop sliding on the table? Newton's first law says that an unbalanced force must be acting on the book. Otherwise, the book would keep sliding in a straight line. The force is called friction. **Friction** is a force between two surfaces that are touching that makes it difficult for the two surfaces to move past each other. Friction always acts opposite to the direction of motion. When friction acts on an object, you have to keep pushing or pulling on the object to overcome the force of friction. ☑

The amount of the friction force depends on the surfaces involved. Rough surfaces have more friction than smooth surfaces. For example, when you hit a hockey puck on smooth ice, it moves a long way before it stops. If you hit the puck with the same force on rough carpet, it will barely move.

Think it Over

3. Explain How does Newton's first law explain why a book stays sitting on a table without moving?

_____

_____

_____

✔ Reading Check

4. Explain What is the force that stops the sliding of the book?

_____

What is inertia and how is it related to mass?

You know that it is hard to move a heavy object, like a refrigerator. What if a heavy object were rolling toward you? Could you easily stop it? Heavy objects are hard to move and hard to stop moving because of inertia. **Inertia** is the tendency of an object to resist change in motion. The word tendency means a way that something usually behaves. ☑

You already know that it is hard to move or stop a heavy object. It is easier to move and stop a light object. The more matter, or mass, an object has, the harder it is to move or stop. The more mass an object has, the greater its inertia.

Newton's Second Law

Newton's second law of motion states that if a net force is applied to an object, the object will accelerate in the direction of the net force. The acceleration equals the net force divided by the mass. You can use Newton's second law to calculate acceleration. ☑

$$\text{acceleration (in m/s}^2\text{)} = \frac{\textbf{net force (in N)}}{\textbf{mass (in kg)}}$$

$$a = \frac{F_{net}}{m}$$

How are mass and acceleration related?

An object's acceleration depends on its mass. The more mass an object has, the more inertia it has. The more inertia an object has, the harder it is to accelerate. Therefore, the more mass an object has, the harder it is to accelerate. Imagine that you push on an empty shopping cart. Then you push on a shopping cart that is full of soda cans with the same force. The full cart will have a smaller acceleration than the empty cart.

Newton's Third Law

Suppose you push on a wall. Did you know the wall pushes back on you? Newton's third law states that when one object applies a force on a second object, the second object applies an equal force in the opposite direction. What does this mean? When you walk, you push back on the floor. The floor pushes forward with an equal force. The forward force makes you move.

✔ **Reading Check**

5. Define What is inertia?

_____

_____

✔ **Reading Check**

6. Identify According to Newton's second law, what is acceleration equal to?

_____

_____

💡 **Think it Over**

7. Apply Imagine you were buying a bicycle and you wanted one that accelerated quickly. Would you buy a heavy bike or light bike? Explain.

_____

_____

_____

Picture This

8. Label Write *action force* and *reaction force* above the correct arrows in the figure.

_____

_____

_____

Think it Over

9. Summarize How does jumping from a boat explain Newton's third law?

_____

_____

_____

_____

✔ Reading Check

10. Identify Which of Newton's laws explains why a tool that is pushed by an astronaut would keep going in a straight line?

_____

The force applied by the first object is the action force. The force applied by the second object is the reaction force. In the figure, the action force is the swimmer pushing on the pool wall. The reaction force is the pool wall pushing on the swimmer. The action and reaction forces are equal, but in opposite directions.

Why don't pairs of forces cancel?

How does anything move if forces always happen in equal and opposite pairs? Won't the forces acting on an object always cancel each other? Remember that, according to Newton's third law, two objects apply equal but opposite forces to each other. When you walk, you apply a force to the floor. The floor applies a force on you. Because the forces act on different objects, they don't cancel.

What are examples of Newton's third law?

If you jump from a small boat, the boat moves back. You push the boat back with your feet. The boat pushes you forward with the same force. You have more mass than the boat, so the boat accelerates more than you. If you jump from a big boat with a large mass, the force you apply to the boat gives it only a tiny acceleration. Your mass is much less than the boat's, so you accelerate more than the big boat.

How do Newton's laws work in space?

Newton's laws are sometimes easier to understand if you think about their effects in space. In space, little gravity or friction acts on objects. For example, if an astronaut on a spacewalk pushes a tool away, Newton's first law states the tool will keep moving until another force acts upon it. With little gravity and friction, the tool would keep going in a straight line away from the astronaut. ☑

Newton's second law explains why spacecraft stay in orbit. Gravity exerts a force on a spacecraft, causing it to accelerate. This causes the spacecraft's motion to constantly change, so it circles around Earth, instead of flying straight away.

Newton's third law explains how rocket engines work. The spacecraft applies an action force to burning fuels, pushing them out of the engine. The upward force exerted on the rocket by the gases is the reaction force.

◉ After You Read

Mini Glossary

force: a push or a pull

friction: a force between two surfaces that are touching each other that makes it more difficult for the two surfaces to move past each other

inertia: the tendency of an object to resist change in motion

Newton's laws of motion: a set of ideas that explains the motion of objects

1. Review the terms and their definitions in the Mini Glossary. Write a sentence using the terms *force* and *friction*.

_____

_____

2. Match the laws of motion with the correct examples. Write the letter of each law of motion in **Column 2** on the line in front of the example it matches in **Column 1**.

Understanding Newton's Laws of Motion

Column 1	Column 2
____ 1. When you throw a baseball, it accelerates up, then begins to accelerate down until it hits the ground.	a. Newton's first law of motion
____ 2. A boulder sitting in a field does not move until a force acts upon it.	b. Newton's second law of motion
____ 3. When you jump off of a skateboard, you move forward and the skateboard moves backward.	c. Newton's third law of motion

3. If it were possible for your class to go into space, why might it be easier to see examples of Newton's laws of motion in space?

_____

_____

_____

  Visit **red.msscience.com** to access your textbook, interactive games, and projects to help you learn more about Newton's laws of motion.

End of Section

Motion, Forces, and Simple Machines

section ❸ Work and Simple Machines

What You'll Learn

■ how to define work
■ different types of simple machines
■ how machines make work easier

● Before You Read

Did you do work today? Write your own definition of work on the lines below.

_____

_____

_____

Study Coach

Create a Quiz As you read the text under each heading, write questions to help you remember the important information. When you finish reading, answer the questions to quiz yourself on what you learned.

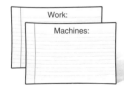

● Compare and Contrast

Make the following note card Foldables out of two half-sheets of paper. Write down information to help you understand how work and machines are related.

> Work:
> Machines:

● Read to Learn

Work

You may think of work as doing chores or even doing your homework. However, in science there is a certain definition for work. In science, **work** is done when a force causes an object to move in the same direction as the force that is applied. Some of what you may think of as work does not include applying a force.

Why doesn't effort always equal work?

If you push against a wall, do you do work? Two things must happen for work to be done. First, a force must be applied to an object. Second, the object must move in the same direction as the force that is applied. If the wall does not move, no work is done.

You do work when you pick a box up from the floor. What happens if you walk forward with the box? Your arms still apply an upward force to the box. But the box does not move up. It moves forward. The motion of the box is not the same as the direction of the force applied by your arms. No work is being done by your arms.

Calculating Work

The amount of work done depends on the amount of force applied and the distance. Does it take more work to lift a shoe or a stack of books 1 m in the air? The distance is the same, but it takes more force to move the stack of books. So more work is done lifting the books. You can calculate work with the following equation.

$$\textbf{work} \text{ (in J)} = \textbf{force} \text{ (in N)} \times \textbf{distance} \text{ (in m)}$$
$$w = Fd$$

Work is measured in joules (J). One joule is about the amount of work it takes to lift a baseball from the ground to your waist.

What is a machine?

How many machines have you used today? A machine is a device that makes work easier. A hand can opener is a machine. It changes a small force applied by your hand into a larger force that makes it easier to open a can.

A **simple machine** is a machine that uses only one movement. A screwdriver is a simple machine. The pulley, lever, wheel and axle, inclined plane, wedge, and screw are all simple machines. A **compound machine** is a combination of simple machines. The hand can opener is a compound machine. Machines make work easier in two ways. They can change the size of the force you apply. They also can change the direction of the force.

What is mechanical advantage?

Some machines can increase the force you apply. The **mechanical advantage** (MA) of a machine is the number of times the applied force is increased by the machine. The force you apply to a machine is the input force (F_i). On a can opener, the input force is the force you apply when turning the handles. The can opener changes your input force to the force pushing the blade into the metal can. The force applied by a machine is the output force (F_o). The mechanical advantage of a machine is the ratio of the output force to the input force. ☑

$$\text{mechanical advantage} = \frac{\text{force out (in N)}}{\text{force in (in N)}}$$
$$MA = \frac{F_o}{F_i}$$

Copyright © Glencoe/McGraw-Hill, a division of The McGraw-Hill Companies, Inc.

> ### 💡 Think it Over
>
> 1. **Compare and Contrast** What is the difference between a simple machine and a compound machine?
>
> _____
>
> _____
>
> _____

> ### ☑ Reading Check
>
> 2. **Explain** Is mechanical advantage the number of times the applied force by a machine is increased or decreased?
>
> _____

3. **Recognize Cause and Effect** When a machine increases force, what must change?

_____

_____

What is an ideal machine?

In a simple machine, the input force and the output force do work. An ideal machine is one in which there is no friction. The work done by the input force is equal to the work done by the output force in an ideal machine.

How do machines increase force?

Simple machines can change a small input force into a large output force. How is this possible? Work equals force times distance—$W = Fd$. Look at the equation. If a machine increases force, but work stays the same, then the distance over which the force was applied must change. ✔

So how does a machine change distance? Think of a can opener. When you apply force to the handles, they might move 1 cm. But when the blade punches through the metal, it might move only 1 or 2 mm. The distance decreased, so the force increased. The amount of work done stays the same.

In real machines, friction always happens when parts move. Friction changes some input work to heat. So for a real machine, work out (W_{out}) is always less than work in (W_{in}).

The Pulley

When you raise a window blind, you use a pulley. A **pulley** is an object, like a wheel, that has a groove with a rope or cable running through it. It changes the direction of the input force. Look at the first figure below. The pulley does not change the size of the input force. So, its mechanical advantage is 1.

With more than one pulley, mechanical advantage increases. The pulley system in the second figure has a mechanical advantage of 2. Each supporting rope holds half of the weight. So the input force needed to lift the block is half as large as with one pulley.

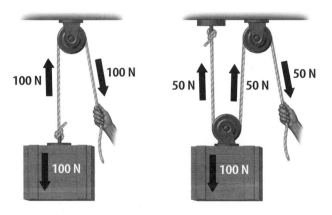

FOLDABLES™

ⓓ Organize Information
Make six half-book Foldables like the one below to help you organize information about simple machines. Label the Foldables *Pulley, Lever, Wheel and Axle, Inclined Plane, Wedge,* and *Screw.*

Pulley

Picture This

4. **Explain** Why is the force needed to lift the box only 50 N when two pulleys are used?

_____

_____

The Lever

The lever might be the first simple machine invented by humans. A **lever** is a rod or plank that pivots about a fixed point. The pivot point is called the fulcrum. Levers increase force, or increase the distance over which a force is applied. There are three types, or classes, of levers. The three classes are shown in the figure below.

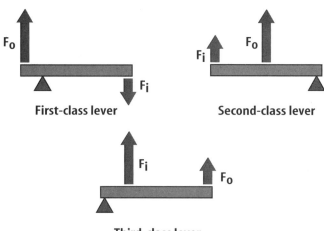

First-class lever

Second-class lever

Third-class lever

First Class In a first-class lever, the fulcrum is between the input force and the output force. A first class lever is usually used to increase force. Using a screwdriver to pry open the lid of a paint can is an example of a first class lever.

Second Class In a second-class lever, the output force is between the input force and the fulcrum. The output force is always greater than the input force. A wheelbarrow is an example of a second-class lever.

Third Class In third-class levers, the input force is between the output force and the fulcrum. Third-class levers increase the distance over which input force is applied. A hockey stick is a third-class lever.

What is a wheel and axle?

Try turning a doorknob by holding the narrow base of the knob. It is much easier to turn the larger knob. A doorknob is a wheel and axle. A wheel and axle is made of two round objects that are attached and rotate together around the same axis, or point. The larger object is the wheel. The smaller object is the axle. To find the mechanical advantage of a wheel and axle, divide the radius of the wheel by the radius of the axle.

<u>Picture This</u>

5. **Identify** In what type of lever is the fulcrum between the input and output forces?

 **Think it Over**

6. **Apply** What is another example of a wheel and axle?

_____

The Inclined Plane

A ramp, or **inclined plane,** is a sloped surface. Inclined planes decrease the input force needed by increasing the distance. Imagine lifting a couch into a truck. It is easier if you use a ramp. It takes less force to push a couch up a ramp than to lift it. Either way, the work needed to move the couch is the same. ☑

The mechanical advantage of an inclined plane is the length of the inclined plane divided by the height of the inclined plane. The longer the ramp, the less force it takes to move the object.

How are wedges and screws related to inclined planes?

A wedge is a moving inclined plane with one or two sloping sides. A basic wedge is shown in the first figure below. Your front teeth are wedges. A wedge changes the direction of an input force. When you bite an apple, the downward input force is changed by your teeth to a sideways force that splits the apple. Axes and knives are also wedges.

A screw is an inclined plane wrapped around a post, as shown in the second figure below. The inclined plane forms the screw threads. A screw changes the direction of the force you apply. It also increases the distance over which the force is applied. The turning input force is changed to a pulling output force that pulls the screw into the material. Friction between the threads and material holds the screw in place.

Copyright © Glencoe/McGraw-Hill, a division of The McGraw-Hill Companies, Inc.

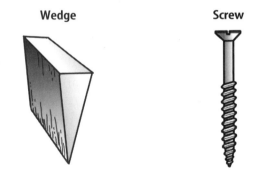

Wedge   Screw

✔ Reading Check

7. Summarize How do inclined planes decrease the input force needed?

_____

_____

Picture This

8. Highlight In the figure showing a screw, use a highlighter to trace the inclined plane wrapped around the post.

⬤ After You Read

Mini Glossary

compound machine: a combination of simple machines

inclined plane: a sloped surface, sometimes called a ramp

lever: a rod or plank that pivots about a fixed point. The pivot point is called the fulcrum

mechanical advantage: (of a machine) the number of times the applied force is increased

pulley: an object, like a wheel, that has a groove with a rope or cable running through it

simple machine: a machine that uses only one movement

work: is done when a force causes an object to move in the same direction as the force that is applied

1. Review the terms and their definitions in the Mini Glossary. Give an example of a simple machine and how you would use it.

_____

_____

2. Match the examples with the correct simple machine. Write each simple machine on the line by the example it matches. Use each simple machine only once.

pulley   wheel and axle   lever   inclined plane   wedge   screw

1. _____

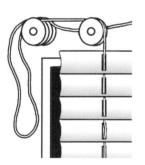

2. _____

3. _____

4. _____

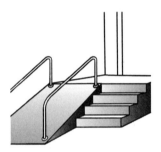

5. _____

6. _____

3. How would touching or using some of the simple machines that you read about in this lesson help you learn more about them?

_____

_____

End of Section

Science Online Visit **red.msscience.com** to access your textbook, interactive games, and projects to help you learn more about work and simple machines.

section ❶ Energy Changes

● Before You Read

On the lines below, write what you think it means when someone says they have a lot of energy.

_____

_____

● Read to Learn

Energy

Energy is a word you probably use every day. You might say eating a snack gives you energy. You might say a soccer player has a lot of energy. Did you know that a burning fire also has energy? A tank of gas and a bouncing ball have energy too.

What is energy?

The word _energy_ comes from the ancient Greek word _energos,_ which means "active." You probably have used the word _energy_ to mean active. **Energy** is the ability to cause change. Energy can change the temperature of a pot of water. Energy can change the speed and direction of a baseball. Energy in a thunderstorm makes lightning and thunder. You use energy when you change the speed of a bicycle by pedaling harder to go faster and by putting on the brakes. Energy also can change the arrangement of atoms in molecules and cause chemical reactions to happen.

Forms of Energy

Energy comes in different forms and from many different places. Food has chemical energy. Your body changes food into energy it needs to move, think, and grow. Nuclear power plants use energy in the nucleus of the atom to make electricity.

What You'll Learn

- what energy is
- about different forms of energy
- about kinetic energy and potential energy

◀ **Mark the Text**

Underline Underline different kinds of energy as you read about them. Then highlight an example of how that type of energy is used.

FOLDABLES™

Ⓐ Compare and Contrast
Use two quarter-sheets of notebook paper to compare and contrast information about kinetic energy and potential energy.

What is an energy transformation?

An energy transformation happens when energy changes from one form to another. Energy transformations, or changes, happen all around you all the time. They even happen inside you. You have chemical energy stored in your muscles. When you push on a bicycle pedal, this chemical energy changes to energy of motion.

What happens to a car sitting in sunlight? The energy in sunlight changes to heat energy. The heat energy warms the inside of the car. Rub your hands together quickly. What happens? Your hands feel warm. The energy you use to move your hands changes to heat energy.

When energy is transformed, the total amount of energy does not change. Energy cannot be lost or gained. Energy only changes form.

How are energy transformations used?

Early humans used the chemical energy in wood when they learned to build fires. They used the energy to cook and stay warm. Today, a gas stove changes the chemical energy in natural gas to heat energy. Heat energy from a gas stove is used to cook food.

You use energy transformations in other ways, too. A hair dryer changes electrical energy into heat energy. A lightbulb changes electrical energy into light and heat energy. The table shows some ways energy transformations are used.

Type of Energy	Device	How Energy Is Transformed
Chemical	Stove	Energy from natural gas is changed to heat and light energy.
Electrical	Lightbulb	Energy from an electric current is changed into heat energy.
Solar	Solar energy collector	Energy from sunlight is changed into heat energy.

Kinetic Energy

Suppose you are bowling. You roll the bowling ball down the lane toward the bowling pins. The moving bowling ball has energy because it can cause change. When the moving bowling ball hits the bowling pins, it causes the bowling pins to fall. The energy an object has because of its motion is **kinetic energy.** A football thrown by a quarterback has kinetic energy. A leaf falling from a tree also has kinetic energy. ☑

Think it Over

1. **Explain** How is sunlight an example of energy transformation?

_____

_____

Picture This

2. **Use a Table** What kind of energy does natural gas turn into?

_____

_____

What affects kinetic energy?

All moving objects have kinetic energy. Not all moving objects have the same amount of kinetic energy. The amount of kinetic energy an object has depends on the mass and the speed of the object.

Mass Suppose a small rock and a large boulder are rolling down a hill at the same speed. Which has more kinetic energy? What would happen if they hit something at the bottom of the hill? Would the boulder cause more damage, or the rock? The boulder would cause more damage. The boulder has more kinetic energy because it has more mass.

Speed The kinetic energy of an object also depends on speed. Imagine two bowling balls that are the same size rolling down two bowling lanes. One ball is rolling much faster than the other. The bowling ball that is rolling faster knocks down more pins, even though both bowling balls hit the pins at the same place. When more pins are knocked down, a greater change has happened. The bowling ball that rolls faster has more kinetic energy. Kinetic energy increases as speed increases.

How is kinetic energy transferred?

When objects hit each other, kinetic energy can be moved, or transferred, from one object to the other. Think about the energy in a bowling ball when it hits the pins. The bowling ball does not have to touch all of the pins to knock them all down. The kinetic energy of the bowling ball is transferred to a few pins. Then, these pins fall and bump into other pins. Kinetic energy of the ball transfers from pin to pin until all of the pins fall down.

Look at the figure. A transfer of kinetic energy takes place when dominoes fall. Tapping only the first domino in the row makes it fall against the next domino. The kinetic energy from the first domino is transferred to the second domino. Kinetic energy is transferred from domino to domino until the last one falls. The kinetic energy of the last domino is transferred to the table.

💡 **Think it Over**

4. **Predict** Two balls are rolling at the same speed. One ball has a mass of 5 kg. Another ball has a mass of 4 kg. Which ball has the greater kinetic energy?

_____

_____

Picture This

5. **Explain** What happens to the kinetic energy when you tap the first domino in a row of dominos?

_____

_____

Think it Over

6. **Explain** Why doesn't a skier standing at the top of a hill have any kinetic energy?

_____

_____

_____

Potential Energy

Look at the figure below. The ski lift takes a skier to the top of a hill. When the skier is standing at the top of the hill, she has no kinetic energy. But as she skis down the hill and moves faster, her kinetic energy increases.

Where does kinetic energy come from?

Gravity pulls the skier down the hill. If she were standing at the bottom of the hill, gravity would not start her moving. When the skier is standing at the top of the hill, she has a form of energy called potential energy. **Potential energy** is energy that is stored in an object because of the object's position. As the ski lift takes the skier up the hill, her potential energy increases. Potential energy is stored inside the skier before gravity pulls her down the hill. Changing her position increased her potential energy. The skier's potential energy gradually changes into kinetic energy as she skis down the hill.

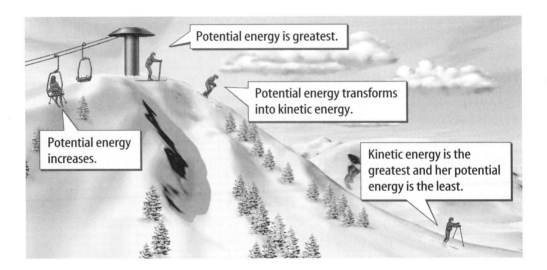

Potential energy is greatest.

Potential energy transforms into kinetic energy.

Potential energy increases.

Kinetic energy is the greatest and her potential energy is the least.

Picture This

7. **Explain** At what point on the hill is the skier's potential energy the least?

_____

_____ .

How can potential energy be increased?

When you lift an object higher than it was, it has the potential to fall. If it does fall, it has kinetic energy. To lift an object, you have to transfer energy to the object. The ski lift uses energy when it takes a skier up a hill. It transfers some energy to the skier. This energy is stored as potential energy in the skier. The potential energy changes to kinetic energy when the skier goes down the hill. The skier's potential energy would increase if she took a ski lift that went higher. The higher an object is lifted above Earth, the greater its potential energy.

Converting Potential and Kinetic Energy

Potential energy is transformed to kinetic energy when a skier skis down a hill. Kinetic energy can be transformed into potential energy. Suppose you throw a ball straight up into the air. Your muscles cause the ball to leave your hand and move up. The ball has kinetic energy because it is moving. Look at the figure below. As the ball gets higher, its potential energy increases. The ball slows down, and its kinetic energy decreases.

What happens when the ball reaches its highest point? It is hard to see, but the ball stops for an instant. The ball has no more kinetic energy when it stops. The kinetic energy it had when it left your hand has all changed into potential energy. Then, the ball falls back down. As the ball falls, its potential energy changes back into kinetic energy. If you catch the ball at the same height that you threw it from, the ball's kinetic energy is the same as when it left your hand.

Picture This

8. Interpret an Illustration Look at the figure. When does the kinetic energy of the ball increase? Circle your answer.

a. before it is thrown
b. right after it is thrown
c. when it reaches its highest point
d. as it is falling

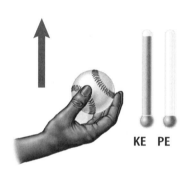

As the ball leaves the person's hand, it is moving the fastest and has greatest kinetic energy.

As the ball moves upward, it slows down as its kinetic energy is transformed into potential energy.

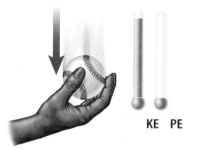

As the ball moves downward, it speeds up as its potential energy is transformed into kinetic energy.

How does energy change in falling water?

Have you ever stood close to a waterfall and listened to the roaring water? The water at the top of a waterfall has potential energy. The potential energy is transformed into kinetic energy as the water falls. ☑

The kinetic energy of falling water can be used to make, or generate, electricity. Dams are built on rivers. Water backs up behind a dam and forms a lake. The water near the top of the dam falls downward. Then, the water's kinetic energy spins generators that produce electricity. The water's potential energy behind the dam is transformed into kinetic energy and then into electrical energy.

✔ Reading Check

9. Determine What kind of energy does the water at the top of a waterfall have?

_____

10. Analyze When a ball that is rolling across a field stops, energy is lost. Is this sentence true or false? Explain.

_____

_____

_____

Conservation of Energy

Keeping track of energy as it is transformed can be hard. Sometimes it seems like energy disappears or is lost. But, that does not happen. In 1840, a scientist named James Joule showed that energy cannot be made or lost. The <u>law of conservation of energy</u> states that energy cannot be created or destroyed, but can only be transformed from one form to another. The total amount of energy in the universe never changes. Energy only changes form.

Kinetic energy can be changed into heat energy. This happens when two objects rub against each other. Suppose you push a book across a table. It will slow down and stop. But its kinetic energy is not lost. The book's kinetic energy is changed into heat energy as the book rubs against the table.

How can you keep track of energy changes?

Look at the figure. It shows how energy flows when a soccer ball is kicked. The soccer player's leg muscles have chemical energy. Chemical energy changes into kinetic energy when the soccer player swings her leg. The kinetic energy is transferred to the ball when she kicks the ball. After the ball rolls for a while, it stops. It seems like the kinetic energy of the ball has disappeared. But it has not. The ball's kinetic energy changed into heat energy. This happened when the ball rubbed against the grass as it rolled.

Picture This

11. Draw Conclusions
When is the kinetic energy of the soccer ball greatest—right after the ball is kicked, or as the ball rubs against the grass?

_____

_____

A moving soccer player has kinetic energy. Kinetic energy from the player's moving leg is transferred to the ball.

When the ball rolls, its kinetic energy is transformed by friction into heat as the ball rubs against the grass.

● After You Read

Mini Glossary

energy: ability to cause change

kinetic energy: energy an object has because of its motion

law of conservation of energy: energy cannot be created or destroyed, it can only be transformed from one form to another

potential energy: energy that is stored in an object because of the object's position

1. Read the vocabulary terms and their definitions in the Mini Glossary. Explain how potential energy can change to kinetic energy.

   _____

   _____

   _____

2. The figure below shows a marble on a ramp. In the boxes, describe the ways the potential energy and kinetic energy of the marble are changing.

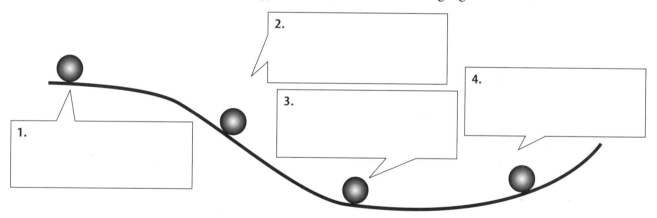

3. You were asked to underline different kinds of energy and then highlight an example of each. Did this strategy help you learn about the different forms of energy? Why or why not?

   _____

   _____

Science●nline Visit **red.msscience.com** to access your textbook, interactive games, and projects to help you learn more about energy changes.

End of Section

chapter 6

Energy

section ② Temperature

What You'll Learn
- the difference between temperature and heat
- ways heat is used
- how heat is transferred

Mark the Text

Identify Concepts Look at the section headings. Highlight each heading that asks a question as you read. Then, use a different color to highlight the answers to those questions.

FOLDABLES

B Organize Information
Make the three-tab Foldable to write information about conduction, convection, and radiation.

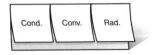

● Before You Read

Is it hot or cold today? On the lines below, explain why it feels hot or cold outside.

_____

_____

● Read to Learn

Temperature

You may have used the outside air temperature to decide what to wear. Some days are so hot you do not need to wear a jacket. Other days are so cold you want to bundle up. *Hot* and *cold* are words people use to describe temperature. But these words mean different things to different people. You might think it is hot when your friend thinks it is just right.

What is temperature?

Remember, any material or object is made up of atoms or molecules. These particles are always moving. Even the particles in your pencil and your desktop are moving. Particles move in all directions. In a gas, particles are spread far apart and can move freely. In a liquid, particles are closer together. They cannot move as far. In solids, particles are even closer together than in liquids. They vibrate, or move back and forth.

The particles in solids, liquids, and gases have kinetic energy because they are moving. The faster the particles are moving, the more kinetic energy they have.

Temperature is a measure of the average kinetic energy of the particles in an object. Gas molecules at a low temperature move slowly. Gas molecules at a higher temperature move faster. At the higher temperature, the molecules are moving faster and have more kinetic energy.

Measuring Temperature

You cannot measure temperature by how something feels. What feels warm to some people feels cool to other people. Recall that temperature is a measure of the average kinetic energy of the particles in an object. You cannot measure the kinetic energy of every atom. There are too many of them. Instead, thermometers are used to measure temperature.

What is the Fahrenheit scale?

The Fahrenheit (FAYR un hite) scale is a common temperature scale used in the United States. On this scale, the freezing point of water is 32°F. The boiling point of water is 212°F. There are 180 degrees between the freezing point and boiling point of water. Each degree is an equal amount.

What is the Celsius scale?

The Celsius (SEL see us) scale is used more widely throughout the world. On this scale, the freezing point of water is 0°C. The boiling point of water is 100°C. There are 100 degrees between the boiling and freezing points of water on the Celsius scale. Therefore, a temperature change of one Celsius degree is bigger than a change of one Fahrenheit degree.

Heat

What is heat? **Heat** is the transfer of energy from one object to another due to a difference in temperature. Heat only flows from warmer objects to cooler ones. ☑

Suppose you held a glass of ice water. The water soon warms up. Why? Your hand is warmer than the ice water. Heat flows out of your hand and into the glass. The temperature of the water increases. The temperature of your skin touching the glass decreases. Heat stops flowing from your hand to the glass when both are the same temperature.

Heat and Temperature

How warm will a colder object get when heat is transferred to it? That depends on two things. The first is the amount of material in the object. The second is the kinds of atoms the material is made of. For example, water has to absorb a lot of heat before its temperature rises by one degree. This is why water is used to cool things. Water in a car's radiator carries a large amount of heat away from the engine to keep the engine from overheating.

Copyright © Glencoe/McGraw-Hill, a division of The McGraw-Hill Companies, Inc.

💡 **Think it Over**

1. **Compare and Contrast** Describe one way that the Fahrenheit scale is different from the Celsius scale.

_____

_____

_____

☑ **Reading Check**

2. **Conclude** Does heat flow from warmer objects to cooler objects or from cooler objects to warmer objects?

_____

_____

How do temperatures of water and land differ?

How does the temperature of water in a lake compare to the temperature of the surrounding air on a hot summer day? How do these temperatures compare at night when the air has cooled off? The water in the lake is cooler than the air on a hot day. The water is warmer than the air at night. This is because it takes longer for a large body of water to warm up or to cool down than the air and land around the body of water.

Heat on the Move

Remember that if a warm area touches a cooler area, heat moves from the warmer area to the cooler area. Heat is transferred in three ways—conduction, convection, and radiation. Conduction transfers heat mainly through solids and liquids. Convection transfers heat through liquids and gases. Radiation transfers energy through space. ☑

What is conduction?

Conduction (kun DUK shun) is the transfer of energy through a material by atoms in the material bumping into each other. What happens when you put a metal spoon into a cup of hot cocoa? The spoon gets hot. The part of the spoon in the hot cocoa becomes warmer. The atoms and molecules move faster. These particles hit other slower-moving particles in the spoon. Kinetic energy transfers from the faster-moving particles to the slower-moving particles farther up the spoon's handle.

Conduction transfers kinetic energy from particle to particle in a solid. The figure shows how the particles move back and forth in place, bumping into one another. Energy is transferred from fast-moving (warmer) particles to slower-moving (colder) particles when they bump.

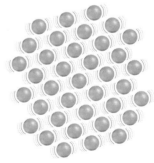

What are thermal conductors?

Thermal conductors are materials that transfer energy easily. Most metals are good conductors of heat. Gold, silver, and copper are the best thermal conductors. Some cooking pans are made of steel but have copper bottoms. A copper bottom conducts heat more evenly. It helps spread the heat across the bottom of the pan so that the food is cooked more evenly.

Copyright © Glencoe/McGraw-Hill, a division of The McGraw-Hill Companies, Inc.

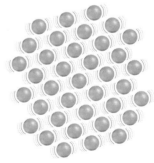

✔ **Reading Check**

3. Summarize What are the three ways heat can be transferred?

_____

_____

Picture This

4. Describe how particles in a solid move during conduction.

_____

_____

Think it Over

5. Apply Which of these would be the best conductor? Circle your answer.

a. a plastic spoon
b. a wooden chopstick
c. a silver fork
d. a rubber spatula

What are insulators?

You use an oven mitt to take a hot pan out of the oven. The oven mitt keeps the heat from moving from the pan to your hands. The oven mitt is a thermal insulator. Insulators are materials that do not transfer heat easily. When you are cold, you can put a blanket over you. The blanket is an insulator that makes it hard for heat to leave your body. Other good insulators are wood, rubber, plastic, and even air.

What is convection?

Convection (kun VEK shun) transfers heat when particles move between objects or areas that have different temperatures. Convection is most common in liquids and gases. As temperature increases, particles move faster and spread farther apart. So the density of the material decreases. Colder, more dense material forces the warmer, less dense material upward.

The figure shows a thermal. Thermals help some birds stay in the air for a long time without flapping their wings. A thermal is a column of warm air forced up by colder air around it. It is a convection current in the air. The Sun heats the ground. The air near the ground gets warmer and becomes less dense. The cooler, denser air pushes the warmer air up. As the air cools, it sinks and pushes more warm air up.

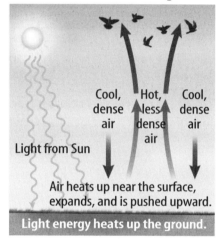

Cool, dense air

Hot, less dense air

Cool, dense air

Light from Sun

Air heats up near the surface, expands, and is pushed upward.

Light energy heats up the ground.

Convection also occurs in liquids. In a pot of boiling water, the warmer, less dense water is forced up as the cooler, denser water sinks. When all the water is warmed to the boiling point, you can see the movement in the boiling water.

What is radiation?

Radiation (ray dee AY shun) is the transfer of energy by waves. When waves hit an object, the object absorbs their energy and its temperature rises. Radiation can travel through air or through a vacuum, like space. Earth gets energy from the Sun through radiation. Your body is warmed by radiation when you stand by a fire or a radiator. You can also use radiation to cook food. A microwave oven uses microwave radiation to transfer energy to the food. ☑

Picture This

6. Label Write "thermal" at its location in the figure.

✔ **Reading Check**

7. Identify In what way is energy transferred in a microwave oven?

_____

_____

● After You Read

Mini Glossary

conduction: transfer of energy by atoms in a material bumping into each other

convection: transfer of heat when particles move between objects or areas that have different temperatures

heat: transfer of energy from one object to another due to a difference in temperature; flows from warmer objects to cooler objects

radiation: transfer of energy by waves

temperature: measure of the average kinetic energy of the particles in an object

1. Review the terms and their definitions in the Mini Glossary. Explain the term *temperature* in your own words.

_____

_____

2. Complete the graphic organizer to give an example of each type of heat transfer.

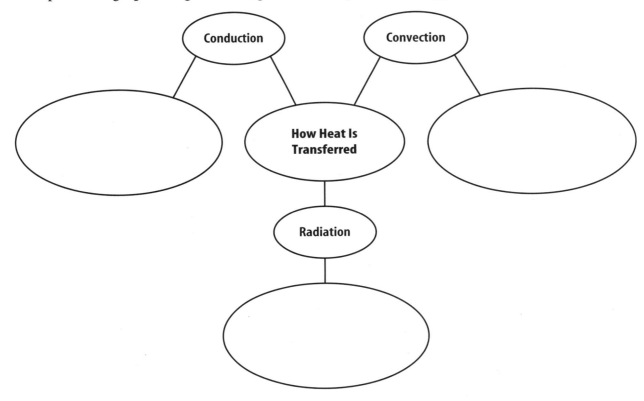

Science Online Visit **red.msscience.com** to access your textbook, interactive games, and projects to help you learn more about temperature and heat.

Energy

section ❸ Chemical Energy

● Before You Read

Have you ever seen fireflies at night in the summer? They make a blinking light. How do you think they make this light?

_____

_____

What You'll Learn
■ how chemical energy is changed
■ how to make a chemical reaction go faster or slower

● Read to Learn

Chemical Reactions and Energy

Have you ever seen light sticks? They glow for a short time. Energy in the form of light comes from a chemical reaction that happens inside the stick. The same thing happens when you turn on a gas stove. A chemical reaction takes place, and energy in the form of heat and light are given off. You use energy from chemical reactions every day.

What is a chemical reaction?

Some chemical reactions happen when atoms or molecules come together and form new compounds. A chemical reaction also can break the bonds between atoms. These atoms can then join with other atoms. For example, a chemical reaction happens when a fire burns. Bonds between atoms in the compounds of the wood break. Then, the atoms join with other atoms to make new compounds.

What are chemical bonds?

Energy is stored in the chemical bonds between atoms in a compound. The energy is a kind of potential energy called chemical energy. The chemical energy stored in coal, gas, and oil is an important energy source that you use every day. Chemical energy stored in food is a source of energy for your body to move and grow. Muscles change chemical energy into kinetic energy and heat when they move. ☑

Study Coach

State the Main Ideas As you read this section, stop after each paragraph and write down the main idea in your own words.

✔ Reading Check

1. **Name** three sources of chemical energy.

_____

_____

_____

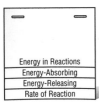

Ⓒ Organize Information
Use two sheets of notebook paper to make the following layered book. Use it to organize information about energy in reactions.

| Energy in Reactions |
| Energy-Absorbing |
| Energy-Releasing |
| Rate of Reaction |

Picture This

2. Highlight Use a highlighter to indicate where sugar is stored after photosynthesis.

Energy in Reactions

Transformations in energy happen in every chemical reaction. Energy must be added to break chemical bonds. When bonds form, energy is released. Energy often is added to begin a reaction. A lighted match placed in a mixture of hydrogen gas and oxygen gas will cause the mixture to explode and water will form. The heat from the flame of the match is the energy needed to start the chemical reaction. Hydrogen and oxygen atoms will bond together to make water molecules. The energy that is released when the atoms bond results in the explosion.

After atoms bond to form water molecules, it is hard to break the water molecules apart. Energy in the form of electricity, heat, or light, is needed to break chemical bonds.

What is an energy-absorbing reaction?

Some chemical reactions need energy all the time or they will stop. These reactions absorb, or take in, energy. An **endothermic** (en duh THUR mihk) **reaction** is a chemical reaction that absorbs heat energy. Endothermic reactions take place during cooking and baking.

Chemical reactions occur when sunlight hits a plant's leaves. The figure shows how plants use sunlight to make food. This process is called photosynthesis (foh toh SIHN thuh sus). Chemical reactions change the energy in sunlight into chemical energy in sugar that plants produce. Plants use carbon dioxide, water, and sunlight to make oxygen and sugar through photosynthesis.

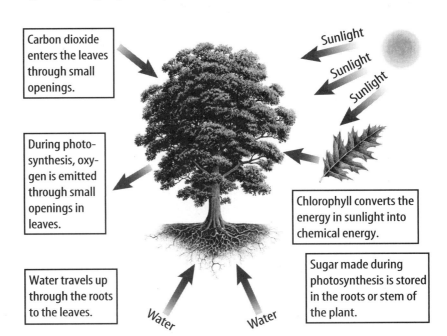

Carbon dioxide enters the leaves through small openings.

During photosynthesis, oxygen is emitted through small openings in leaves.

Water travels up through the roots to the leaves.

Sunlight

Chlorophyll converts the energy in sunlight into chemical energy.

Sugar made during photosynthesis is stored in the roots or stem of the plant.

Water   Water

What is an energy-releasing reaction?

Endothermic chemical reactions, like photosynthesis, are important because they make compounds such as oxygen and food. Other reactions are important because they make energy. **Exothermic** (ek soh THUR mihk) **reactions** are chemical reactions that give off heat energy. When you add a piece of wood to a fire, it burns. Atoms in the wood join with oxygen atoms in the air. An exothermic reaction takes place, and heat energy and light energy are released. This kind of exothermic reaction is called combustion. Burning oil, coal, and gas produces much of the energy needed to heat homes and schools.

How fast do chemical reactions happen?

Chemical reactions can happen at different rates, or speeds. When fireworks explode, chemical reactions happen very fast. When metal is left outside for a long time, it gets rusty. Metals rust when they join with oxygen. Rusting is a kind of chemical reaction that happens much more slowly than a fireworks explosion.

Many chemical reactions happen in your body every second. The reactions happen at different rates. Your body controls the rates of these reactions so that your body will work correctly and stay healthy.

Can the rate of a chemical reaction change?

You can change the rate of a chemical reaction two ways. One way is to change the temperature. For example, if you leave cake batter in a pan on the counter for many hours, nothing happens. If you put the pan in a hot oven, it turns into a cake. Raising the temperature of the cake batter makes the chemical reactions happen more quickly.

Another way to change the rate of a reaction is to add a compound called a catalyst. A **catalyst** (KA tuh list) is something that changes the rate of a chemical reaction without changing itself. Catalysts in your body called enzymes help you grow, breathe, and digest food. The saliva in your mouth has an enzyme in it. When you chew a piece of bread, this enzyme helps break down the starches in bread into smaller molecules. Enzymes help turn the food into the energy your body needs. ✔

Other chemical reactions use catalysts to go faster. These reactions include the production of vegetable shortening, synthetic rubber, and high-octane gasoline.

Copyright © Glencoe/McGraw-Hill, a division of The McGraw-Hill Companies, Inc.

Think it Over

3. Infer Which of the following is an example of an exothermic reaction?

  a. candle burning
  b. bread baking
  c. ice melting
  d. photosynthesis

✔ **Reading Check**

4. Define What is a catalyst?

_____

_____

_____

● After You Read

Mini Glossary

catalyst: substance that changes the rate of a chemical reaction without changing itself

endothermic reaction: chemical reaction that absorbs heat energy

exothermic reaction: chemical reaction that gives off heat energy

1. Review the terms and their definitions in the Mini Glossary. In your own words, explain the difference between an endothermic reaction and an exothermic reaction.

_____

_____

_____

2. In the table below, write if each reaction is exothermic or endothermic.

Chemical Reaction	Endothermic or Exothermic?
Exploding fireworks	
Photosynthesis	
Baking cookies	Endothermic
Burning gas	
Hydrogen and oxygen combining to form water	

3. You were asked to write the main idea of each paragraph as you read this section. How did you decide which is the main idea for each paragraph?

_____

_____

_____

End of Section

Science Online Visit **red.msscience.com** to access your textbook, interactive games, and projects to help you learn more about chemical energy.

 **Electricity and Magnetism**

section ❶ Electric Charge and Forces

● Before You Read

What are two examples of how you use electricity?

_____

_____

What You'll Learn

- how electrical charges apply forces
- what an electrical field is
- how objects become electrically charged
- how lightning happens

● Read to Learn

Electric Charges

Many things use electrical energy. Electrical energy comes from the forces between the electric charges found in atoms.

Where are the charges found in atoms?

Matter around you is made of atoms. Atoms are particles that are too small to be seen. They are less than a billionth of a meter in size. Every atom has electrons. The electrons move around a nucleus, as shown in the figure. The nucleus contains protons and neutrons. An atom has the same number of protons as electrons.

Protons and electrons have electric charge. Protons have positive charge. Electrons have negative charge. The amount of positive charge on a proton is equal to the amount of negative charge on an electron. Neutrons have no electric charge.

When is an object electrically charged?

An atom has equal amounts of positive and negative charge because it has equal numbers of protons and electrons. The positive and negative charges cancel each other out. An atom can become electrically charged if it gains or loses electrons. An object is electrically charged if the amounts of positive and negative charge are not equal.

Study Coach

Create a Quiz After you have read this section, create a quiz based on what you have learned. After you have written the quiz questions, be sure to answer them.

FOLDABLES

Ⓐ **Organize Information** Make the following Foldable to organize information about protons, neutrons, electric charges, and electric fields.

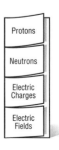

Protons

Neutrons

Electric Charges

Electric Fields

Copyright © Glencoe/McGraw-Hill, a division of The McGraw-Hill Companies, Inc.

Copyright © Glencoe/McGraw-Hill, a division of The McGraw-Hill Companies, Inc.

The Forces Between Charges

Two objects that are electrically charged exert forces on each other. These electric forces can bring objects together, or attract them. They also can push objects apart, or repel them. Look at the figure. If two objects are positively charged, they repel each other. If two objects are negatively charged, they also repel each other. But if one object is positively charged and the other is negatively charged, they attract each other. Like charges repel and unlike charges attract.

Picture This

1. **Highlight** Highlight the direction of the forces in each example in the figure.

Like charges repel.   Like charges repel.

Unlike charges attract.

How does distance affect electric force?

The distance between two charged objects affects the electric force between them. As the distance between charged objects increases, the electric force between them decreases. Suppose two electrons are moving apart. As they move farther apart, the force that repels them decreases.

Think it Over

2. **Apply** When two electrons move closer together, how does the force between them change?

_____

_____

How does charge affect electric force?

The amount of charge on two objects affects the electric force between them. If the amount of charge on either object decreases, so does the electric force. If the amount of charge increases, the electric force increases.

Electric Field and Electric Forces

Electric charges can exert forces on each other even when they are not touching. What happens when you rub a balloon on your hair and then hold the balloon a little away from your hair? Your hair moves toward the balloon. The balloon and your hair are not touching, but they are exerting forces on each other.

How do electric charges exert forces if they are not touching?

An electric charge is surrounded by an area called an electric field. The electric field exerts a force on other electric charges. Every proton and electron is surrounded by an electric field that exerts a force on all other protons and electrons. ☑

☑ **Reading Check**

3. **Identify** What parts of an atom are surrounded by electric fields?

_____

_____

How can you describe an electric field?

The electric field surrounding an electric charge is invisible. The figures show a way to describe an electric field for a positive charge and a negative charge. The arrows show the direction of the force the electric field exerts. The figures show the electric field at only a few points in space surrounding a charge, but the electric field is at every point in space surrounding a charge.

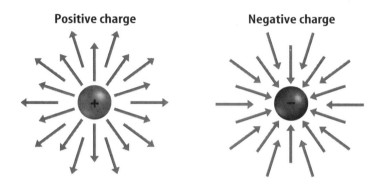

Positive charge   Negative charge

Picture This

4. Compare How are the electric fields of positive and negative charges different?

_____

_____

_____

_____

Making Objects Electrically Charged

A balloon becomes electrically charged when you rub it on your hair. The balloon no longer has an equal number of protons and electrons. Electric charges move from your hair to the balloon. This is how the balloon becomes electrically charged.

How does touch make an object electrically charged?

When you rub the balloon on your hair, the atoms in your hair and in the balloon are close together. Electrons move from atoms in your hair to atoms in the balloon. This is an example of charging by contact. **Charging by contact** is the movement of electric charges between objects that are touching, or in contact. ☑

The balloon gains electrons from your hair making it have more electrons than protons. Remember electrons have a negative charge, so the balloon is negatively charged. Your hair loses electrons to the balloon making it have more protons than electrons. Since protons are positively charged, your hair is positively charged. The amount of negative charge gained by the balloon equals the amount of positive charge left on your hair.

✔ **Reading Check**

5. Summarize For charging by contact, what must two objects do?

_____

Static Cling Another example of charging by contact is the static cling your clothes can get when they are in a dryer. Your clothes rub against each other when they tumble in a dryer. Electrons move from one piece of clothing to another. This can cause pieces of clothing to stick to each other.

Are there other ways to charge objects?

What happens when you rub a balloon on your hair and then try to stick it to a wall? It sticks. Why? You make the balloon negatively charged by rubbing it on your hair. But the wall does not have a charge. Look at the figure. As the balloon gets close to the wall, the electric field around the balloon repels electrons in the wall. The electrons are pushed away from their atoms. This makes the part of the wall close to the balloon positively charged. The negatively charged balloon is attracted to the positively charged part of the wall.

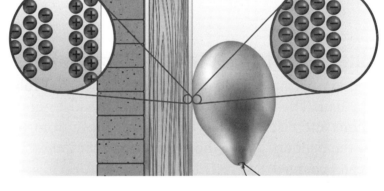

<u>Charging by induction</u> is the rearrangement of electric charge because of the presence of an electric field. One part of the object becomes positively charged and another part becomes negatively charged. However, the whole object stays electrically neutral.

Insulators and Conductors

<u>Insulators</u> are materials in which electric charges cannot move easily. Electrons in insulators are held tightly by the atoms and cannot move easily. Plastics, glass, rubber, and wood are examples of materials that are insulators. <u>Conductors</u> are materials in which electric charges can move easily. Electrons in conductors are not held tightly and can move rather easily. The best conductors are metals such as copper and gold.

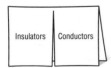
Right margin: Copyright © Glencoe/McGraw-Hill, a division of The McGraw-Hill Companies, Inc.

Static Charge

When charging by contact happens, the object that loses electrons has more positive charge than negative charge. The object that gains electrons has more negative charge than positive charge. The imbalance of electric charge on an object is **static charge**.

What is electric discharge?

Have you ever walked across a carpet and then touched a metal doorknob? Did you feel an electric shock or see a spark? The spark is an example of an electric discharge. An **electric discharge** is the movement of static charge from one place to another. The spark you saw was the result of a static charge.

How did this happen? Electrons move from the carpet to your body. Your hand then has an electric field that repels electrons in the doorknob. The electrons in the doorknob move away. This leaves a positively charged place on the doorknob. If the attractive electric force on the extra electrons is strong enough, these electrons can be pulled from your hand to the doorknob. The spark you see and the shock you feel are caused by this quick movement of electrons. ☑

What is lightning?

Lightning is an example of an electric discharge. Air currents in storm clouds sometimes cause electrons to move from the top of the cloud to the bottom. The electric field surrounding the bottom of the cloud repels electrons in the ground. This makes the ground positively charged. Lightning is the quick movement of the charges between the ground and the cloud.

What is grounding?

A lightning flash has a lot of electrical energy. If lightning hits a tree, it can start a fire. If it hits a building, the building can be damaged or burn. Buildings are protected from lightning by metal lightning rods on their roofs. A thick wire is connected to each lightning rod. The other end of the wire is connected to the ground. If lightning hits the lightning rod, the electrical charges go through the wire into the ground. Earth can be a conductor. Earth is so big that it can absorb a lot of extra electrical charge. The charge from the lightning goes into the ground and not the building. Making a path for electrical charge to go into the ground is called grounding. ☑

Copyright © Glencoe/McGraw-Hill, a division of The McGraw-Hill Companies, Inc.

✔ **Reading Check**

7. Identify What moves from your hand to a doorknob when you get a shock?

_____

✔ **Reading Check**

8. Identify What acts as a conductor for a lightning rod?

_____

● After You Read

Mini Glossary

charging by contact: the movement of electric charges between objects that are touching, or in contact

charging by induction: the rearrangement of electric charge because of the presence of an electric field

conductors: materials in which electric charges can move easily

electric discharge: the movement of static charge from one place to another

insulators: materials in which electric charges cannot move easily

static charge: the imbalance of electric charge on an object

---

1. Read the key terms and definitions in the Mini Glossary above. On the lines below, explain how the terms *charging by induction* and *static charge* are related.

_____

_____

2. Write the letter of each statement in the correct location in the Venn diagram to compare and contrast charging by induction to charging by contact.

   a. Objects must be touching
   b. Makes part of an object positively charged and part negatively charged
   c. Move electric charge
   d. Objects are not touching
   e. Makes the charge of an object positive or negative

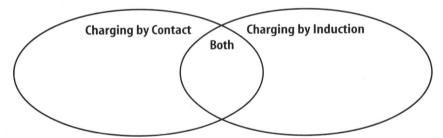

Charging by Contact   Both   Charging by Induction

3. You were asked to create a quiz and answer the quiz questions after you read this section. How did this help you learn the material in this section?

_____

_____

End of Section

 **Science** Online Visit **red.msscience.com** to access your textbook, interactive games, and projects to help you learn more about electric charge and forces.

 **chapter 7 Electricity and Magnetism**

section ❷ Electrical Current

● Before You Read

When you turn on a lamp, where does the light come from?

_____

_____

Copyright © Glencoe/McGraw-Hill, a division of The McGraw-Hill Companies, Inc.

● Read to Learn

Electric Current

A TV produces light waves and sound waves. Where does this energy come from? An electrical outlet provides electrical energy. Electrical energy is available only when an electric currant flows in the TV. The TV changes the electrical energy into sound and light.

What is an electric current?

An **electric current** is the flow of electric charges. An electric current flows in a wire when electrons move along the wire.

A wire is electrically neutral. It has the same number of protons and electrons. The electrons move along the wire when electric current flows in the wire. At the same time, electrons flow into one end of the wire and flow out of the other end of the wire. The number of electrons that flow into one end is the same as the number of electrons that flow out of the other end. This keeps the wire electrically neutral. ☑

What is the unit for current?

The amount of electric current in a wire is the amount of electric charge that flows into and out of the wire every second. The SI unit for electric current is the ampere (A). One ampere of electric current means a huge number of electrons (about six billion billion) are flowing into and out of the wire every second.

What You'll Learn
- about electric current
- how electrical energy is moved to a circuit
- current, voltage, and resistance

◄ **Mark the Text**

Locate Information
Underline every heading in the reading that asks a question. Then, use a different color to highlight the answers to those questions.

☑ **Reading Check**

1. **Determine** What keeps a wire electrically neutral?

_____

_____

_____

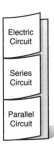
✔ **Reading Check**

2. Summarize What kind of reactions make an electric field in a battery?

_____

Picture This

3. Draw In the figure, draw arrows along the wire that show the flow of the electric current when the circuit is closed.

A Simple Electric Circuit

When lightning flashes, electric energy turns into heat energy, sound energy, and light energy. This happens in an instant. When you watch TV, electricity must be turned into light energy and sound energy for as long as you have the TV on. An electric current must keep flowing in the TV.

Electric current will flow only if the charges can flow in a closed, or non-stopping, path. A closed path in which electric charges can flow is an **electric circuit**. The figure at the bottom of the page shows a simple electric circuit. Current flows in this circuit as long as the conducting path between the battery, wires, and lightbulb is not broken. If the switch is open, the path is broken and the current will not flow. Also, if a wire or the filament in the lightbulb is broken, the path is broken and current will not flow.

Making Electric Charges Flow

A force must be exerted on electric charges to make them flow. Remember that a force is exerted on an electric charge by an electric field. To make electric charges flow in a circuit, there must be an electric field in the circuit that moves electrons in one direction.

What can make charges flow?

The battery in the figure produces the electric field that can make electrons flow. Chemical reactions happen in the battery when it is connected in a circuit. These chemical reactions cause one post, or the negative terminal, of the battery to become negatively charged and the positive terminal to become positively charged. The negative and positive charges on the battery terminals make the electric field in the circuit. The electric field causes electrons to flow from the negative terminal toward the positive terminal. ✔

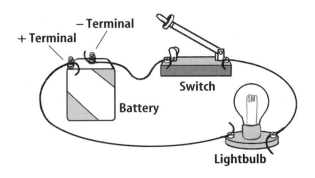

− Terminal

+ Terminal

Switch

Battery

Lightbulb

What is electric resistance?

Electrons are always hitting atoms and other electric charges as they flow. This causes electrons to change direction. But the electric field in the circuit keeps the electrons moving in the direction the current is flowing.

A measure of how hard it is for electrons to flow in an object is **electric resistance**. The resistance of insulators is usually much higher than the resistance of conductors. The unit for electric resistance is the ohm (Ω).

How can you model electron flow?

Look at the figure of a ball bouncing down a flight of stairs. The ball hits the steps and changes its direction many times. Its overall motion is in one direction—downward. The ball is like an electron moving through an electric circuit. Electrons in a circuit change direction after they hit atoms and other electric charges. But their overall motion is in one direction—the direction of the current flow.

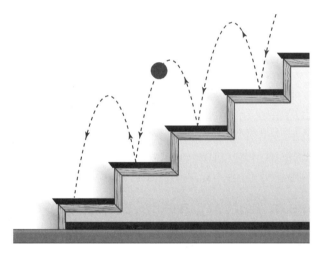

Why do electrons flow slowly in a wire?

If the ball had fallen without bouncing, it would have gotten to the bottom of the stairs much faster. Changing directions from bouncing on the steps slowed the ball down. In the same way, electrical resistance in a wire causes electrons to flow slowly. An electron in a circuit may take several minutes to move only a centimeter. If that is true, why does a lighbulb light up as soon as you flip a switch? When you flip a switch, you close a circuit. An electric field moves through the circuit at the speed of light. The electric field causes electrons in the lightbulb to start flowing almost immediately after the switch is flipped.

Picture This

4. **Analyze** Draw an arrow to show the overall direction of the ball in the figure.

 Think it Over

5. **Apply** How would turning on a light be different if the electric field were much slower?

_____

_____

Transferring Electrical Energy

When a current flows in a material, kinetic energy moves to the material. This is because the electrons and atoms bump into each other. The energy that flowing electrons move to the circuit also is called electrical energy. Electrical energy is changed into other forms of energy. When current flows to a lightbulb, it is changed to heat and light.

Electrical Energy and the Electric Field

The electrical energy that electrons move to a circuit depends on the strength of the electric field. If the electric field becomes stronger, the electric force exerted on electrons increases as they move from one point to another in the circuit. This causes electrons to move faster between hitting other atoms and electric charges. Since the speed of the flowing electrons increases as the electric field gets stronger, their kinetic energy also increases. A stronger electric field causes more electrical energy to move to the circuit.

Voltage

Have you seen a sign that says "Danger! High Voltage?" **Voltage** is a measure of how much electrical energy is moved by an electric charge as it moves from one point to another in a circuit. You can measure the voltage between two points with a voltmeter. The voltage between any two points in the circuit increases when the electric field in the circuit increases. The SI unit for voltage is the volt (V).

How does a battery make electrical energy?

The electric field in a circuit causes flowing electrons to have electrical energy. If a battery is connected in a circuit, chemical reactions in the battery make the electric field. In a battery, chemical energy is changed into electrical energy. This electrical energy can be changed into other forms of energy in the circuit. The battery is the source of energy.

What is battery voltage?

Battery voltage is the voltage between the positive and negative terminals of a battery. The battery voltage is related to how much electrical energy an electron would move to a circuit from the negative terminal to the positive terminal. When the voltage of a battery increases, more electrical energy is moved to a circuit. The voltage a battery makes depends on the chemical reactions in the battery. ☑

Think it Over

6. Apply What happens to voltage in a circuit when the electric field decreases?

_____

✔ Reading Check

7. Summarize What happens when the voltage of a battery increases?

_____

What happens if the voltage in a circuit is increased?

The voltage, current, and resistance in a circuit are all related. If the voltage in a circuit increases, the electric field in the circuit increases. Electrons speed up between bumping into atoms and other electric charges. This makes the current in a circuit increase. If the resistance in a circuit increases, it increases the number of times that electrons bump into atoms and other electric charges every second. This makes it harder for electrons to flow in the circuit. Because of this, increasing the resistance reduces the current.

What is Ohm's law?

The relationship between the voltage, current, and resistance of a circuit is known as Ohm's law. Ohm's law can be written as the following equation.

$$\begin{array}{ccc} \textbf{voltage} & = & \textbf{current} & \times & \textbf{resistance} \\ \text{(in volts)} & & \text{(in amperes)} & & \text{(in ohms)} \end{array}$$

$$V = IR$$

Series and Parallel Circuits

There are probably a lot of devices connected to circuits in your home. There are two ways that devices can be connected in a circuit. One way is a series circuit, shown in the top figure. The other way is a parallel circuit, shown in the lower figure.

In a **series circuit**, there is only one closed path for the current to follow. If any part of the path is broken, the current will not flow in the circuit. In a **parallel circuit**, there is more than one closed path for current to follow. If the current flow is broken in one path, current will still flow in other paths in the circuit. The electric circuits in your house are parallel circuits. This means you can switch off the light in one room without turning off the lights in the whole house.

Series Circuit

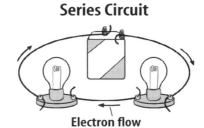

Electron flow

Parallel Circuit

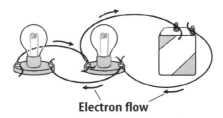

Electron flow

Applying Math

8. Apply The current in a circuit is 0.10A. The resistance of the circuit is 30.0 Ω. What is the voltage in the circuit? Show your work.

_____

_____

_____

Picture This

9. Observe Look at the lightbulb in the middle in the parallel circuit. How many closed paths is it a part of?

_____

● After You Read

Mini Glossary

electric circuit: a closed path in which electric charges can flow

electric current: the flow of electric charges; measured in amperes (A)

electric resistance: a measure of how hard it is for electrons to flow in an object; unit is the ohm (Ω)

parallel circuit: a circuit where there is more than one closed path for current to follow

series circuit: a circuit where there is only one closed path for the current to follow

voltage: a measure of how much electrical energy is moved by an electric charge as it moves from one point to another in a circuit

---

1. Review the terms and their definitions in the Mini Glossary. Write a sentence comparing and contrasting a parallel circuit and a series circuit.

_____

_____

2. Complete the flow chart about how electrons flow to make a lightbulb glow.

Electrical Energy in a Circuit

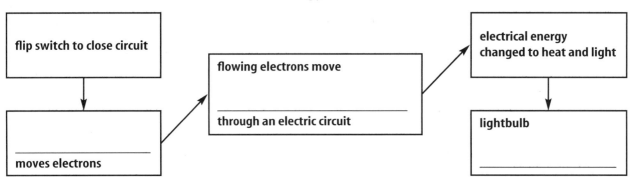

3. You were asked to underline the headings that were questions and then highlight the answers to each question. How did this help you understand more about electric current?

_____

_____

Science Online Visit **red.msscience.com** to access your textbook, interactive games, and projects to help you learn more about electric current.

End of Section

Electricity and Magnetism

section ❸ **Magnetism**

● Before You Read

What happens when you put a paper clip close to a magnet?

_____

_____

What You'll Learn
■ how magnets exert forces on each other
■ why some materials are magnetic
■ how an electric generator works

● Read to Learn

Mark the Text

Magnets

Did you use a magnet today? If you have watched TV or used a computer, you used a magnet. Magnets are a part of TVs, computers, and other devices. Magnets can exert forces on objects that are made from, or contain, magnetic materials. Magnets also can exert forces on other magnets. The forces of magnets make them very useful.

Identify Specific Ideas
As you read through this section, highlight information about how magnets exert forces.

What are magnetic poles?

Every magnet has two ends or sides. Each of these ends or sides is called a magnetic pole. There are two kinds of magnetic poles. One is a north pole. The other is a south pole. Every magnet has a north pole and a south pole.

How do magnets exert forces on each other?

Magnetic Poles Magnetic poles of a magnet exert forces on magnetic poles of other magnets. Look at the figure at the top of the next page. If two north poles or two south poles are near each other, they repel or push away. If the north pole of one magnet is near the south pole of another magnet, they attract. Like poles repel and unlike poles attract.

Copyright © Glencoe/McGraw-Hill, a division of The McGraw-Hill Companies, Inc.

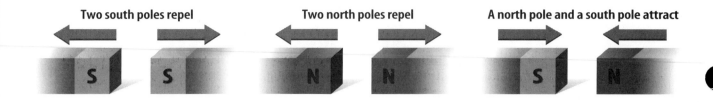

Two south poles repel   **Two north poles repel**   **A north pole and a south pole attract**

S   S   N   N   S   N

Picture This

1. **Compare** In the figure, how are the magnets whose unlike poles are near each other different from the magnets whose like poles are near each other?

_____

_____

💡 Think it Over

2. **Determine** Which of these will stick to a magnet?

   a. drinking glass
   b. pencil
   c. sewing needle
   d. plastic cup

Distance The magnetic forces between two magnets get stronger as the magnets get closer. The magnetic forces between two magnets get weaker as the magnets get farther apart.

What is a magnetic field?

Have you ever held like poles of two magnets near each other? They push each other apart. You can feel this even when they are not touching. Recall that electric charges exert forces on each other even when they are not touching. This is because an electric charge is surrounded by an electric field. In the same way, a magnet is surrounded by a magnetic field. It exerts a force on other magnets.

If iron filings are sprinkled around a bar magnet, they will line up in a pattern of curved lines. These lines are called magnetic field lines. They help show the direction of the magnetic field around a magnet. The magnetic field lines are closest together at the magnet's poles. This is where the magnetic field is strongest.

Magnetic Materials

A paper clip will stick to a magnet if you hold a magnet near it. But a piece of aluminum foil will not stick to a magnet. Both are made of metal. Why is one attracted to the magnet and not the other?

Not all metals are attracted to magnets. Only metals that contain the elements iron, nickel, cobalt, and a few other rare-earth elements are attracted to magnets. Materials that contain these elements are magnetic materials. Magnets contain one or more of these metals. The steel paper clip contains iron, so it is a magnetic material.

Why are some materials magnetic?

Atoms of magnetic elements, like iron, nickel, and cobalt, also are tiny magnets. Each atom has a north pole and a south pole. If an element is not magnetic, its atoms are not magnets. Objects that are made of elements that are not magnetic will not be affected by a magnetic field.

What are magnetic domains?

In a magnetic material, forces that atoms exert on each other cause the magnetic fields around atoms to line up. So the atoms have their magnetic poles pointing in the same direction. A group of atoms that have their magnetic poles pointing in the same direction is called a **magnetic domain**. ☑

The magnetic fields of all the atoms in a magnetic domain add together. This means each magnetic domain has a south pole and a north pole. Each magnetic domain also is surrounded by a magnetic field. One magnetic domain may have trillions of atoms. But it is still too small to see. There may be billions of magnetic domains in a small piece of iron.

Do domains line up in permanent magnets?

What happens if you hold two paper clips together? They both are made of magnetic material. But they do not attract or repel each other. Why do they stick to a magnet and not each other? The magnetic domains in a paper clip point in all different directions. As a result, the magnetic fields around each magnetic domain cancel each other out and the paper clip does not have a magnetic field. ☑

In a permanent magnet, like a bar magnet, most of the magnetic domains point in the same direction. The magnetic fields around each magnetic domain do not cancel each other out. They add together to make a stronger magnetic field. The magnetic field that surrounds the magnet is a combination of the magnetic fields around the magnetic domains.

Why are magnetic materials attracted to a magnet?

A paper clip is not a magnet. But it has magnetic domains that are small magnets. Usually the domains point in all directions. But when a permanent magnet gets close to a paper clip, the magnetic field of the magnet exerts forces on the magnetic domain of the paper clip. These forces make the magnetic poles of the domains in the paper clip line up. The magnetic poles point in a single direction when a permanent magnet is nearby. The nearby pole of the permanent magnet is always next to the opposite poles of the magnetic domains. This causes the paper clip to be attracted to the magnet.

Because the magnetic fields of the domains are lined up, they do not cancel each other out. When the paper clip is attached to the magnet, it is a temporary magnet. It has a north pole and a south pole.

✔ **Reading Check**

3. Explain Why do atoms in a magnetic material have their magnetic fields pointing in the same direction?

_____

_____

_____

✔ **Reading Check**

4. Summarize Why won't two paper clips attract or repel each other?

_____

_____

_____

FOLDABLES

D Compare Make the following Foldable to help you compare different kinds of magnets.

Electromagnetism

Electricity and magnetism are related. A wire carrying an electric current is surrounded by a magnetic field. Any moving electric charge also is surrounded by a magnetic field. The connection between electricity and magnetism is called electromagnetism.

What are electromagnets?

You can make the magnetic field of a wire that is carrying a current stronger by wrapping it around an iron core. A wire, carrying a current, wrapped around an iron core is an **electromagnet**. The figure shows an electromagnet. An electromagnet has a north pole and a south pole. If the direction of current flow in the wire coil of an electromagnet is changed, the north pole and the south pole switch places.

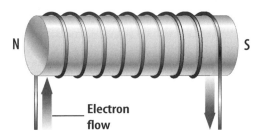

Electron flow

The strength of a magnetic field made by an electromagnet depends on the amount of current in the wire coil. Increasing the amount of current increases the magnetic field strength. If there is no current, there will be no magnetic field. So, an electromagnet is a temporary magnet. The properties of an electromagnet can be controlled. Electromagnets are used in doorbells and telephones.

Generating Electric Current

An electric current makes a magnetic field. Can a magnetic field make an electric current? The answer is yes. If a magnet is moved through a wire loop that is part of a circuit, it will make an electric current flow through the circuit. The current flows only as long as the magnet is moving. It also would work if the magnet was still, but the wire loop was moving. The making of an electric current by moving a magnet through a wire loop or moving a wire loop around the magnet is **electromagnetic induction**. Electromagnetic induction makes an electric field in a circuit that causes electrons to flow. This is just like a battery.

Picture This

5. Observe From which pole does the electric current flow in the electromagnet?

_____

Think it Over

6. Apply If the amount of current in an electromagnet decreases, what will the electric field do?

_____

What is an electric generator?

What makes the electrical energy in an electrical outlet? It is made by an electric generator. The figure shows a simple electric generator.

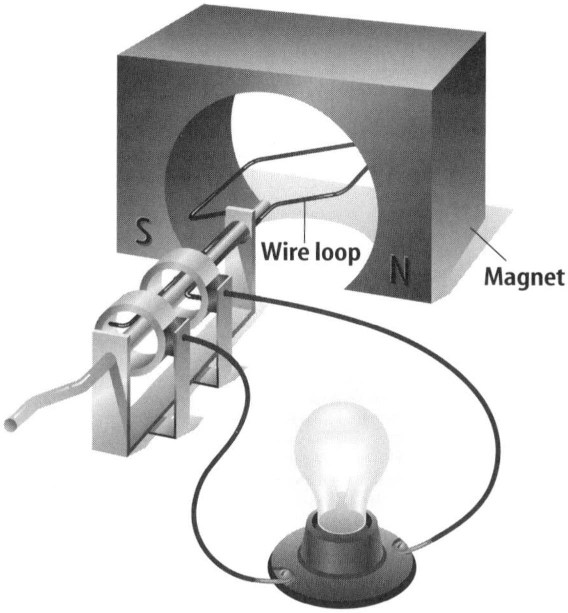

Picture This

7. Locate Where is the magnetic field strongest in the simple generator?

____

____

In an electric generator, a wire loop is rotated within a magnetic field. The movement of the wire loop in the magnetic field makes an electrical field in the wire. This electrical field causes a current to flow. The current flows as long as the wire loop is rotating. How can you keep the wire loop rotating? Mechanical energy is used to keep the wire loop rotating. The generator turns mechanical energy into electrical energy. ☑

Reading Check

8. Identify On the lines below, write the words that make this sentence true: An electric generator changes ___a___ energy, in the form of kinetic energy, into ___b___ energy.

a. ______________________

b. ______________________

Where does electricity you use come from?

The electrical energy in an electrical outlet comes from generators in electric power plants. Electromagnets are rotated past wire coils in these generators. Power plants use mechanical energy to rotate the electromagnets. The mechanical energy is usually in the form of kinetic energy. Moving water or moving steam provide the kinetic energy to make electrical energy.

Some power plants burn fossil fuels like gas and coal. The fossil fuels heat water and make steam that spins generators. In hydroelectric power plants, water flowing from behind a dam provides mechanical energy. This mechanical energy is turned into electrical energy.

Copyright © Glencoe/McGraw-Hill, a division of The McGraw-Hill Companies, Inc.

● After You Read

Mini Glossary

electromagnet: a wire, carrying current, wrapped around an iron core

electromagnetic induction: the making of an electric current by moving a magnet through a wire loop, or moving a wire loop around the magnet

magnetic domain: a group of atoms that have their magnetic poles pointing in the same direction

1. Review the terms and their definitions in the Mini Glossary. Describe electromagnetic induction in your own words.

_____

_____

2. The figures show the magnetic domains of a permanent magnet and a paper clip. Using information you learned about magnetic domains, label the magnet and the paper clip.

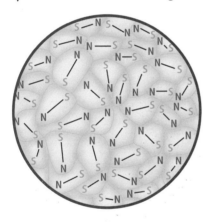   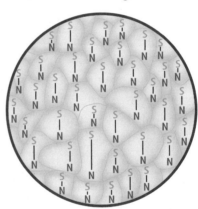

_____   _____

3. You were asked to highlight information you read about how magnets exert forces. How did this help you to understand more about magnets?

_____

_____

_____

End of Section

 **Science Online** Visit **red.msscience.com** to access your textbook, interactive games, and projects to help you learn more about magnetism.

122 Electricity and Magnetism

Waves

section ❶ What are waves?

● Before You Read

Describe what comes to mind when you think of waves.

_____

_____

Copyright © Glencoe/McGraw-Hill, a division of The McGraw-Hill Companies, Inc.

● Read to Learn

What is a wave?

Imagine that you are floating on an air mattress in a swimming pool and someone jumps into the pool near you. You and your air mattress bob up and down after the splash. What happened? Energy from the person jumping in made your air mattress move. But the person did not touch your air mattress. The energy from the person jumping in moved through the water in waves. **Waves** are regular disturbances that carry energy without carrying matter. The waves disturbed, or changed the motion of, your air mattress.

What do waves do?

Water waves carry energy. Sound waves also carry energy. Have you ever felt a clap of thunder? If so, you felt the energy in a sound wave. You also move energy when you throw a ball. But, there is a difference between a moving ball and a wave. A ball is made of matter. When you throw a ball, you move matter as well as energy. A wave moves only energy.

A Model for Waves

How can a wave move energy without moving matter? Imagine several people standing in a line. Each person passes a ball to the next person. The ball moved, but the people did not. Think of the ball as the energy in a wave and the people as the molecules that move the energy.

What You'll Learn

- how waves, energy, and matter are related
- the difference between transverse waves and compressional waves

Study Coach

Create a Quiz As you read this section, write quiz questions based on what you have learned. After you write the quiz questions, answer them.

FOLDABLES

ⓐ Identify Make the following Foldable from a sheet of notebook paper to help you organize information about waves.

What are waves?

Mechanical Waves

In the model of the wave, the ball (energy) could not be moved if the people (molecules) were not there. The same thing happens when a rock is thrown into a pond. Waves form where the rock hits the water. The molecules in the water bump into each other and pass the energy in the waves. The energy of a water wave cannot be moved or transferred if there are no water molecules.

Waves that use matter to move or transfer energy are **mechanical waves.** Water waves are mechanical waves. The matter that a mechanical wave travels through is called a medium. In a water wave, the medium is water. Solids, liquids, and gases are also mediums. For example, sound waves can travel through air, water, solids, and other gases. Without one of these mediums, there would be no sound waves. There is no air in outer space, so sound waves cannot travel in space.

What are transverse waves?

One kind of mechanical wave is a transverse wave. Transverse means to pass through, across, or over. In a **transverse wave,** the energy of the wave makes the medium move up and down or back and forth at right angles to the direction the wave moves. Think of a long rope stretched out on the ground. If you shake one end of the rope up and down, you make a wave that seems to slide along the rope, like the wave shown in the figure.

Picture This

2. **Draw and Label** In the figure, draw a circle around each crest in the wave. Then, use a different color of pen or pencil to draw a square around each trough.

Transverse Wave

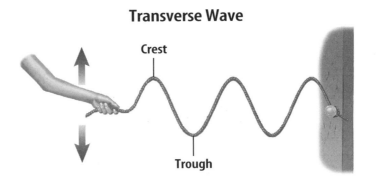

Crest

Trough

It might seem that the rope is moving away from you, but only the wave is moving away from your hand. The energy of the wave travels through the rope. But the matter in the rope does not move. Look at the figure. You can see that the wave has peaks and valleys that are spaced apart at even and regular distances. The high points of transverse waves are called crests. The low points are called troughs.

What are compressional waves?

Mechanical waves can be either transverse or compressional. Compress means to press or squeeze together. In a **compressional wave,** matter in the medium moves forward and backward along the same direction that the wave travels.

An example of a compressional wave made with a coiled spring is shown in the figure. A string is tied to the spring to show how the wave moves. Some coils on one end are compressed and then let go. As the wave begins, the coils near the end are close together. The other coils are far apart. The wave travels along the spring.

Compressional Wave

The coils and string move only as the wave passes them. Then, they go back to where they were. Compressional waves carry only energy forward along the spring. The spring is the medium the wave moves through, but the spring does not move along with the wave.

Sound Waves Sound waves are compressional waves. How do you make sound waves when you talk or sing? Hold your fingers against your throat while you hum. You can feel your vocal cords vibrating, or moving back and forth very quickly. You can also feel vibrations when you touch a stereo speaker while it is playing. All waves are made by something that is vibrating. ☑

Picture This

3. **Describe** Look at the figures. Describe the coils of the spring when the wave passes through them. Are they close together or far apart?

_____

✔ **Reading Check**

4. **Identify** What kind of waves are sound waves?

_____

FOLDABLES

B **Compare and Contrast**
Make the following Foldable to compare and contrast the characteristics of sound waves and electromagnetic waves.

Picture This

5. Identify Look at the figure. What do the dots above the drum represent?

_____

☑ Reading Check

6. Classify What is radiant energy?

_____

_____

Making Sound Waves

A vibrating object causes the air molecules around it to vibrate. Look at the figure. When the drum is hit, the drumhead vibrates up and down. When the drumhead moves up, the air molecules next to it are pushed closer, or compressed, together. The group of compressed molecules is called a compression. The compression moves away from the drumhead.

When the drumhead moves down, the air molecules near it have more room and can spread apart. This group of molecules is a rarefaction. Rarefaction means something that has become less dense. The rarefaction also moves away from the drumhead. As the drumhead vibrates up and down, it makes a series of compressions and rarefactions in the air molecules that make up a sound wave.

 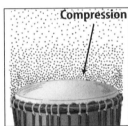 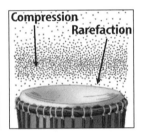

Electromagnetic Waves

<u>**Electromagnetic**</u> (ih lek troh mag NEH tik) <u>**waves**</u> are waves that can travel through space where there is no matter. There are different kinds of electromagnetic waves, such as radio waves, infrared waves, visible light waves, ultraviolet waves, X rays, and gamma rays. These waves can travel in matter or in space. For example, radio waves from TV and radio stations travel through air. They can be reflected from a satellite in space. Then, they travel through air and the walls of your house to your TV or radio.

How does the Sun emit light and heat?

The Sun emits electromagnetic waves that travel through space and reach Earth. The energy carried by electromagnetic waves is called radiant energy. Almost 92 percent of the radiant energy that reaches Earth from the Sun is carried by infrared and visible light waves. Infrared waves make you feel warm. Visible light waves make it possible for you to see. Some of the Sun's radiant energy is carried by ultraviolet waves. These are the waves that can cause sunburn. ☑

● After You Read

Mini Glossary

compressional wave: a type of mechanical wave in which matter in the medium moves forward and backward along the same direction that the wave travels

electromagnetic waves: waves that can travel through space where there is no matter

mechanical waves: waves that use matter to move energy

transverse wave: a type of mechanical wave in which the energy of the wave makes the medium move up and down or back and forth at right angles to the direction the wave travels

waves: regular disturbances that carry energy without carrying matter

1. Read the key terms and definitions in the Mini Glossary above. Write a sentence using the term *mechanical wave* on the lines below.

_____

_____

2. Use the Venn diagram to compare and contrast transverse and compressional waves. Arrange the characteristics of the waves according to whether they are true for transverse waves, compressional waves, or both.

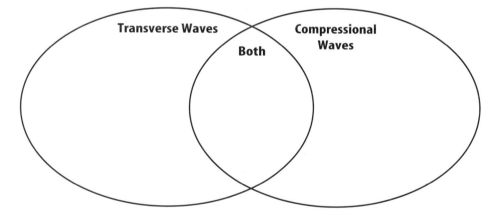

Transverse Waves   Both   Compressional Waves

3. How did the examples of the rope and the spring toy help you understand the difference between transverse and compressional waves?

_____

_____

_____

Science Online Visit **red.msscience.com** to access your textbook, interactive games, and projects to help you learn more about waves.

End of Section

Waves

section ❷ Wave Properties

What You'll Learn

- about the frequency and the wavelength of a wave
- why waves travel at different speeds

Underline Terms As you read this section, underline each property of a wave. Then, highlight information about each property in a different color.

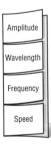

FOLDABLES™

❻ **Organize Information** Make the following Foldable to help you organize information about the different properties of waves.

Amplitude

Wavelength

Frequency

Speed

● Before You Read

Think about waves in an ocean and waves in a pond. How would you describe each kind of wave?

_____

_____

● Read to Learn

Amplitude

To describe a water wave, you might say how high the wave rises above, or falls below, a certain level. This distance is called the wave's amplitude. The **amplitude** of a transverse wave is one-half the distance between a crest and a trough, as shown in the figure.

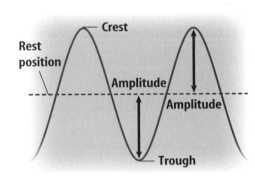

In a compressional wave, the amplitude depends on how close together the particles of the medium are. The amplitude is greater when the particles of the medium are squeezed closer together in each compression and spread farther apart in each rarefaction.

How are amplitude and energy related?

A wave's amplitude is related to the energy that the wave carries. For example, electromagnetic waves of bright light carry more energy and have greater amplitudes than electromagnetic waves of dim light. Loud sound waves carry more energy and have greater amplitudes than soft sound waves. A very loud sound can carry enough energy to damage your hearing.

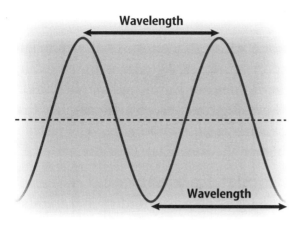

Transverse Wave

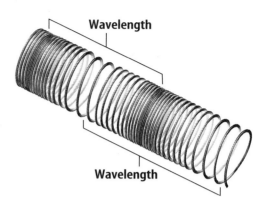

Compressional Wave

Wavelength

You also can describe a wave by its wavelength. Look at the figure above. For a transverse wave, **wavelength** is the distance from the top of one crest to the top of the next crest, or from the bottom of one trough to the bottom of the next trough. For a compressional wave, the wavelength is the distance between the center of one compression and the center of the next compression, or from the center of one rarefaction to the center of the next rarefaction.

The wavelengths of electromagnetic waves can vary from extremely short to longer than a kilometer. X rays and gamma rays have wavelengths that are smaller than the diameter of an atom.

This range of wavelengths is called the electromagnetic spectrum. The figure at the right shows the names given to different parts of the electromagnetic spectrum. Visible light, or light you can see, is only a small part of the electromagnetic spectrum. The wavelength of visible light gives light its color. For example, red light waves have longer wavelengths than green light waves.

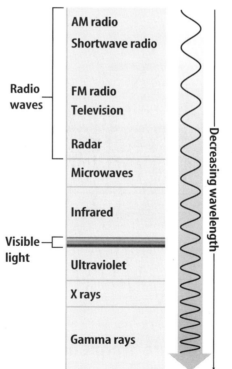

Copyright © Glencoe/McGraw-Hill, a division of The McGraw-Hill Companies, Inc.

Picture This

1. **Describe** Look at the figure of the transverse wave. Compare the wavelengths between two crests to the wavelength between two troughs. Describe what you find.

_____

_____

Picture This

2. **Use Graphs** Which of the following has the greatest wavelength?
   a. microwaves
   b. X rays
   c. AM radio waves
   d. FM radio waves

Frequency

The **frequency** of a wave is the number of wavelengths that pass a given point in 1 s. Frequency is measured in hertz (Hz). Hertz are the number of wavelengths per second. So, 1 Hz means one wavelength per second. Remember that waves are made by something that vibrates. The faster the vibration is, the higher the frequency is of the wave. ☑

How can you model frequency?

You can use a model to help you understand frequency. If two waves travel with the same speed, their frequency and wavelength are related. Look at the figure below. Imagine people on two moving sidewalks next to each other. One sidewalk has four people on it. They are spaced 4 m apart. The other sidewalk has 16 people on it. They are spaced 1 m apart.

Imagine both sidewalks are moving at the same speed. The sidewalks move toward a pillar. On which sidewalk will more people go past the pillar? The sidewalk with 16 people on it has a shorter distance between people. Four people on this sidewalk will pass the pillar for every one person on the other sidewalk.

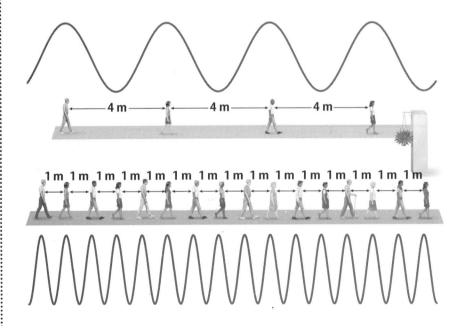

How are frequency and wavelength related?

Suppose that each person on the sidewalks represents the crest of a transverse wave. The movement of the people on the first sidewalk is like a wave with a 4 m wavelength. For the second sidewalk, the wavelength would be 1 m.

Copyright © Glencoe/McGraw-Hill, a division of The McGraw-Hill Companies, Inc.

Reading Check

3. **Summarize** Write the correct words to complete the sentence on the lines below.

Waves that vibrate fast have ____a.____ frequencies. Waves that vibrate slowly have ____b.____ frequencies.

a._____

b._____

Picture This
4. **Use Models** On the bottom sidewalk, circle groups of four people each. Then draw a line from each group of four people to one person on the top sidewalk.

Applying Math

5. **Calculate** If three people on the top sidewalk pass the pillar, how many people on the bottom sidewalk will have passed the pillar?

_____

The sidewalk with the longer, 4 m, wavelength carries a person past the pillar less frequently. Longer wavelengths have lower frequencies. On the second sidewalk, people pass the pillar more frequently. There, the wavelength is shorter—only 1 m. Shorter wavelengths have higher frequencies. This is true for all waves that travel at the same speed. As the frequency of a wave increases, its wavelength decreases.

What makes different colors and pitches?

The color of a light wave depends on the wavelength or the frequency of the light wave. For example, blue light has a higher frequency and shorter wavelength than red light.

Pitch is how high or how low a sound seems to be. Either the wavelength or the frequency determines the pitch of a sound wave. The pitch and frequency increase from note to note when you sing a musical scale. High-sounding pitches have higher frequencies. As the frequency of sound waves increases, their wavelengths decrease. Lower pitches have lower frequencies. As the frequency of a sound wave decreases, their wavelengths increase. ☑

Wave Speed

You have probably watched a thunderstorm on a hot summer day. You see lightning flash between a dark cloud and the ground. If the thunderstorm is far away, it takes many seconds before you will hear the sound of the thunder that goes with the lightning. This happens because light travels much faster in air than sound does. Light travels through air at about 300 million m/s. Sound travels through air at about 340 m/s. You can calculate the speed of any wave using this equation. The Greek letter lambda, λ, represents wavelength.

Wave Speed Equation

wave speed (m/s) = **frequency** (Hz) × **wavelength** (m)
$$v = f\lambda$$

Mechanical waves, such as sound, and electromagnetic waves, such as light, change speed when they travel in different mediums. Mechanical waves usually travel fastest in solids and slowest in gases. Electromagnetic waves travel fastest in gases and slowest in solids. For example, the speed of light is about 30 percent faster in air than in water.

☑ **Reading Check**

6. **Summarize** What determines color and pitch? Circle your answer.
   a. wavelength
   b. frequency
   c. wavelength and frequency
   d. wavelength or frequency

Applying Math

7. **Use an Equation** What is the speed in m/s of a wave with a frequency of 50 Hz and wavelength of 2 m? Show your work.

_____

_____

_____

● After You Read

Mini Glossary

amplitude: transverse wave—one-half the distance between a crest and a trough; compressional wave—how close together the particles of the medium are

frequency: the number of wavelengths that pass a given point in 1 s

wavelength: transverse wave—the distance from the top of one crest to the top of the next crest, or from the bottom of one trough to the bottom of the next trough; compressional wave—the distance between the center of one compression and the center of the next compression, or from the center of one rarefaction to the center of the next rarefaction

1. Review the terms and their definitions in the Mini Glossary. Explain in your own words how wavelength and frequency are related.

_____

_____

2. Label the parts of the transverse wave in the diagram below.

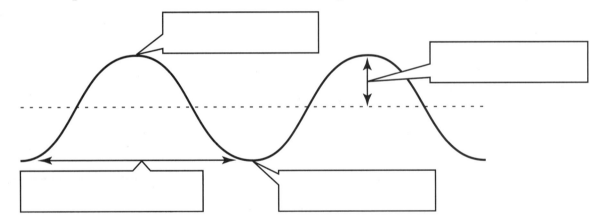

3. You were asked to underline properties of waves and highlight information about them. How did this help you understand and learn about properties of waves?

_____

_____

_____

End of Section

 **Science Online** Visit **red.msscience.com** to access your textbook, interactive games, and projects to help you learn more about properties of waves.

chapter 8 Waves

section 3 Wave Behavior

Before You Read

Have you ever shouted and heard an echo? On the lines below, write about what you think causes an echo.

____

____

What You'll Learn

- how waves can reflect
- how waves change direction
- how waves can bend around barriers

Read to Learn

Reflection

You can see yourself in a mirror because waves of light are reflected. Reflect means to throw back. **Reflection** happens when a wave hits an object or surface and bounces off. Light waves from the Sun or a lightbulb bounce off of your face. The light waves hit the mirror and reflect back to your eyes. So you see your reflection in the mirror.

You can see your reflection in the smooth surface of a pond, too. But, if the water has ripples or waves, it is harder to see your reflection. You cannot see a sharp image when light reflects from an uneven surface like ripples on the water. This is because the reflected light goes in many different directions.

Mark the Text

Identify Details Highlight each question head. Then use another color to highlight the answer to each question.

Refraction

A wave changes direction when it reflects from a surface. Waves can also change direction in another way. Have you ever tried to grab a sinking object in a swimming pool, but missed it? You were probably sure you grabbed right where it was. But, the light waves from the object changed direction when they moved from the water to the air. The bending of a wave as it moves from one medium to another is **refraction.**

FOLDABLES™

D Organize Information Use four quarter-sheets of paper to take notes about reflection, refraction, diffraction, and interference as you read.

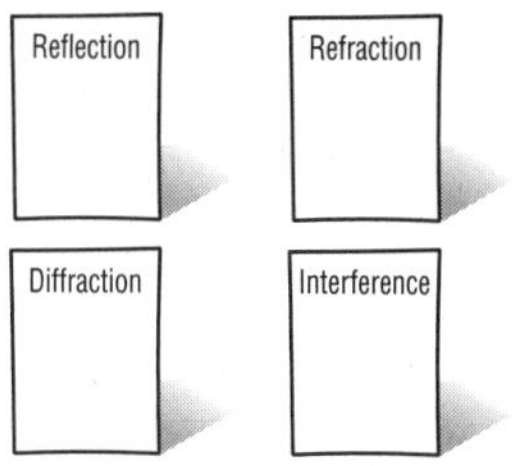

Copyright © Glencoe/McGraw-Hill, a division of The McGraw-Hill Companies, Inc.

How are refraction and wave speed related?

Remember that the speed of a wave can be different in different materials. For example, light waves travel faster in air than in water. Refraction happens when the speed of a wave changes as it moves from one medium to another.

Picture This

1. **Display** In the water of the first figure, draw an arrow from the light ray to the normal that shows how the light ray bends toward the normal.

   In the air of the second figure, draw an arrow from the normal to the light ray to show how the light ray bends away from the normal.

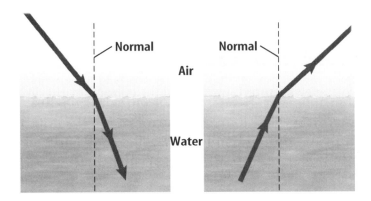

Wave Speed The figures above show how a light wave bends when it passes from air to water and water to air. A line that is perpendicular to the water's surface is called the normal. A light ray slows down and bends toward the normal when it passes from air into water. A light ray speeds up and bends away from the normal when it passes from water into air. If the speed of the wave changes a lot between mediums, the direction of the wave will change a lot too.

Refraction The figure below shows refraction of a fish in a fishbowl. Refraction makes the fish appear to be closer to the surface. It also appears farther away from you than it really is. Light rays reflected from the fish are bent away from the normal as they pass from water to air. Your brain assumes that light rays always travel in straight lines. So, the light rays seem to be coming from a fish that is closer to the surface.

Picture This

2. **Use an Illustration** In the figure, trace the line that shows how the light would travel if light rays did not travel at different speeds in water and air.

Refraction

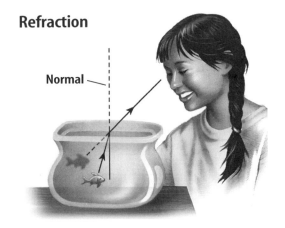

How does refraction make color?

Recall that different wavelengths make different colors. You can separate the colors in sunlight using a prism. A prism is an object or medium used to break light into its different wavelengths. Light is refracted twice when it passes through a prism—once it when it enters and once when it leaves. Since each color has a different wavelength, each color is refracted by a different amount. The colors of light are separated when they leave the prism. Violet light has the shortest wavelength. It is refracted, or bent, the most. Red light has the longest wavelength. It is refracted the least.

How are the colors of a rainbow made?

Each raindrop is a tiny prism. Light rays refract when they enter and again when they leave a raindrop. The colors refract at different angles because they have different wavelengths. The wavelengths separate into all the colors you can see. The colors you see in a rainbow are in order of decreasing wavelength: red, orange, yellow, green, blue, indigo, and violet.

Diffraction

Why can you hear music from the band room when you are down the hall? Sound waves bend as they pass through an open doorway. This is why you can hear the music. This bending is caused by diffraction. **Diffraction** is the bending of waves around a barrier. ☑

Light waves can diffract, too. But, they cannot diffract as much as sound waves. You can hear the band playing music when you are down the hall, but you cannot see the musicians until you actually look inside the band room door.

How are diffraction and wavelength related?

The wavelengths of light are much shorter than the opening of the band room door. This is why the light waves do not diffract as much as the sound waves do when they pass through the door. Light waves have wavelengths that are very short—between about 400 and 700 billionths of a meter. The doorway is about 1 m wide. The wavelengths of sound waves you can hear can be as long as 10 m. Sound waves are much closer in measurement to the opening of the door. A wave diffracts more when its wavelength is similar to the size of the barrier or opening.

💡 Think it Over

3. **Explain** why the color violet is refracted the most.

_____

_____

✔ Reading Check

4. **Define** What is diffraction?

_____

_____

_____

💡 Think it Over

5. **Communicate** A garage door is 3 m wide. Which sound waves will diffract most easily when they pass through the door—ones with a wavelength of 2 m or ones with a wavelength of 0.2 m?

_____

Can water waves diffract?

Imagine water waves in the ocean. What happens when the waves hit a barrier like an island? They go around the island. If the wavelength of the water waves is close to the size and spacing between the islands, the water waves diffract around the islands and keep moving. If the islands are bigger than the wavelength of the water waves, the water waves diffract less.

What happens when waves meet?

Suppose you throw two pebbles into a still pond. Waves spread out from where each pebble hits the water. When two waves meet, will they hit each other and change direction? No, they pass right through each other and keep moving. ☑

How do waves interfere with each other?

What happens when two waves overlap? The two waves add together, or combine, and make a new wave. The ability of two waves to combine and make a new wave when they overlap is __interference__. There are two kinds of interference— constructive and destructive as shown in the figure.

Constructive Interference In constructive interference, the crest of one wave overlaps the crest of another wave. They form a larger wave with greater amplitude. Then the original waves pass through each other and keep traveling as they were before.

Constructive Interference

Destructive Interference In destructive interference, the crest of one wave overlaps the trough of another. The amplitudes of the waves combine to make a wave with a smaller amplitude. If the waves have equal amplitudes, they will cancel each other out while the waves overlap. Then the original waves pass through each other and keep traveling as they were before.

Destructive Interference

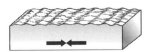

☑ **Reading Check**

6. Infer What happens when two waves meet?

_____

_____

Picture This

7. Conclude Look at the figure of destructive interference. When can two waves cancel each other out?

How are particles and waves different?

Diffraction When light travels through a small opening, it spreads out in all directions on the other side of the opening. What would happen if particles were sent through the small opening? They would not spread out. They would keep going in a straight line. Diffraction, or spreading, happens only with waves.

Interference Interference does not happen with particles, either. When waves meet, they interfere and then keep going. If particles meet, either they hit each other and scatter, or miss each other. Interference and diffraction both are properties of waves but not particles. ☑

How can noise be reduced?

A lawn mower and a chain saw make loud noises. These loud noises can damage hearing.

Ear Protectors That Absorb Noise Loud sounds have waves with larger amplitudes than softer sounds. Loud sound waves carry more energy than softer sound waves. You have cells in your ears that vibrate and send signals to your brain. Energy from loud sound waves can damage these cells and can cause you to lose your hearing. Ear protectors can help prevent loss of hearing. The protectors absorb, or take in, some of the energy from sound waves. The ear is protected because less sound energy reaches it.

Ear Protectors That Interfere With Noise Pilots of small planes have a similar problem. The airplane's engine makes a lot of noise. But, pilots cannot wear ear protectors to shut out all of the engine's noise. If they did, they would not be able to hear instructions from air-traffic controllers.

Instead, pilots wear special ear protectors. These ear protectors have electronic circuits. The circuits detect noise from the airplane. Then they make sound frequencies that destructively interfere with the noise. Remember that destructive interference makes a smaller wave. The frequencies interfere only with the engine's noise. Pilots can still hear the air-traffic controllers. So, destructive interference can be helpful.

8. Determine What two properties do waves have that particles do not have?

_____

_____

💡 **Think it Over**

9. Explain How do the ear protectors some pilots wear work?

_____

_____

_____

● After You Read

Mini Glossary

diffraction: the bending of waves around a barrier

interference: the ability of two waves to combine and make a new wave when they overlap

reflection: occurs when a wave hits an object or surface and bounces off

refraction: the bending of a wave as it moves from one medium to another

1. Review the terms and their definitions in the Mini Glossary. Write one or two sentences describing how refraction can make a rainbow.

   _____

   _____

   _____

2. In the graphic organizer below, name the four different wave properties. Give an example of each.

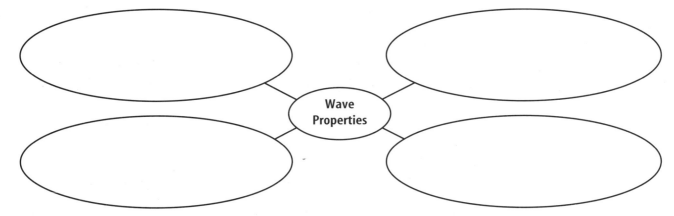

3. You were asked to highlight each question head and the answer to each question as you read this section. Name another strategy that would help you learn the properties of wave.

   _____

   _____

   _____

End of Section

Science Online Visit **red.msscience.com** to access your textbook, interactive games, and projects to help you learn more about wave behavior.

 **Rocks and Minerals**

section ❶ **Minerals—Earth's Jewels**

Before You Read

Think about a gem, such as a diamond, and a rock that you have seen. How are gems and rocks the same and how are they different?

_____

_____

_____

What You'll Learn

■ how rocks and minerals are different
■ what properties are used to identify minerals

Read to Learn

What is a mineral?

Suppose you wanted to look for minerals (MIH nuh rulz). Would you have to crawl into a cave or go down into a mine to find them? No. You could find minerals just walking around outdoors. You can even find minerals in your home. Things you use every day, such as pots, glasses, and the salt you sprinkle on food, are all made from minerals. Minerals and products made from them are all around you.

How are minerals defined?

A <u>mineral</u> is a solid, inorganic material found in nature. Inorganic means that minerals are not made from living things such as plants or animals. Every mineral has its own particular chemical makeup and its own unique arrangement of atoms. An X-ray of a mineral would reveal the orderly arrangement of its atoms, often seen in the mineral's crystal structure. Every mineral's distinct crystal structure gives it unique properties. These properties can be used to identify minerals. So far, more than 4,000 minerals have been identified. <u>Rocks</u> usually are made up of two or more minerals.

Study Coach

Sticky-note Discussions
As you read this section, use sticky notes to mark pages you find interesting or you have a question about. Share the information or question with another student in your class or your teacher.

FOLDABLES

Ⓐ **Find Main Ideas** Make a layered Foldable from four sheets of paper as shown to help you understand the properties of minerals.

Properties of Minerals
Crystals
cleavage and fracture
color
streak or luster
hardness
specific gravity
other properties

How do minerals form?

Minerals form in several ways. Some minerals form from melted rock inside Earth called magma. As magma cools, atoms combine in orderly patterns to form minerals. Minerals also form when magma reaches Earth's surface. Magma at Earth's surface is called lava.

Some minerals form from evaporation of water. For example, ocean water has salt dissolved in it. If the water evaporates, salt crystals remain. Many kinds of minerals are dissolved in water. When the water evaporates, the minerals form crystals.

Minerals also form from a process called precipitation (prih sih puh TAY shun). Water can hold only a certain amount of dissolved minerals. Any extra minerals separate from the water and fall out of solution. The extra minerals are deposited as crystals. For example, large areas of the ocean floor are covered with manganese nodules that formed in this way. The manganese fell out of solution and formed round deposits of manganese crystals.

What are some clues to mineral formation?

Sometimes just by looking at a mineral you can tell how it formed. Some minerals have large grains that fit together like the pieces of a puzzle. Large mineral grains usually form in open spaces within the rocks. They may have formed in these big spaces as magma cooled very slowly. When magma cools slowly, mineral grains have more time to grow.

Some crystals grow from solutions rich in dissolved minerals. To figure out how a mineral was formed, first look at the size of the mineral crystals, then look at how the crystals fit together.

Properties of Minerals

Imagine you are walking down the street. You think you see a friend walking ahead of you. The person is the same height and weight and has the same hair color as your friend. Is it your friend? Then the person turns around and you see her face and recognize her features right away. You've identified your friend by physical properties that set her apart from other people.

Each mineral also has unique properties. You can identify minerals by their unique properties in the same way you identify friends by their physical properties. ✔

What are crystals?

All minerals have an orderly pattern of atoms. These atoms are arranged in a repeating pattern. A **crystal** is a solid material that has an orderly, repeating pattern of atoms. Sometimes crystals have smooth growth surfaces, called crystal faces.

What are cleavage and fracture?

One clue to a mineral's identity is the way it breaks. Some minerals split into pieces with smooth, flat planes that reflect light. Minerals that break this way have cleavage (KLEE vihj). The mica in the figure below shows cleavage because it splits into thin sheets. ☑

Some minerals do not show cleavage when they break. These minerals break into uneven pieces with rough edges. Minerals that break into uneven chunks have fracture (FRAK chur). The figure below shows the fracture of the mineral flint.

Mica   Flint

How does color help identify minerals?

Copper is a mineral that has a reddish-gold color. The reddish-gold color of a penny tells you it is made of copper. Sometimes a mineral's color helps you identify it.

Sometimes, though, a mineral's color can fool you. The common mineral pyrite (PI rite) has a shiny gold color similar to the color of the mineral gold. During the California Gold Rush of the 1800s, miners sometimes thought pyrite was gold. Pyrite has little value, while gold is extremely valuable.

While different minerals may look similar in color, the same mineral may be found in several different colors. For example, the mineral calcite can occur in different colors depending on what other materials are mixed in with it.

✔ **Reading Check**

3. **Describe** If a mineral has cleavage, how does it break?

_____

_____

Picture This

4. **Compare** How is mica different from flint in the way it breaks?

_____

_____

_____

What are streak and luster?

Scraping a mineral across an unglazed white tile, called a streak plate, produces a streak of color. The color of a mineral's streak is another way to identify it. Oddly, a mineral's streak is not always the same color as the mineral itself. Yet a mineral's streak color is a more accurate way of identifying a mineral. For example, pyrite has a green-black or brown-black streak. Gold has a yellow streak. If the gold miners had used streak tests to identify the minerals they found, they might not have confused pyrite with gold.

Some minerals are shiny. Others are dull. Another property of minerals is luster. A mineral's luster describes how light reflects off its surface. If a mineral shines like metal, the mineral has a metallic (muh TA lihk) luster. A mineral with a nonmetallic luster looks dull, glassy, pearly, or earthy. Together, a mineral's color, streak, and luster help identify it. ☑

How is a mineral's hardness measured?

Some minerals are harder than others. Talc is a mineral that is so soft, it can be scratched with a fingernail. Diamond is the hardest mineral. Diamond can be used to scratch or cut almost anything else.

In 1822, Austrian geologist Friedrich Mohs developed a way to classify mineral hardness. The Mohs scale is shown in the figure below.

Mohs Scale		
Mineral	Hardness	Hardness of Common Objects
Talc	1 (softest)	
Gypsum	2	fingernail (2.5)
Calcite	3	copper penny (3.0)
Fluorite	4	iron nail (4.5)
Apatite	5	glass (5.5)
Feldspar	6	steel file (6.5)
Quartz	7	streak plate (7)
Topaz	8	
Corundum	9	
Diamond	10 (hardest)	

✔ **Reading Check**

5. **Identify** What is the term for the way a mineral reflects light?

Picture This

6. **Analyze** Look at the table showing the Mohs scale. If harder minerals can scratch softer minerals, what mineral can gypsum scratch?

How is the Mohs scale used?

A mineral with the number 1 on the Mohs scale is the softest mineral, talc. A mineral with the number 10 is the hardest mineral, diamond.

A mineral's hardness is determined by scratching it with other minerals. For example, fluorite (number 4 on the Mohs scale) will scratch calcite (number 3 on the Mohs scale). But fluorite cannot scratch apatite (number 5 on the Mohs scale).

You can use objects you have at home to determine a mineral's hardness. Look at the table on the previous page. The hardness of several common objects is listed. Using common objects can help you determine the hardness of the mineral. Knowing a mineral's hardness will help you identify that mineral.

What is specific gravity?

Imagine two 3 cm cubes. One is made out of wood and the other is made out of lead. Which one is heavier? Though both cubes are the same size, the lead cube is much heavier than the wooden cube. Some minerals are much heavier for their size than others. Specific gravity compares the weight of a mineral with the weight of an equal volume of water. For example, pyrite is about five times heavier than water. Pure gold is more than 19 times heavier than water. You could feel the difference by holding each one in your hand. Measuring specific gravity is another way you can identify minerals. ☑

What other properties help identify minerals?

Some minerals have other unusual properties that can help identify them. For example, the mineral magnetite acts like a magnet. A piece of magnetite will attract metal paper clips just like a magnet.

The mineral calcite has two unusual properties. When it comes into contact with an acid like dilute HCl, calcite begins to fizz. Calcite also changes a single ray of light into a double ray of light. If you look through a piece of calcite, you will see a double image.

Halite is a mineral that has a salty taste. Scientists sometimes use taste to identify a mineral. You should not do this because some minerals are harmful to the body. ☑

Together, all the properties you have read about are used to identify minerals. Learn to use them and you can identify most minerals you find.

✔ Reading Check

7. Determine Specific gravity compares the weight of a mineral with what ?

_____

_____

✔ Reading Check

8. Identify What unusual property does the mineral halite have?

_____

Common Minerals

Rocks that make up huge mountain ranges are made of minerals. But of the 4,000 known minerals, only a few make up most of the rocks. These minerals are known as the rock-forming minerals. If you learn to recognize these common minerals, you will be able to identify most rocks.

What are silicates?

Most rock-forming minerals are silicates (SIH luh kaytz). Silicates contain the elements silicon and oxygen. Quartz is a mineral that is pure silica (SiO_2). Feldspar is a silicate mineral in which silica is combined with iron. More than half of the minerals in Earth's crust are types of feldspar. ✔

What are carbonates?

Other important rock-forming minerals are carbonates. Carbonates are compounds containing the elements carbon and oxygen. The carbonate mineral calcite makes up most of the common rock limestone.

Other common minerals can be found in rocks formed on the bottom of ancient seas. When these seas evaporated, the mineral gypsum remained. Rocks that contain the mineral gypsum are found in many places.

The mineral halite, or rock salt, is found beneath the surface of much of the Midwest. The mineral halite formed when the ancient seas that covered the Midwest evaporated.

What are gems?

Which type of ring would you rather have—a quartz ring or a diamond ring? Of course, you would rather have a diamond ring. Diamond is a gem that is often used in jewelry. A **gem** is a rare, valuable mineral that can be cut and polished, giving it a beautiful appearance. To have the quality of a gem, a mineral must be clear. It should not have any flaws, defects, or cracks. A gem must also have a beautiful luster or color. Few minerals meet these high standards. That is why the ones that do are rare and valuable.

Why are gems so rare?

Gems are rare because they are made under special conditions. Scientists have learned to make synthetic diamonds by using very high pressure. This pressure is greater than any found in Earth's crust. For this reason, scientists think diamonds form deep inside Earth's mantle.

✔ **Reading Check**

9. Identify What two elements do all silicates contain?

_____

_____

💡 **Think it Over**

10. Classify What qualities must a mineral have in order to be considered a gem?

_____

_____

_____

What are ores?

An **ore** is a mineral that contains enough of a useful substance that it can be mined and sold for a profit. Many metals that humans use every day come from ores. For example, the iron used to make steel comes from the mineral hematite. The lead used in batteries comes from galena, and the magnesium in vitamins comes from dolomite.

Ores of these useful metals must be removed from Earth in a process called mining. Mining is an expensive process. To offset the costs and be profitable, ores must be found in large deposits or rich veins.

How can minerals be conserved?

Because minerals often take millions of years to form, there are limited amounts of them in Earth's crust. As a result, minerals are considered a nonrenewable resource. For this reason, scrap metal is often reused or recycled. Old, used metal products are melted down and made into new products. Conserving metal in this way decreases the need for mining and saves mineral resources. Recycling also limits the amount of land that is disturbed by mining. Do you recycle? The figure below shows some common items collected and recycled.

How are ores processed?

After an ore is mined, it must be processed to remove the useful mineral or element. Smelting is the process used to obtain copper. In the smelting process, the ore is melted and unwanted materials are removed. After smelting, the copper is refined, or purified. Then it is made into many types of products used in homes, businesses, and industry. Copper products include electrical wiring, pots and pans, and most electronics. ☑

Think it Over

11. Apply Why is it important to recycle metal products?

____

____

____

Reading Check

12. Name one everyday product that contains copper.

____

Copyright © Glencoe/McGraw-Hill, a division of The McGraw-Hill Companies, Inc.

● After You Read

Mini Glossary

crystal: solid material with atoms arranged in an orderly, repeating pattern

gem: rare, valuable mineral that can be cut and polished

mineral: solid, inorganic material found in nature that always has the same chemical makeup, atoms arranged in an orderly pattern, and unique properties

ore: material that contains enough of a useful metal that it can be mined and sold for a profit

rock: solid inorganic material that is usually made up of two or more minerals

1. Review the terms and their definitions in the Mini Glossary. Write one sentence about minerals. Use at least two terms in your sentence.

_____

_____

_____

2. Compare minerals and gems using this Venn diagram.

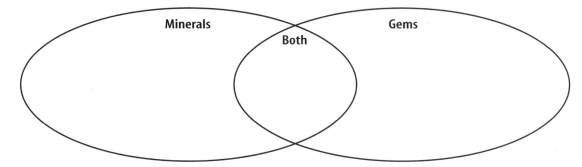

3. As you read, you used sticky notes to mark interesting pages or questions. How did this strategy help you understand the information you learned about minerals?

_____

_____

_____

End of Section

 **Science Online** Visit **red.msscience.com** to access your textbook, interactive games, and projects to help you learn more about minerals.

 **Rocks and Minerals**

section ❷ Igneous and Sedimentary Rocks

● Before You Read

Think about an erupting volcano. Often, there is red-hot material exploding out of it. What do you think happens to the material when it cools?

_____

_____

● Read to Learn

Igneous Rock

Rocks are constantly changing. Slowly, over time, rocks are worn away and new rocks form. These processes produce the three main kinds of rocks—igneous, sedimentary, and metamorphic.

Deep inside Earth, it is hot enough to melt rock. **Igneous** (IHG nee us) **rock** forms when melted rock from inside Earth cools and hardens. When melted rock material cools on Earth's surface, it is called **extrusive** (ehk STREW sihv) igneous rock. When melted rock material cools beneath Earth's surface, it is called **intrusive** (ihn TREW sihv) igneous rock.

What is igneous rock made from?

The chemicals in the melted rock determine the color of the rock that forms. Melted rock that contains a lot of silica will produce an igneous rock with a light color. Light-colored igneous rocks are call granitic (gra NIH tihk) rocks. Melted rock that contains more iron, magnesium, or calcium, will produce an igneous rock that has a dark color. Dark-colored igneous rocks are called basaltic (buh SAWL tihk) rocks. Intrusive igneous rocks are often granitic. Extrusive igneous rocks are often basaltic.

What You'll Learn

- how intrusive and extrusive igneous rocks are different
- how different types of sedimentary rocks form

Study Coach

Two Column Notes As you read, organize your notes in two columns. In the left column, write the main ideas of each paragraph. Next to it, in the right column, write details about it.

FOLDABLES

Ⓑ Classify Make the following Foldable to help you organize information about rocks made from lava and magma.

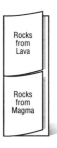

How do rocks form from lava?

When melted rock reaches Earth's surface, it is called lava. Extrusive igneous rocks form from lava that cools on Earth's surface. Since lava cools quickly, large mineral crystals, or grains, do not have time to form. As a result, extrusive igneous rocks usually have small mineral crystals that are hard to see and a smooth, sometimes glassy, appearance.

Extrusive igneous rocks can form in two ways. They may form when a volcano erupts and shoots lava and ash into the air or onto the surface. Extrusive igneous rocks also may form from cracks in Earth's crust called fissures (FIH shurz). When a fissure opens, lava oozes out onto the ground or into water. This is called a lava flow.

How do rocks form from magma?

Melted rock inside Earth is called magma. Intrusive igneous rock forms when magma cools below the surface of Earth. They form when a huge glob of magma inside Earth is forced upward but never reaches the surface. The glob of magma sits under the surface and cools slowly. Over millions of years, the magma cools and hardens into igneous rock. The cooling process is so slow, minerals in the magma have time to form large crystals. The figure below shows where intrusive and extrusive igneous rocks form around a volcano.

Think it Over

1. **Describe** What would you look for to determine if a rock is an intrusive or an extrusive igneous rock?

_____

_____

_____

Picture This

2. **Identify** Use a blue pencil to trace the path of the magma to the area where the extrusive igneous rock forms. Use a red pencil to circle the area where the intrusive igneous rock forms.

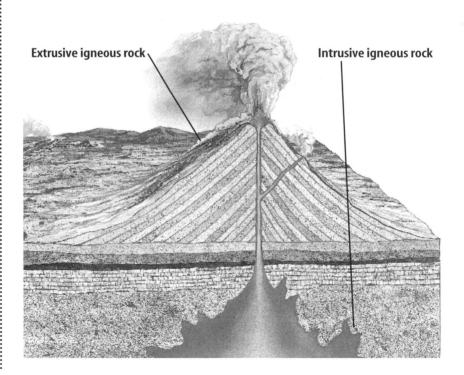

Extrusive igneous rock

Intrusive igneous rock

Sedimentary Rocks

Tiny pieces of rock, shells, mineral grains, and other materials are called sediment (SE duh munt). For example, the sand at the beach is a type of sediment.

Sediment is made and transported in several ways. Wind, water, and ice break down pieces of rock or rock mineral grains. Wind, water, and ice can also carry these sediments from one place to another. When the sediments settle, they form a thin layer. **Sedimentary** (sed uh MEN tuh ree) **rock** is made from sediment that collected in layers to form rock layers. It takes many thousands or even millions of years for sedimentary rock to form. Because rock is being worn away all the time, sedimentary rock forms continuously. There are three main categories of sedimentary rock—detrital, chemical, and organic.

How are detrital rocks formed?

Some sedimentary rocks are made of mineral grains or tiny pieces of rocks that have been worn away by wind, water, or ice. Sedimentary rocks that form from tiny mineral grains or other rock particles are called detrital (dih TRI tuhl) sedimentary rocks. Wind, gravity, ice, or water carry these tiny particles of sediment and deposit them in layers. Layer upon layer of mineral grain sediment is deposited. As the layers pile up, top layers press down, or compact, lower layers. Other minerals dissolved in water act like cement to bind the layers of sediment together into rock. Sandstone is a common detrital sedimentary rock.

How are detrital rocks identified?

To identify detrital sedimentary rock, you use the size of the grains that make up the rock. The smallest, clay-sized grains feel slippery when they are wet. These clay-sized grains make up a rock called shale.

Silt-sized grains are slightly larger than clay-sized grains and feel rough. Siltstone is a detrital sedimentary rock made up of silt-sized grains.

Sand-sized grains are even larger. Rough sedimentary rocks, such as sandstone, are made of sand-sized grains.

The roughest detrital sedimentary rock is made up of pebbles. Pebbles that are mixed and cemented together with other sediments form detrital rocks called conglomerates (kun GLAHM ruts).

FOLDABLES

B Classify Make a four-tab Foldable as shown to help you learn about sedimentary rocks.

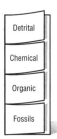

Detrital

Chemical

Organic

Fossils

Think it Over

3. Classify Write the four grain sizes in order from smallest to largest.

_____

_____

_____

_____

How do chemical sedimentary rocks form?

Chemical sedimentary rocks can form in different ways. Sometimes chemical sedimentary rocks form from ocean water that is rich in minerals. When the water evaporates, mineral layers are left behind. Over time, the layers form chemical sedimentary rock.

Some chemical rocks form from geysers or hot springs. At a geyser or hot spring, hot, mineral-rich water reaches the surface from deep underground. As the hot water evaporates on the surface, layers of minerals are left behind. Eventually, the layers of minerals form chemical sedimentary rocks. ☑

Have you ever sat in the Sun after swimming in the ocean? If you have, you may have noticed tiny crystals forming on your skin as the Sun warms and dries you. When the ocean water on your skin evaporated, it left behind crystals of salt, or halite. The halite was dissolved in the ocean water. When the water evaporated, mineral crystals remained.

How do organic sedimentary rocks form?

Think about the chalk your teacher uses to write on the chalkboard. Did you know that chalk may also be a sedimentary rock? Another sedimentary rock is the coal that is used as a fuel to produce electricity.

Chalk and coal are examples of organic sedimentary rocks. When living matter dies, the remains pile up in layers. Over millions of years, the layers are pressed together to form rock. If the rock is formed from layers of dead plant material, then coal forms. If the rock is formed from layers of dead animal material, such as bits of seashells, then chalk may form. Organic sedimentary rock made from seashells in the ocean can also form limestone. ☑

Are fossils found in sedimentary rocks?

Chalk, limestone, and other types of organic sedimentary rocks are made from the fossils of millions of tiny organisms. Fossils are the remains or traces of once-living plants and animals. Often, the fossils in organic sedimentary rock are extremely small. But sometimes, the fossils are large and reveal much of the body of the once-living plant or animal. For example, dinosaur bones and footprints are fossils that have been found in sedimentary rocks.

Copyright © Glencoe/McGraw-Hill, a division of The McGraw-Hill Companies, Inc.

✔ **Reading Check**

4. Draw Conclusions
What must happen to water in order for its dissolved minerals to be deposited?

_____

_____

✔ **Reading Check**

5. Identify What organic material forms coal?

_____

_____

● After You Read

Mini Glossary

extrusive: igneous rocks that have small or no crystals and form when melted rock cools quickly on Earth's surface

igneous rock: intrusive or extrusive rock that forms when melted rock from inside Earth cools and hardens

intrusive: igneous rocks that usually contain large crystals and form when magma cools slowly beneath Earth's surface

sedimentary rock: type of rock made from pieces of other rocks, dissolved minerals, or plant and animal matter that collect to form rock layers

1. Review the terms and their definitions in the Mini Glossary. Then write one sentence about igneous rock and one sentence about sedimentary rock.

_____

_____

_____

2. Fill in the blanks in the boxes below.

TWO TYPES OF ROCK

_____ rock forms from magma deep inside Earth.

_____ rock forms from layers of sediment.

| _____ forms from cooling lava on the surface. | _____ forms from cooling magma underground. | _____ forms from mineral grains or tiny parts of rock. | _____ forms from mineral dissolved in water that evaporates. | _____ forms from the remains of once-living plants and animals. |

3. Did the two column notes you made help you understand the information about sedimentary rock? Would you use this strategy again to learn new information?

_____

_____

Science Online Visit **red.msscience.com** to access your textbook, interactive games, and projects to help you learn more about igneous and sedimentary rocks.

End of Section

section ❸ Metamorphic Rocks and the Rock Cycle

What You'll Learn
- the conditions needed for metamorphic rock to form
- that all rocks are linked by the rock cycle

Mark the Text

Underline As you read, underline the key words and ideas in each paragraph to help you understand new information.

FOLDABLES™

D Organize Make the following Foldable to help you understand how rocks change.

● Before You Read

Imagine that someone leaves a hat on a chair and you accidentally sit on it. Describe how the pressure of your body changes the hat.

_____

_____

_____

● Read to Learn

New Rock from Old Rock

Rocks on Earth are constantly changing because of different physical processes. Sedimentary rocks are formed by low temperature processes that break down and wear away bits of rock. Igneous rocks are formed by high temperature conditions that form molten rock material. There are other conditions on Earth that also produce new rocks.

How do pressure and temperature change rock?

Deep inside Earth, rock is under great pressure. Just as the pressure of your body can change a hat you sit on, pressure inside Earth can cause certain changes in rock. Changes in pressure and temperature can change the chemicals that make up rock and the size of the mineral grains in rock.

It can take millions of years for rocks to change. It may take that long for pressure to build up while rocks are buried deeply or continents collide. Sometimes rocks are cooked by magma moving up into Earth's crust. The heat of the magma doesn't melt the rock, but it does change the rock's mineral crystals. All these events make new rock out of old rock.

How do metamorphic rocks form?

Do you recycle your plastic milk jugs? Have you ever thought about what happens to these jugs after you put them in the recycling bin? First the jugs are collected, sorted, and cleaned. Then they are heated and squeezed into pellets. The pellets later can be made into useful new products.

Rocks are recycled too, in a process that takes millions of years. Most rocks are recycled deep inside Earth, where great pressure and high temperatures process them into new rocks. **Metamorphic** (me tuh MOR fihk) **rock** is new rock that forms when existing rock is heated or squeezed, but not melted. The new rock that forms not only looks different, but it might be chemically changed, too. Sometimes the minerals in the new rock line up in a distinct way. ☑

The word *metamorphic* means "change of form." This is a good word for rocks that get a new look when they are under great pressure and high temperature.

How are metamorphic rocks grouped?

New metamorphic rocks can form from any other type of rock—sedimentary, igneous, or even other metamorphic rock. One way to identify and group rock is by its texture. A rock's texture is a physical property that refers to how the rock looks. Texture helps to divide metamorphic rock into two main groups—foliated (FOH lee ay tud) and nonfoliated.

What are foliated rocks?

Foliated rocks have visible layers of minerals. The word *foliated* comes from a Latin word that means "leafy." Foliated minerals have been heated and squeezed into layers, like the pages, or leaves, of a book. Many foliated rocks have bands of different-colored minerals. Slate, gneiss (NISE), phyllite (FIH lite), and schist (SHIHST) are examples of foliated rocks. Some walkways and roofs are made of slate, a foliated metamorphic rock. ☑

What are nonfoliated rocks?

Nonfoliated rocks do not have distinct layers or bands. They are usually more evenly colored than foliated rocks. Often mineral grains can't be seen in nonfoliated rocks. If the mineral grains are visible at all, they are not lined up in any particular way. Soapstone and marble are nonfoliated rocks. Quartzite is a nonfoliated rock made from quartz sand grains. When the sand grains are squeezed and heated, they form the new kind of crystals found in quartzite.

☑ **Reading Check**

1. Identify What type of rock forms when existing rock is heated or squeezed?

_____

☑ **Reading Check**

2. Identify What would you look for to identify a foliated rock?

_____

_____

The Rock Cycle

Rocks are constantly changing from one type to another. Scientists have made a model to show how all rocks are related to one another and how different processes constantly change rocks. The **rock cycle** is the model that shows the slow continuing process of rocks changing from one type to another. Every rock on Earth is on an endless journey through the rock cycle. A rock's trip through the rock cycle can take millions of years. The rock cycle is shown below.

Picture This

3. **Circle** the three types of rock in the Rock Cycle.

The Rock Cycle

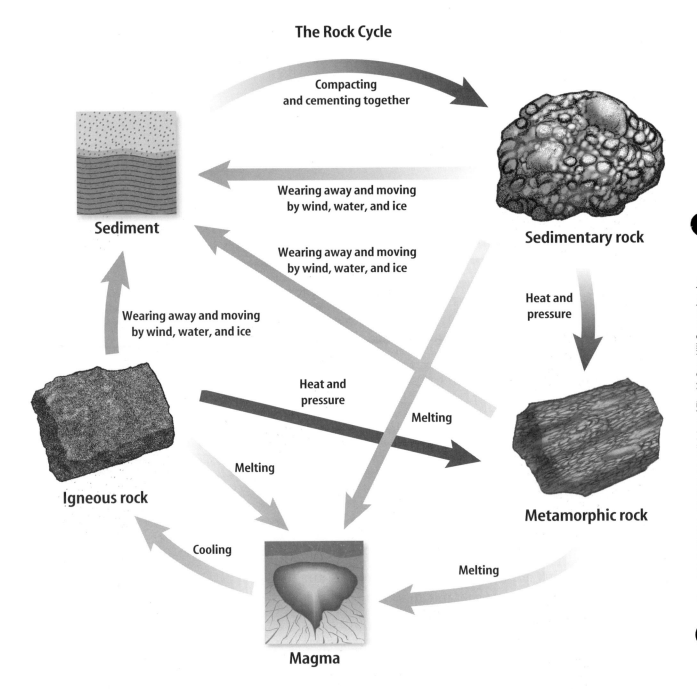

Compacting and cementing together

Sediment

Sedimentary rock

Wearing away and moving by wind, water, and ice

Wearing away and moving by wind, water, and ice

Heat and pressure

Wearing away and moving by wind, water, and ice

Heat and pressure

Melting

Igneous rock

Melting

Metamorphic rock

Cooling

Melting

Magma

What is the journey of a rock?

Look at the figure of the rock cycle on the previous page. Pick any spot on the rock cycle model. What form of rock is on the spot you chose? From that spot, follow the rock through the rock cycle. Notice the processes that act on the rock and change it. These processes include heat and pressure, wearing away, moving, melting, cooling, compacting, and cementing together. Look at the types of rock they become through these different processes. You can see that any rock can turn into any other type of rock.

What forms from magma?

Now start tracing the rock cycle from the magma at the bottom of the figure. The magma rises to the surface as a glob of lava. The lava cools and forms an igneous rock.

What changes igneous rock?

Wind, rain, and ice slowly wear away bits of the igneous rock, breaking off some of its tiny mineral grains, or sediment. The sediment is carried by the wind or by a river or maybe even by ice. Eventually, the sediment is deposited in thin layers. Over time, the layers build up. The weight of the top layers presses down on lower layers compacting them. The pressure acts like glue, cementing the layers together to form a sedimentary rock.

What other changes occur?

Deep inside Earth, the sedimentary rock is under great pressure and high temperature. Slowly, over millions of years, the sedimentary rock is changed into metamorphic rock. The metamorphic rock may eventually be melted to form magma. When magma cools below Earth's surface, intrusive igneous rock forms. When magma explodes out of a volcano and lava flows onto Earth's surface, extrusive igneous rock forms.

The cycle of change continues. The processes that are part of the rock cycle change rocks slowly over time. These processes are taking place right now.

Think it Over

4. Think Critically Is magma the source of all rocks on Earth? Explain your answer.

_____

_____

_____

Think it Over

5. Predict How can one sedimentary rock be changed into another sedimentary rock?

_____

_____

_____

After You Read

Mini Glossary

foliated: metamorphic rocks that have visible layers of mineral

metamorphic rock: new rock that forms when existing rock is heated or squeezed

nonfoliated: metamorphic rocks that do not have distinct layers or bands

rock cycle: model that shows the slow continuing process of rocks changing from one type to another

1. Review the terms and their definitions in the Mini Glossary. Then write one sentence about metamorphic rocks. Use at least two vocabulary words in your sentences.

____

____

2. Fill in the blanks in the chart below to show how rocks change.

The Rock Cycle

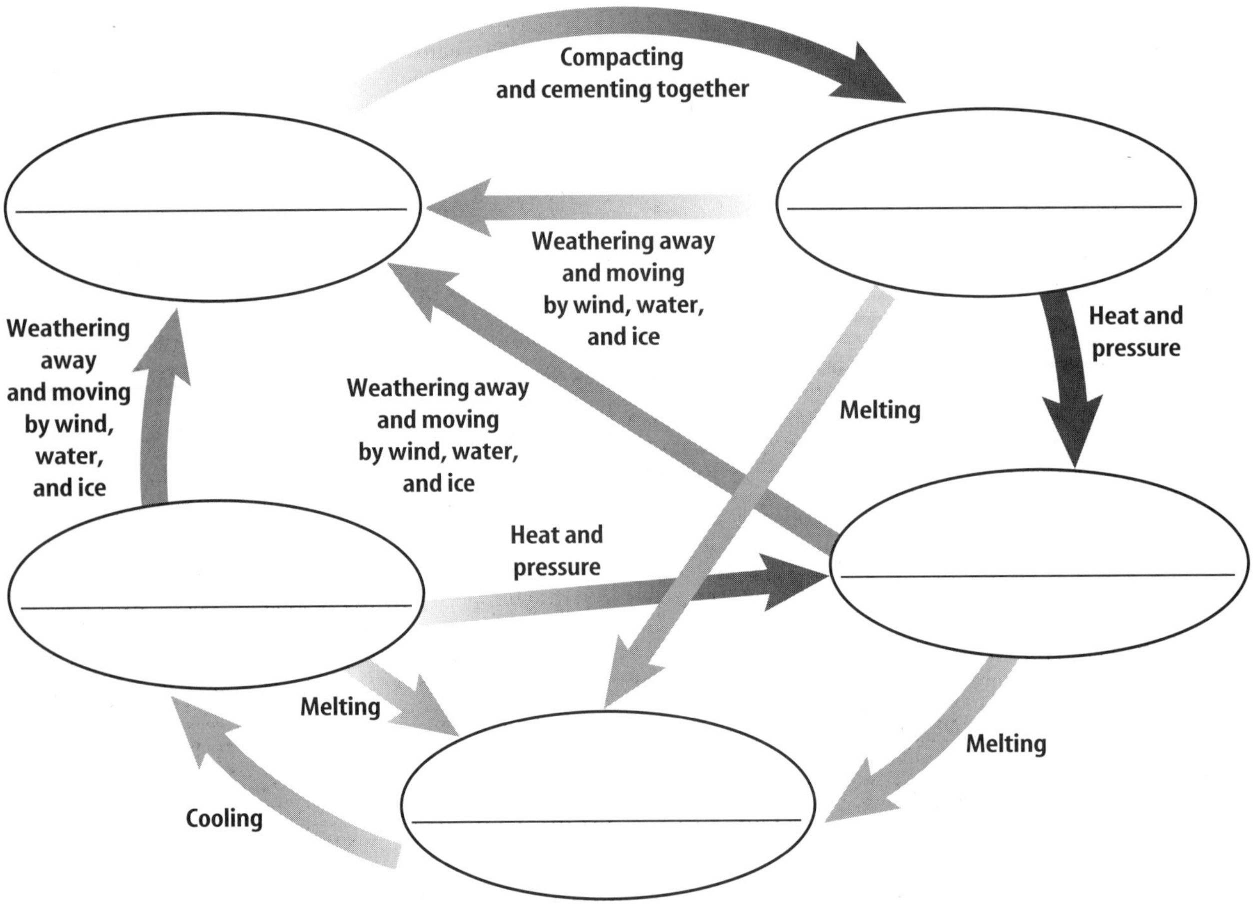

End of Section

Science Online Visit **red.msscience.com** to access your textbook, interactive games, and projects to help you learn more about metamorphic rocks and the rock cycle.

Forces Shaping Earth

section ❶ Earth's Moving Plates

Before You Read

Think of a time you saw or dug a very deep hole in the ground. Describe what the soil was like as the hole went deeper into the ground.

What You'll Learn

- about Earth's interior layers
- how and why Earth's plates move

Read to Learn

Clues to Earth's Interior

If someone gives you a wrapped present, how can you figure out what it is? You might hold it and shake it gently to find some clues. Even though you can't see what's inside, these clues can help you figure out what it might be. The observations you make are called indirect observations.

Scientists do the same thing when they try to learn about Earth's interior. Since it is not possible to directly observe what is deep inside Earth, scientists gather clues from earthquakes and rocks on the surface of Earth. These clues are indirect evidence about Earth's interior.

What are seismic waves?

What happens if you throw a rock into a pond? Waves travel out in all directions from the spot where the rock hit the water. These waves carry some of the rock's energy away. The same thing happens when an earthquake occurs. Seismic waves carry energy as they travel out in every direction from the focus, or center, of the earthquake.

Seismic waves travel at different speeds through different materials. Waves travel faster in solid rock than in liquid. By looking at the speed of the waves and the paths that they take, scientists can get clues about how the planet is put together.

Study Coach

Sticky-note Discussion
As you read, use sticky notes to mark pages you find interesting or have a question about. Share the interesting fact or question with another student in your class or your teacher.

Copyright © Glencoe/McGraw-Hill, a division of The McGraw-Hill Companies, Inc.

What do rocks tell about Earth's interior?

Certain rocks are found in different places on Earth's surface. The material in these rocks is similar to the material scientists think exists deep inside Earth. The rock formed far below the surface. Forces inside Earth pushed the rocks near the surface. There they were exposed by erosion. The rock clues and the clues from seismic waves suggest that the Earth is made up of layers of different kinds of materials.

Earth's Layers

Based on evidence from seismic waves and exposed rocks, scientists have made a model of Earth's interior. The model shows that Earth's interior has four different layers. These layers include the inner core, the outer core, the mantle, and the crust.

In some ways, Earth's structure is similar to a peach, as shown in the figure. A peach has a thin skin covering the thick, juicy part that you eat. Under that is a large pit that surrounds a seed in the center.

What is the inner core?

The pit and the seed are like the two parts of Earth's core. One part of Earth's core is liquid and one part is solid. The **inner core** is the solid, innermost layer of Earth's interior. It is the hottest part of Earth and has the greatest amount of pressure. This part of the core is made up mostly of solid iron. When seismic waves reach the inner core, they speed up. This clue tells scientists that the inner core is solid. ☑

The temperature is extreme in the inner core. Its temperature is about 5,000°C, making it the hottest part of Earth. The core is under a great amount of pressure. This is because of the weight of the rock surrounding it. Pressure increases the deeper you go beneath Earth's surface. More material pushes towards Earth's center because of gravity. This is why the inner core has the greatest amount of pressure.

Picture This

1. **Identify** The peach pit has a seed inside. Color the center of the pit red to show where the seed lies. This is similar to where Earth's inner core is located.

Reading Check

2. **Recall** What is the inner core made of?

_____

Copyright © Glencoe/McGraw-Hill, a division of The McGraw-Hill Companies, Inc.

What is the outer core?

The <u>outer core</u> is the layer of Earth that lies above the inner core and is thought to be made up mostly of molten metal. Since the outer core slows down some seismic waves and stops others, scientists concluded that the outer core is a liquid.

The location of the outer core is similar to the location of the pit in the peach example. Even the wrinkled surface of the pit is like the uneven boundary between the outer core and the mantle, which lies above it.

What are Earth's mantle and crust like?

The layer in Earth's interior just above the outer core is the mantle. In the model of the peach, the mantle would be the large, juicy, inside part that you eat. The <u>mantle</u> is the largest layer of Earth's interior. Even though the mantle is solid, it can move and flow slowly.

Earth's outermost layer is the <u>crust</u>. In the peach model, this layer would be the fuzzy skin of the peach. The crust is thinnest under the oceans and thickest through the continents. All the features of Earth's surface—mountains, rivers, and canyons—are part of Earth's crust.

The figure below shows Earth's four layers: inner core, outer core, mantle, and crust.

Earth's Four Layers

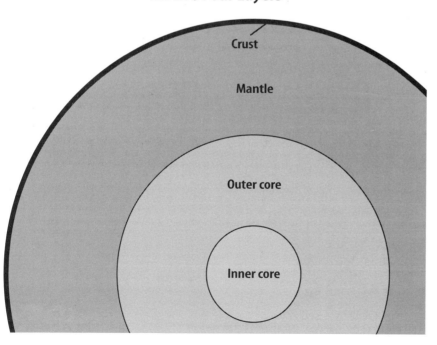

Crust

Mantle

Outer core

Inner core

Think it Over

3. **Explain** How did scientists determine that Earth's outer core is liquid?

_____

_____

_____

Picture This

4. **Interpret and Label** Which of Earth's layers is thinnest? Mark it with an X.

_____

Earth's Structure

As you have learned, Earth's structure is made up of four layers. It can also be divided into other layers. These layers are based on physical properties that change with depth beneath the surface. Density, temperature, and pressure are three properties that change as depth changes. These three properties are lowest in the crust and greatest in the core. ☑

Earth's Plates

Even though the crust is separated from the mantle, the rigid uppermost part of the mantle moves with the crust. The rigid upper part of Earth's mantle and the crust is called the **lithosphere.** The lithosphere is broken into about 30 sections, called plates. A **plate** is a section of Earth's lithosphere that moves around slowly on another part of the mantle, called the asthenosphere. Plates can move because the asthenosphere below them is liquid and plasticlike. The figure below shows the lithosphere which is composed of crust and the uppermost part of the mantle. The asthenosphere, a plastic-like layer, is also shown.

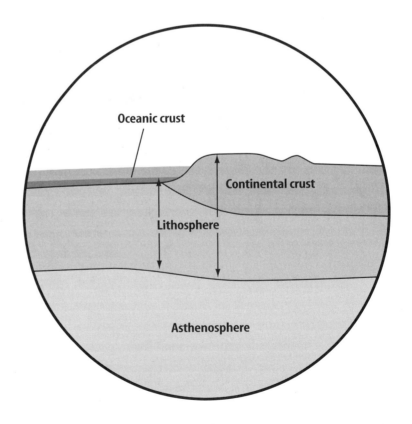

✔ **Reading Check**

5. Identify Name the three properties that change as you go deeper inside Earth.

_____

_____

_____

Picture This

6. Identify Outline the lithosphere in red. Color the asthenosphere blue.

How do Earth's plates move?

Earth's plates move very slowly. Sometimes it takes more than a year for a plate to move only a few centimeters. A plate might only move 2 centimeters per year, but over thousands of years, it can move a long distance. Over time, the plates have changed shape, size, and location. Antarctica now covers the south pole, but it used to be near the equator. At one time, North America was joined with Africa and Europe. Today, tools such as lasers and satellites help scientists measure small plate movements. The map below shows where Earth's plates are now located. The arrows show how the different plates are moving.

FOLDABLES

A **Organize Information**
Construct a half-book Foldable as shown to record information about why plates move.

Why do plates move?

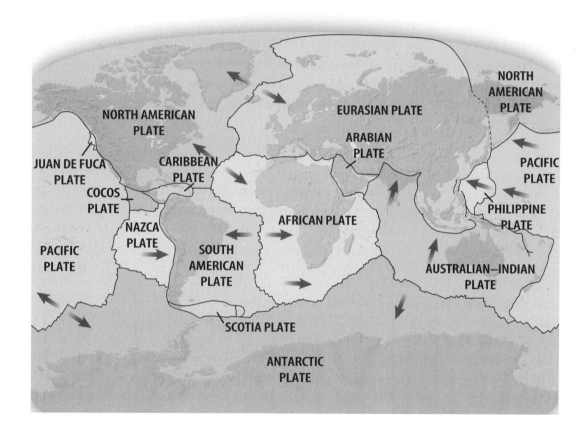

Plate Boundaries

The places where the edges of different plates meet are called plate boundaries. The constant movement of plates creates forces that affect Earth's surface at the boundaries of the plates. At some boundaries, the forces are strong enough to cause mountains to form. At other boundaries, rift valleys and volcanoes form. At a third type of boundary, faults form. A **fault** is a large break in rocks along which movement occurs. The movement can cause earthquakes.

Picture This

7. **Locate and Label** On the map, circle a place where two plates are moving apart. Draw a box around a place where two plates are moving together.

B Organize Information
Construct a three-tab Foldable to help organize information about how Earth's plates move.

Plates that Collide | Plates that Move Apart | Plates that Slide Past

✔ **Reading Check**

8. Identify What is the force that causes rock layers to crumble and fold?

What happens when plates move apart?

Sometimes two plates move away from each other because of pulling forces that act in opposite directions on each plate. This pulling force is called tension. If tension continues to pull two plates apart, large slabs of rock may sink. This forms an area called a rift valley.

Another result of plates separating is the formation of new crust. New crust forms in gaps where the plates pull apart. As tension continues along these boundaries, new gaps form. Then the gaps are filled in by magma that is pushed up from Earth's mantle. Over time, the magma in the gaps cools to become new crust. This process of plates separating and new crust forming takes place under the oceans at places called mid-ocean ridges.

What happens when plates collide?

When plates move toward each other, they collide. The result of the collision depends on the density of the two plates that collide. The crust that forms ocean floors is denser than the crust that forms continents.

If two continental plates collide, they have a similar density. They are both less dense than the mantle under them. As a result, the collision causes the crust to pile up. When rocks come together like this, the force is called compression. Compression causes the rock layers on both plates to crumble and fold. Imagine putting a piece of cloth on your desk. If you push the edges of the cloth toward each other, the cloth will crumble and fold over on itself. This is similar to what occurs when plates crash into each other, causing mountains to form. ☑

Flat rock layers are pushed up into folds. Sometimes the folding is so severe that rock layers bend completely over on themselves, turning upside down. As rock layers fold, they pile up and form mountains.

What is plate subduction?

When one oceanic plate collides with another oceanic plate or with a continental plate, the plate that is more dense goes under the other one. As a result, a deep trench forms. **Subduction** is a type of plate movement that occurs when one plate sinks beneath another. When a plate subducts, it sinks into the mantle. Earth's crust does not grow larger. As new crust material is formed, older crust material subducts into, or sinks below, the mantle.

Copyright © Glencoe/McGraw-Hill, a division of The McGraw-Hill Companies, Inc.

What happens when plates slide past each other?

You have learned that plates move toward each other and away from each other. Plates can also slide past one another. The boundary where these plates meet is called a transform boundary. As the plates move past each other in opposite directions, the edges grind and scrape. When a force pushes two plates in opposite directions, it is called shearing. Shearing causes the area between the plates to form faults and have many earthquakes.

Why do plates move?

Earth's plates are large. It takes a massive amount of energy to move them. Scientists are not sure where this energy comes from, but they have many theories. Most of these theories suggest that gravity is the force that provides the energy. Gravity pulls things toward the center of the Earth. But plates move sideways across the globe. How does gravity make something move across the surface of Earth?

One theory to explain plate movement is convection of the mantle. As the figure on the right shows, rock in the mantle is 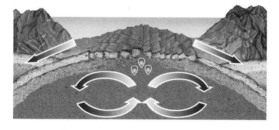 heated by the core. The hotter rock rises towards Earth's surface. Then it cools and sinks deep into the mantle. After it sinks into the mantle, it is heated again. This cycle causes rock material to circulate. The convection theory suggests that plates move as material in the mantle circulates.

What other factors cause plates to move?

At mid-ocean ridges, plates may move because of ridge-push. Mid-ocean ridges are higher than the ocean floor around them. Because of gravity, the plate that is higher moves down the slope. This is called ridge-push.

Slab-pull occurs as plates move away from a mid-ocean ridge. They become cooler which makes them denser. A plate can get so dense that it sinks when it collides with another plate. If a dense plate sinks, it is easier for it to move across Earth's surface. ☑

Picture This

9. Identify Color the parts of the arrows red that show hot rock rising. Color the parts of the arrows blue that show cooled rock sinking.

☑ Reading Check

10. Determine When plates become cooler, do they become more dense or less dense?

_____

Copyright © Glencoe/McGraw-Hill, a division of The McGraw-Hill Companies, Inc.

● After You Read

Mini Glossary

crust: Earth's outermost layer that is thinnest under the oceans and thickest through the continents

fault: large breaks in rocks along which movement occurs

inner core: solid, innermost layer of Earth's interior that is the hottest part of Earth and has the greatest amount of pressure

lithosphere: rigid layer of Earth made up of the crust and the upper part of the mantle

mantle: largest layer of Earth's interior that lies above the outer core

outer core: layer of Earth that lies above the inner core and is thought to be made up mostly of molten metal

plate: section of Earth's lithosphere that moves around slowly on the asthenosphere

subduction: type of plate movement that occurs when one plate sinks beneath another one

1. Review the terms and their definitions in the Mini Glossary above. Write a sentence explaining how each of the following pairs of words is related.

   a. crust and fault _____

   _____

   b. subduction and plate _____

   _____

2. Label Earth's layers in the figure below.

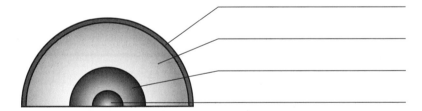

3. You used sticky-notes to mark pages that had interesting or difficult information. Did this strategy help you learn about Earth's layers and plates? Explain why or why not.

   _____

   _____

   _____

End of Section

  Visit **red.msscience.com** to access your textbook, interactive games, and projects to help you learn more about Earth's moving plates.

164 Forces Shaping Earth

 **chapter 10** **Forces Shaping Earth**

section ⊜ Uplift of Earth's Crust

● Before You Read

Picture a mountain range you have seen either in person or in a picture. How do you think these mountains formed? Write your ideas about how mountains may form.

_____

_____

_____

What You'll Learn

- how different types of mountains form
- forces that shape Earth's mountains

● Read to Learn

Building Mountains

Mountains tower over the surrounding land, offering spectacular views from their tops or from the areas around them. The highest mountain peak in the world is Mount Everest in the Himalaya in Asia. It is more than 8,800 m above sea level. In the United States, the highest mountain is more than 6,000 m high. There are four main types of mountains—fault-block, folded, upwarped, and volcanic. Since they form in different ways, these mountains have different looks and sizes.

How old are different mountains?

Some mountains are tall and jagged with snow covered peaks. Other mountains are rounded and have gentle slopes. This difference depends on whether or not the mountains are still forming. The Himalaya, which are forming at the rate of several centimeters per year, are jagged and steep. Mountain ranges that formed millions of years ago have had time to erode. The Ouachita Mountains in Arkansas stopped forming millions of years ago. They have large, gently rolling hills.

Study Coach

Two-Column Notes As you read, organize your notes in two columns. In the left-hand column, write the main idea of each paragraph. Next to it, in the right-hand column, write details about the main idea.

FOLDABLES ™

ⓒ Organize Information Make a Foldable as shown to help organize information on each kind of mountain.

fault-block mountain	folded mountain
unwarped mountain	volcanic mountain

Copyright © Glencoe/McGraw-Hill, a division of The McGraw-Hill Companies, Inc.

1. Identify Use a marker to highlight the sharp peaks that are formed by tension forces.

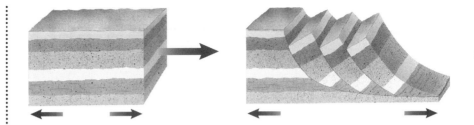

How do fault-block mountains form?

Sometimes, tension forces pull Earth's plates in opposite directions. As a result, surface features such as rift valleys and faults are formed. Fault-block mountains also form from these pulling forces. **Fault-block mountains** are sharp, jagged mountains made of huge, tilted blocks of rock that are separated from surrounding rocks by faults. As the figure above shows, tension forces pull the level layers of rock from opposite directions. Large blocks slide downward forming peaks and valleys.

If you hold a candy bar between your hands and pull it apart, cracks may form. When rocks are pulled apart, faults form. Unlike rocks deep inside Earth, rocks at Earth's surface are hard and break easily. When they are pulled apart, large blocks of rock can move along the faults. The Sierra Nevada in California and the Teton Range in Wyoming have sharp, jagged peaks that are typical of fault-block mountains.

How do folded mountains form?

Imagine holding a flat piece of clay between your hands and then pushing your hands together. What happens? As you push your hands together, the clay begins to bend and fold over itself. If you travel through the Appalachian Mountains, you can see rock layers that have been folded just like the clay was when it was squeezed or compressed. When two of Earth's plates moved together, compression forces squeezed the rock layers from opposite sides. This caused the rock layers to buckle and fold, forming folded mountains. **Folded mountains** are mountains formed by the folding of rock layers caused by compression. ☑

The Appalachian Mountains are folded mountains that formed millions of years ago. At one time, they were high, steep mountains, even higher than the Rocky Mountains. But they have been weathered and eroded over time, so now they are small compared to other mountain ranges.

✔ Reading Check

2. Recall What kind of force causes folded mountains to form?

How do upwarped mountains form?

The Adirondack Mountains in New York, the southern Rocky Mountains in Colorado and New Mexico, and the Black Hills in South Dakota are all examples of upwarped mountains. **Upwarped mountains** form when forces inside Earth push up the crust. Over time, the sedimentary rock layers on top erode. Then the metamorphic and igneous rocks underneath are exposed. These can erode further to form peaks and ridges. ☑

How do volcanic mountains form?

At times, magma from inside Earth reaches the surface. Magma that flows out onto Earth's surface is called lava. When lava flows onto the surface, volcanic mountains can form. Layer upon layer of lava piles up and cools until a cone-shaped feature called a **volcanic mountain** forms.

Some volcanic mountains form at plate boundaries, where one plate subducts into the mantle. As the plate sinks into the mantle, it melts. This melted material, or magma, is less dense, so it rises to the surface over time. If it reaches the surface, it can erupt as lava and ash. Layers of lava and ash pile up over time to form a new volcanic mountain.

The figure below shows a volcanic mountain and the path magma follows as it rises to Earth's surface and erupts as lava.

Copyright © Glencoe/McGraw-Hill, a division of The McGraw-Hill Companies, Inc.

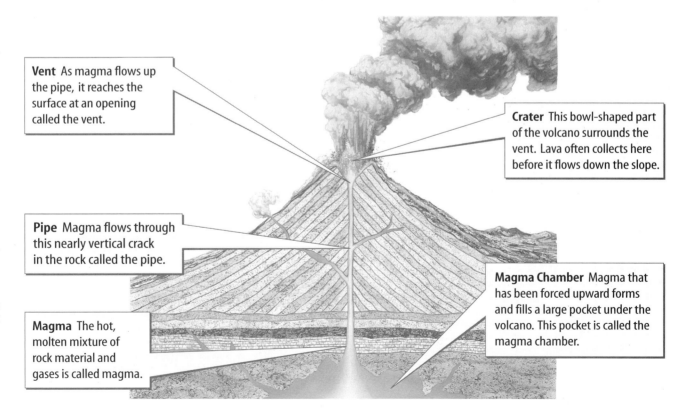

Vent As magma flows up the pipe, it reaches the surface at an opening called the vent.

Pipe Magma flows through this nearly vertical crack in the rock called the pipe.

Magma The hot, molten mixture of rock material and gases is called magma.

Crater This bowl-shaped part of the volcano surrounds the vent. Lava often collects here before it flows down the slope.

Magma Chamber Magma that has been forced upward forms and fills a large pocket under the volcano. This pocket is called the magma chamber.

☑ Reading Check

3. Identify What type of mountains form when forces inside Earth push up the crust ?

_____

_____

Picture This

4. Use Scientific Illustrations Trace the path magma follows when the volcano erupts.

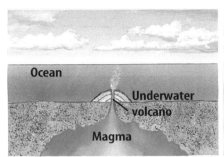 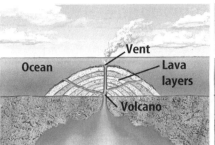 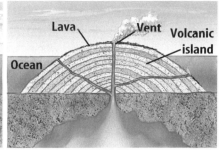

Picture This

5. Identify Circle the point at which magma becomes lava.

How do underwater volcanic mountains form?

You know that volcanic mountains form on land. Did you know that volcanic mountains also form on the ocean floor? The figure above shows this process. Underwater eruptions form mountains under the sea. Magma rises up and then flows out as lava. Over time, as the layers of lava build up, mountains rise above sea level. This is how the Hawaiian Islands formed.

Volcanic mountains like the Hawaiian Islands are different from volcanic mountains that form when one plate subducts into the mantle. The Hawaiian Islands didn't form at a plate boundary. They formed over a hot spot. Hot rock that is forced up through Earth's mantle melts to form a hot spot in Earth's crust. When plates move over the hot spot, a series of volcanoes form. The Hawaiian Islands are a series of volcanic mountains that formed as lava erupted onto the ocean floor.

There are some differences between hot spot volcanoes and subduction volcanoes. Magma from subduction volcanoes forms closer to Earth's surface. Hot spot volcanoes are much larger and have more gently sloping sides than subduction volcanoes.

Other Types of Uplift

If you place wooden blocks of different thicknesses in a bucket of water, you will notice that different blocks of wood float in the water at different heights. Thicker blocks of wood float higher than thinner blocks do. The buoyant force of the water balances the force of gravity. This is like a process called isostasy (i SAHS tuh see) that occurs in Earth. **Isostasy** is the principle that Earth's lithosphere floats on a plasticlike upper part of the mantle called the asthenosphere. ☑

✔ Reading Check

6. Recall What principle states that Earth's lithosphere floats on the asthenosphere?

How does isostasy affect Earth's crust?

The effects of isostasy were first noticed near large mountain ranges. Earth's crust is thicker under mountains than in other places. If mountains keep getting uplifted, the crust under the mountains becomes thicker and extends farther down into the mantle. This is like the floating wooden blocks. If you pile another wooden block on a block that is already floating, you will see that the new, larger block will sink farther into the water. The new block will also float higher than it did before. ☑

How does gravity affect uplifted crust?

As mountains grow larger, they sink farther into the mantle, just as larger wooden blocks sink farther into water. When mountains stop forming, erosion lowers them. As a result, the crust rises again because weight has been removed. If this process continues, the thicker crust under the mountains will be reduced to the thickness of the crust where there are no mountains.

This is similar to the way icebergs behave, as shown in the figure below. The iceberg is largest when it first breaks off of a glacier. As the iceberg floats, it melts and loses mass. As a result, it rises in the water. Over time, the iceberg will get smaller and smaller and won't extend as deeply into the water.

Reading Check

7. Determine Is Earth's crust thicker or thinner under mountains?

_____

Picture This

8. Observe Is the larger amount of ice in the icebergs above or below the water?

● After You Read

Mini Glossary

fault-block mountain: sharp, jagged mountains made of huge, tilted blocks of rock that are separated from surrounding rocks by faults and that form because of pulling forces

folded mountain: mountains formed by the folding of rock layers caused by compression

isostasy (i SAHS tuh see): principle that Earth's lithosphere floats on a plasticlike upper part of the mantle called the asthenosphere

upwarped mountain: mountains that form when forces inside Earth push up the crust

volcanic mountain: mountain that forms when magma is forced upward and flows onto Earth's surface

1. Review the terms and their definitions in the Mini Glossary. In your own words, explain the principle of isostasy.

_____

_____

2. Complete the chart to show what type of mountain is formed from each type of force.

Forces that form mountains

Compression forces ⟶	
Tension forces ⟶	
Subduction ⟶	
Forces inside Earth push up the crust ⟶	

3. In this section you used two-column notes to help you learn the information. Was this a helpful strategy? Would you use it again? Explain why or why not.

_____

_____

_____

End of Section

Science Online Visit **red.msscience.com** to access your textbook, interactive games, and projects to help you learn more about how mountains form.

 **chapter 11**

Weathering and Erosion

section ❶ Weathering and Soil Formation

Before You Read

Have you ever heard someone describe something as weathered? On the lines below, describe how a weathered object might look.

_____

_____

_____

What You'll Learn

- processes that break rock apart
- processes that chemically change rock
- how soil forms

Read to Learn

Weathering

Have you seen potholes in roadways and broken concrete in sidewalks and curbs? Potholes in roads and broken sidewalks are proof that solid materials can be changed by nature. **Weathering** is a mechanical or chemical process that causes rocks to change by breaking them down into smaller pieces. Rocks can be changed by freezing and thawing, by oxygen in the air, and even sometimes by plants and animals. These things cause rocks to weather and, in some cases, to become soils.

Mechanical Weathering

When a sidewalk breaks apart, a large slab of concrete is broken into many small pieces. The concrete looks the same. It's just broken apart. This is like mechanical weathering of rocks. **Mechanical weathering** is a process that breaks rocks into smaller pieces without changing them chemically. The small pieces of rock are the same as the original rock. There are many causes for mechanical weathering, including ice wedging and living organisms.

Mark the Text

Highlight Highlight the key terms and their meanings as you read this section.

FOLDABLES

A Compare Make a two-tab Foldable as shown below to compare weathering and erosion.

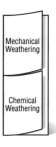

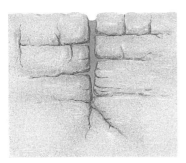

1. Water seeps into cracks.

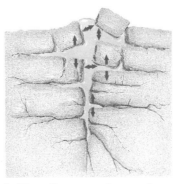

2. Water freezes and expands, opening cracks.

3. Ice melts and the process repeats.

Picture This

Picture This

1. **Highlight** the areas in each figure where water fills in the cracks. What do you notice about the spaces between the rocks in figures 1 and 3?

_____

_____

_____

✔ Reading Check

2. **Identify** What does chemical weathering change in rock?

_____

_____

What is ice wedging?

In some parts of the world, air temperature drops low enough to freeze water. Then, when the temperature rises, the ice thaws. This freezing and thawing cycle breaks up rocks. How can this happen? The figure above shows this process. When it rains or snow melts, water seeps into cracks in rocks. If the temperature drops below freezing, ice forms. As the ice forms, its takes up more space than the water did. That's because water expands when it freezes. As it expands, it puts pressure on the rocks. With enough force, the rocks will crack more. In time, they will break apart. Ice wedging causes potholes to form in roadways.

How do plants and animals cause weathering?

Plants and animals can cause mechanical weathering, too. Plants can grow in the most unlikely places. Sometimes their roots grow deep into cracks in rock where water collects. This puts pressure inside the rock and slowly wedges the rock apart.

Gophers, prairie dogs, and other animals that dig in the ground also cause mechanical weathering. As they burrow through sediment or soft sedimentary rock, these animals break rock apart. Sometimes as they dig, they push rock and sediment to the surface. At the surface, another kind of weathering, called chemical weathering, takes place.

Chemical Weathering

Chemical weathering is a process in which the chemical makeup of rock is changed. This kind of weathering is rapid in tropical areas where it is moist and warm most of the time. On the other hand, in areas that are dry or cold, chemical weathering occurs slowly. ✔

Rates of Weathering	
Climate	**Chemical Weathering**
Hot and dry	Slow
Hot and wet	Fast
Cold and dry	Slow
Cold and wet	Slow

💡 **Think it Over**

3. **Explain** What two conditions speed up the process of chemical weathering?

_____

_____

What causes chemical weathering?

The table above shows the rates of chemical weathering in areas with different climates. You have read that temperature and rainfall are important factors in how quickly chemical weathering occurs. But what causes the process of chemical weathering to begin? Two main causes of chemical weathering are natural acids and oxygen.

How do natural acids affect rocks?

Some rocks react with natural acids in the environment. For example, when water mixes with carbon dioxide in the air or soil, carbonic acid forms. Carbonic acid can change the chemical makeup of rocks. Even though carbonic acid is weak, it reacts with many rocks. When carbonic acid comes in contact with rocks like limestone, dolomite, and marble, they dissolve. Other rocks also weather when exposed to carbonic acid.

How do plant acids affect rocks?

Plant roots also produce acid that reacts with rocks. Many plants produce a substance called tannin. When water and tannin mix, they form tannic acid. This acid dissolves some minerals in rock. When that happens, the rest of the rock is weakened. Over time, it can break into smaller pieces.

How does oxygen affect rocks?

When you see rusty cars, red soil, or red stains on rocks, you are seeing oxidation. Oxidation is the effects of chemical changes caused by oxygen. Oxygen reacts with iron in materials like steel, causing these materials to rust and weaken. Rocks chemically weather in a similar way. When some iron-containing minerals are exposed to oxygen, they can weather into minerals that are like rust. This leaves the rock weakened, and it can break apart. ☑

☑ **Reading Check**

4. **Identify** What can oxygen do to materials that have iron in them?

_____

_____

5. Identify What does soil contain besides rock, water, and air?

_____

Picture This

6. Explain Do you think mountaintops have rich soil or poor soil? Why?

_____

_____

_____

B Explain Make a half-book Foldable from notebook paper to explain soil formation and types of soil.

Soil

Soil

Is soil just dirt under your feet, or does it have more value? **Soil** is a mixture of weathered rock, organic matter, water, and air that supports the growth of plant life. Organic matter is rotted leaves, twigs, roots, and other material. Many things affect the way soil forms including the parent rock, the slope of the land, time, climate, and organisms. ✔

How does parent rock affect soil?

One factor that affects soil formation is the type of parent rock, or original rock, that is being weathered. For example, in places where limestone is chemically weathered, clay soil is common. That's because clay is left behind when the limestone dissolves. In places where sandstone is weathered, sandy soil forms.

How does the slope of the land affect soil?

The **topography,** or surface features, of the land also influence the types of soils that form. On steep hillsides, like those in the figure below, soil has little chance of forming. That's because rock fragments move downhill all of the time. However, in areas where the land is flat, wind and water deposit fine sediments that help form thick soils.

How does time affect soil?

It takes time for rocks to weather. It can take thousands of years for some soils to form. As soils develop, they become less like the rock from which they formed. In young soils, the parent rock determines the characteristics of the soil. As weathering goes on, however, the soil is less and less like the parent rock. Deep, rich soils are found in some places where the weathering has gone on for a long time. For deep soils to form, soil materials must build up slowly on the land and not be eroded.

How does climate affect soil?

Climate affects soil changes, too. If rock weathers rapidly, deep soils can form quickly. This is more likely to happen in tropical areas where the climate is warm and moist.

Climate also affects the amount of organic material in soil. In desert climates, soils contain little organic material. But in warm, humid climates, there is a lot of organic material.

When plants and animals die, they begin to decay. Eventually, humus is formed. Humus is a dark material that helps soil hold water and provides nutrients for plants. A humus-rich soil layer is shown in the figure below.

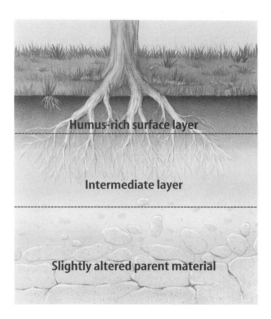

Humus-rich surface layer

Intermediate layer

Slightly altered parent material

Picture This

7. Identify Circle the layer of humus in the figure.

How do organisms affect soil?

Organisms also affect how soil forms. Lichens are small organisms that consist of an alga and a fungus. You may have seen lichens as colorful patches on trees or rocks. Lichens can grow directly on rock. As they grow, they take nutrients from the rock that they are breaking down and form a thin soil. After soil has formed, many other plants can grow, including trees and grasses. ☑

The roots of the plants break down more of the parent rock. Dead plant material, such as leaves, builds up. This adds organic matter to the soil. Some plants provide more organic matter to soil than others. Soil under grassy areas often is richer than soil in forests. Much of the midwestern United States used to be grasslands. This is why it is now some of the best farmland in the country.

✔ Reading Check

8. Explain If lichens grow directly on rock, where do they get nutrients?

_____

_____

_____

● After You Read

Mini Glossary

chemical weathering: process in which the chemical makeup of rock is changed

mechanical weathering: process that breaks rocks into smaller pieces without changing them chemically

soil: mixture of weathered rock, organic matter, water, and air that supports the growth of plant life

topography: surface features of the land that influence the types of soils that form

weathering: mechanical or chemical process that causes rocks to change by breaking them down into smaller pieces

1. Review the terms and their definitions in the Mini Glossary. Then write two sentences explaining how mechanical and chemical weathering are the same and how they are different.

_____

_____

_____

2. Complete the following table by adding the missing information.

Factors That Affect Soil	Mechanical Weathering	Chemical Weathering
Ice wedging		No
Plants		Yes
Animals	Yes	
Natural acids	No	
Plant acids		Yes
Oxygen		

Science Online Visit **red.msscience.com** to access your textbook, interactive games, and projects to help you learn more about weathering and soil.

End of Section

 **chapter 11**

Weathering and Erosion

section ❷ Erosion of Earth's Surface

● Before You Read

Have you ever seen a flood or a picture of a flood? On the lines below, describe how the water looked.

_____

_____

_____

● Read to Learn

Agents of Erosion

Imagine looking over the rim of the Grand Canyon. Far below is the winding Colorado River. Imagine watching a sunset over Utah's famous arches. These stunning views are examples of Earth's natural beauty. But how do canyons and arches form in solid rock?

These and other landforms are a result of erosion of Earth's surface. <u>Erosion</u> is the movement of rock or soil by forces like gravity, ice, wind, and water.

Gravity

Gravity is a force that pulls objects toward other objects. Gravity pulls everything on Earth toward Earth's center. As a result, water flows down hills. Rocks tumble down slopes. When gravity alone causes rock or sediment to move down a slope, the erosion is called <u>**mass movement**</u>.

Mass movements can occur anywhere there are hills or mountains. One place they often occur is near volcanoes. Creep, slump, rock slides, and mudflows are four types of mass movements. They are all caused by gravity.

Study Coach

Make Flash Cards As you read this section, make flash cards for each vocabulary term or unknown word. On one side of the card, write the term or word. On the other side of the card, write the definition.

FOLDABLES™

❻ Compare and Contrast Make the four-tab Foldable as shown below. Use it to record information on causes of erosion.

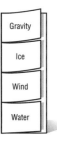

Gravity

Ice

Wind

Water

Copyright © Glencoe/McGraw-Hill, a division of The McGraw-Hill Companies, Inc.

What is creep?

<u>Creep</u> is the process in which sediments move slowly downhill. Creep is common where freezing and thawing occur. As ice expands in soil, it pushes sediments up. Then as soil thaws, the sediments move farther down the slope. The figure below shows how creep can move large amounts of sediment down a slope. Sometimes, creep causes damage to structures.

Picture This

1. **Trace** over the arrow that shows the direction the soil and sediment are moving.

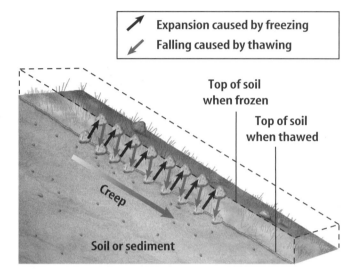

↗ Expansion caused by freezing
↙ Falling caused by thawing

Top of soil when frozen

Top of soil when thawed

Creep

Soil or sediment

What is slump?

A <u>slump</u> occurs when a mass of rock or sediment moves downhill along a curved surface. Slumps are most common in thick layers of loose sediment. They also can form in sedimentary rock. Slumps often occur on slopes that have been worn away by erosion. This often happens at the base of cliffs that have been worn away by waves. Slumps of this kind are common along the coast of Southern California, where they threaten to destroy homes and other buildings. ☑

What is a rock slide?

Can you imagine millions of cubic meters of rock roaring down a mountain at speeds faster than 250 km/h? That is about as fast as a small plane flies. This can happen when a rock slide occurs. During a rock slide, layers of rock break loose from slopes and slide to the bottom. The rock layers often bounce and break apart as they move. This makes a huge, jumbled pile of rocks at the bottom of the slope. Rock slides can destroy whole villages and cause hazards on mountain roads.

2. **Identify** What occurs when a mass of rock or sediment moves downhill along a curved surface?

What are mudflows?

Mudflows can occur where heavy rains or melting snow and ice soak the soil. A mudflow is a mass of wet sediment that flows downhill on top of the ground. Some mudflows are thick. As a result, they flow slowly and only move a few meters per day. Other mudflows are more fluid and move downhill at speeds close to 160 km/h. Fast-moving mudflows are common on some volcanoes.

Ice

In some parts of the world, ice causes erosion. In cold regions, more snow might fall than melt. Over many years, the snow can build up to form large, deep masses of ice called glaciers. When the ice in a glacier becomes thick enough, its own weight makes it flow downhill. It moves because of gravity. As glaciers move over the land, they erode materials from some areas and deposit them in other areas.

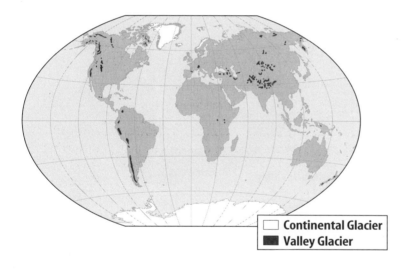

☐ Continental Glacier
■ Valley Glacier

The figure above shows where two kinds of glaciers, continental glaciers and valley glaciers, are found. Continental glaciers are huge ice sheets that can bury whole mountains. They once covered wide areas of Earth, but today they are found just in polar regions. Continental glaciers cover about ten percent of the land. ☑

Valley glaciers are much smaller. They are found in high mountains where the temperature isn't warm enough to melt the ice sheets. Most of the time, these ice sheets only move 0.01 to 2.0 meters per day. But at times, they can flow up to 100 meters per day.

3. Calculate A rock slide may move 250 km/h. A mudflow may move 160 km/h. How much faster might a rock slide be than a mudflow?

_____

_____

Picture This

4. Locate and Infer Outline areas where continental glaciers are found. Why do you think these are the only areas that have continental glaciers?

_____

_____

✔ Reading Check

5. Identify Name the two kinds of glaciers.

_____

_____

How do glaciers cause erosion?

Glaciers can erode rocks in two ways. If the rock under the glacier has cracks in it, the ice can pull out pieces of rock. This causes the rock to erode slowly. Loose pieces of rock freeze into the bottom of the glacier and are dragged along as the glacier moves.

As the rock fragments are dragged over Earth's surface, they scratch the rock below like sheets of sandpaper. This scratching is the second way that glaciers can erode rock. Scratching makes grooves in the rock underneath and can wear rock into a fine powder called rock flour.

How do glaciers change the land?

Glacial erosion is a powerful force that shapes the land. In mountains, valley glaciers can move rock from mountaintops. This forms large bowls, called cirques (SURKS), and steep peaks. When a valley glacier moves into a stream valley, it erodes rock along the valley sides. That makes a wider, U-shaped valley. These features are shown in the figure below.

Picture This

6. Identify Circle the cirque in the figure. Highlight the U-shaped valley.

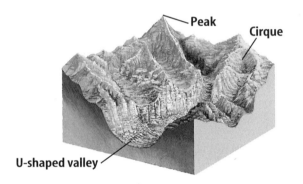

Peak · Cirque · U-shaped valley

Continental glaciers also shape Earth's surface. These ice sheets can completely remove rock layers from the land.

What do glaciers deposit?

Glaciers can deposit sediments. When ice melts from a glacier, the sediment it was carrying gets left behind. This sediment dropped from the ice is called till. Till is a mix of soil and rock particles, ranging in size from small bits of clay to large boulders. ☑

In summer, a lot of melting occurs around glaciers. So much ice can melt that streams often flow away from the glacier. These streams carry and drop sediment. The sand and gravel dropped by streams flowing from glaciers are called outwash. Unlike till, outwash usually is made up of particles of rock that are all about the same size.

Reading Check

7. Identify What is the term for sediment that is dropped from the ice of a glacier?

_____

Wind

If you've had sand blow into your eyes, you understand wind as a cause of erosion. When wind blows across loose sediment, it lifts and carries it. Wind leaves behind particles that are too heavy to move. The erosion of the land by wind is called **deflation**. Deflation can lower the land's surface by several meters.

Wind that is carrying sediment can wear down rocks. It works just like a sandblaster. **Abrasion** is a form of erosion that occurs when wind blows sediments into rocks, makes pits in the rocks, and produces smooth, polished surfaces. ☑

How does wind deposit sediment?

When wind blows around an object, like a rock or plant, it slows down. As the wind slows, it drops the sand it was carrying. If this sand deposit keeps growing, a sand dune might form. Sand dunes move, as shown in the figure, when wind carries sand up one side of the dune and it flows down the other side.

Dune movement

Sometimes, wind carries only fine sediment called silt. When silt is deposited and blankets the surface, it is called loess (LOOS). Loess is as fine as talcum powder. Loess is often dropped downwind of large deserts and glacial outwash deposits.

✔ **Reading Check**

8. **Identify** What form of erosion produces smooth, polished surfaces?

_____

Picture This

9. **Draw** red arrows on the sand dune to show the direction of the wind against it. Draw blue arrows to show how the sand moves over the top of the sand dune and flows down the other side.

Water

You probably have seen muddy water running down a street after a heavy rain. Water that flows over the ground is called **runoff**. Runoff is a key force in erosion, especially if the water is moving fast. The faster water moves, the more material it can carry. Water can flow over the land in a few different ways.

What is sheet flow?

When raindrops hit the ground, they break up clumps of soil and loosen small bits of sediment. If these raindrops fall on a slope, a thin sheet of water might start to move downhill. You have seen something similar if you've ever washed a car and seen sheets of water flowing over the hood. When water flows down a hill as a thin sheet, it is called sheet flow. This thin sheet of water can carry loose sediment with it, causing a type of erosion called sheet erosion. ☑

What are rills and gullies?

Where a sheet of water flows around objects and becomes deeper, rills can form. Rills are small channels cut into sediment on Earth's surface. These channels carry more sediment than sheet flow does. In some cases, a group of rills can form on a slope after just one heavy rain. As runoff keeps flowing through rills, more sediment erodes. Soon, the channel gets wider and deeper. When the channels get to be about 0.5 m across, they are called gullies.

How do streams cause erosion?

Gullies often connect to streams. Streams can be so small that you can jump to the other side or large enough for huge river barges to use them. Most streams have water flowing through them all the time, but some streams only have water part of the year.

In mountains and hills, streams flow down steep slopes. These streams have lots of energy. They often cut into the rock below them. This type of stream often has white-water rapids and may have waterfalls. When streams flow on flatter land, they flow more smoothly. Streams might snake back and forth across their valley, washing away and depositing sediment along their sides. In the end, all streams flow into an ocean or a lake where they drop their load of water and sediment. The level of water in the ocean or lake determines how deeply a river can erode.

☑ **Reading Check**

10. Identify What type of erosion is caused by sheet flow?

_____

_____

💡 **Think it Over**

11. Evaluate Which factors affect the speed of the water in a stream?

_____

_____

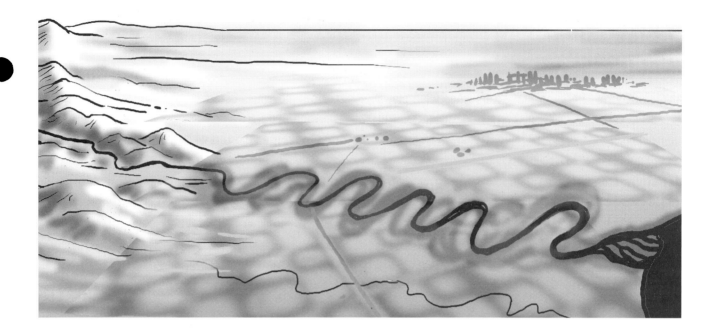

How do streams shape the land?

Streams are the main cause of erosion on Earth. The figure above shows the flow of a stream shaping land. Streams shape more of the land than ice, wind, or gravity. Over time, water moving in a stream can cut canyons into solid rock. Many streams together can shape the land over a wide area, forming valleys and leaving some rock as hills.

Streams also shape the land by depositing sediment. They can form sandbars along their path and build up sheets of sand across their valleys. When rivers enter an ocean or lake, the water slows. Then sediment is deposited, sometimes forming large deposits called deltas. The city of New Orleans is built on a delta formed by the Mississippi River. ☑

Effects of Erosion

All types of erosion change the land. Rock and sediment are removed from some areas and deposited in other areas. Where rock is removed, canyons, valleys, and mountain cirques can form. Where sediment is deposited, deltas, sandbars, sand dunes, and other land features can form.

Picture This

12. **Draw** arrows to show the direction in which the water is moving. Put an X at the spot where the stream flows into the lake and deposits sediment.

 **Reading Check**

13. **Identify** What forms when water slows and deposits sediment where a river enters a lake?

● After You Read

Mini Glossary

abrasion: form of erosion that occurs when wind blows sediments into rocks, makes pits in the rocks, and produces smooth, polished surfaces

creep: process in which sediments move slowly downhill

deflation: erosion of land that occurs when wind blows loose sediments and carries them away, leaving behind particles that are too heavy to move

erosion: movement of rock or soil by forces like gravity, ice, wind, and water

mass movement: occurs when gravity alone causes rock or sediment to move down a slope

runoff: water that flows over the ground

slump: occurs when a mass of rock or sediment moves downhill along a curved surface

1. Review the terms and their definitions in the Mini Glossary. Write two sentences explaining the difference between deflation and abrasion.

_____

_____

_____

2. Complete the following table to compare different types of erosion.

Type of Erosion	Mass Movement?	Caused by What Force?	Affects What?
Abrasion	No	Wind	Exposed rock
Creep			
Deflation	No		
Glacier			
Runoff			
Slump		Gravity	
Stream			

3. In this section you made flash cards. How was this helpful in learning about weathering and erosion?

_____

End of Section

Science●**nline** Visit **red.msscience.com** to access your textbook, interactive games, and projects to help you learn more about erosion of Earth's surface.

chapter 12

The Atmosphere in Motion

section ❶ The Atmosphere

◉ Before You Read

Air is everywhere. It's always there. Without it, Earth would be unfit for life. Have you ever wondered how air keeps us alive? Write your ideas below.

_____

_____

Copyright © Glencoe/McGraw-Hill, a division of The McGraw-Hill Companies, Inc.

◉ Read to Learn

Investigating Air

An Italian scientist named Galileo Galilei (1564–1642) thought that air was more than just empty space. He weighed a container, injected air into it, and weighed it again. He observed that the container weighed more after air had been added. Galileo concluded that air has weight, so it must contain matter.

Today, scientists know other facts about Earth's atmosphere as well. Air stores and releases heat, and it holds moisture. Because air has weight, it can exert pressure. All of these properties, when combined with energy from the Sun, create Earth's daily weather.

Composition of the Atmosphere

The **atmosphere** is the layer of gases surrounding Earth. It provides Earth with the gases that organisms need to live. The atmosphere protects living things from harmful doses of ultraviolet radiation and X-ray radiation. It absorbs heat from the Sun and keeps Earth warm.

The atmosphere is a mixture of gases, water, and tiny particles of solids and other liquids. Gravity keeps the atmosphere around Earth and prevents it from moving into space.

What You'll Learn
- how the atmosphere supports life on Earth
- what makes up the atmosphere
- about the water cycle

Study Coach

Create-a-Quiz As you read the text, create a quiz question for each subject. When you have finished reading, see if you can answer your own questions correctly.

FOLDABLES™

Ⓐ Classify Make the following Foldable to help you organize information about the things that make up Earth's atmosphere.

Gases in the Atmosphere

Aerosols in the Atmosphere

1. Use Percentages
What percentage of Earth's atmosphere is made up of nitrogen and oxygen? What percentage is made up of trace gases? Show your work.

_____

_____

_____

B Organize Information
Make a Foldable to record information about the troposphere, stratosphere, and upper layers.

What gases are in Earth's atmosphere?

Nitrogen makes up about 78 percent of the atmosphere. Oxygen, the gas necessary for human life, makes up about 21 percent. The rest is made up of trace gases or gases that are found in extremely small amounts.

Two of the trace gases have important roles within the atmosphere. Water vapor (H_2O) is critical to weather. It is responsible for clouds and precipitation. The other important trace gas, carbon dioxide (CO_2), is needed for plants to make food. It also absorbs heat and helps keep Earth warm.

What are aerosols?

<u>Aerosols</u> (AR uh sahlz) in the atmosphere are solids such as dust, salt, and pollen, and tiny liquid droplets such as acids. Dust gets into the atmosphere when wind picks tiny soil particles off the ground or when volcanoes release ash. Salt enters the atmosphere when wind blows across the oceans. Pollen is released by plants. Human activities, such as burning coal, also can release aerosols.

Layers of the Atmosphere

The atmosphere is divided into five layers. These layers are based on temperature changes that occur with altitude, or height above Earth's surface. The lower layers are the troposphere and the stratosphere. The upper layers are the mesosphere, the thermosphere, and the exosphere.

What are the lower layers of the atmosphere?

The <u>troposphere</u> (TROH puh sfihr) is the layer of atmosphere closest to Earth's surface. It reaches upward to about 10 km. The troposphere contains about three fourths of the matter in Earth's atmosphere. This is also where nearly all clouds and weather occur. About 50 percent of the Sun's energy passes through the troposphere and reaches Earth's surface. The rest is reflected back to space.

Above the troposphere is the stratosphere (STRAH tuh sfihr). The stratosphere is the layer of atmosphere that exists from about 10 km to about 50 km above Earth's surface. Most of the atmosphere's ozone is in the stratosphere. The ozone in the stratosphere absorbs much of the Sun's ultraviolet radiation. Without the ozone in this layer, too much radiation would reach Earth's surface, causing health problems for plants and animals.

What are the upper layers of the atmosphere?

Above the stratosphere is the mesosphere (ME zuh sfihr). This layer extends from about 50 km to 85 km above Earth's surface. It contains little ozone, so much less heat is absorbed.

The thermosphere (THUR muh sfihr) is above the mesosphere. This layer reaches from about 85 km to 500 km above Earth's surface. Temperatures in the thermosphere can reach more than 1,700°C. This layer helps filter out harmful rays from the Sun.

Parts of the thermosphere and mesosphere contain electrically charged particles called ions. This zone is called the ionosphere (i AH nuh sfihr). The ionosphere can reflect AM radio waves, making long-distance communication possible.

The outermost layer of the atmosphere is the exosphere. It contains few atoms. No clear border separates the exosphere from space.

Earth's Water

Earth often is called the water planet. This is because Earth's surface is about 70 percent water. Water can exist in three separate states—ice, water, and water vapor. The table shows where Earth's water can be found.

Water is found as solid snow or ice in glaciers. In oceans, lakes, and rivers, water exists as a liquid. In the atmosphere, it is a gas called water vapor.

Distribution of Earth's Water	
Location	**Amount of Water (%)**
Oceans	97.2
Ice caps and glaciers	2.05
Groundwater	0.62
Rivers and lakes	0.009
Atmosphere	0.001
Total (rounded)	**100.00**

Applying Math

2. **Convert Percentages to Fractions** Earth's surface is about 70 percent water. What fraction of Earth's surface is water? What fraction is not water? Show your work.

_____

_____

_____

Picture This

3. **Interpret Data** According to the table, where would you find the least amount of Earth's water?

_____

Infer Would you expect more evaporation to occur on a sunny day or a cloudy day?

_____

✔ **Reading Check**

5. **Compare and Contrast** How is evaporation different from condensation?

_____

_____

_____

Picture This

6. **Interpret Scientific Illustrations** How does liquid water become part of the atmosphere?

_____

_____

_____

What is the water cycle?

Earth's water is in constant motion. The **water cycle** is the never-ending cycle of water between Earth's surface and the atmosphere. The Sun's energy powers the water cycle. The water in Earth's oceans, rivers, and streams absorbs the Sun's energy and stores it as heat.

Evaporation and Condensation When water has enough heat energy, it changes from liquid water into water vapor. This process is called evaporation. Water vapor then enters the atmosphere. Water also is transferred into the atmosphere from plant leaves. This process is called transpiration.

As water vapor moves up through the atmosphere, it becomes cooler. The molecules slow down. Eventually, the water molecules change back into droplets of liquid water. This process is called condensation. ☑

Precipitation Water droplets get larger when two or more droplets join together. Eventually, these droplets become large enough to be seen. They form a cloud. If the water droplets continue to get larger, they become too large and heavy to remain in the atmosphere. They fall to Earth as precipitation.

After the water is on the ground, some of it evaporates. Most water enters streams or soaks into the soil. In the soil, it is called groundwater. Much of this water makes its way back to lakes or to the oceans, where more evaporation occurs and the water cycle continues. The figure below shows the water cycle.

As water vapor rises into the air, it cools and forms liquid water again. Tiny water droplets form clouds.

Droplets inside clouds fall as precipitation, such as rain or snow.

Energy for the water cycle is provided by the Sun.

Water evaporates from oceans, lakes, and rivers. Plants release water vapor.

Rain runs off the land into streams and rivers. Plants also take up some of the water.

● After You Read

Mini Glossary

aerosols (AR uh sahlz): solids such as dust, salt, and pollen, and tiny liquid droplets such as acids in the atmosphere

atmosphere: layer of gases surrounding Earth that protects living things from harmful doses of ultraviolet radiation and X-ray radiation and absorbs and distributes warmth

troposphere (TROH puh sfihr): the layer of the atmosphere that is closest to Earth's surface; contains nearly all clouds and weather

water cycle: the never-ending cycle of water between Earth's surface and the atmosphere

1. Review the terms and their definitions in the Mini Glossary above. Choose two of the terms that are related and write a sentence using both terms.

_____

_____

2. Complete the chart to organize information from this section.

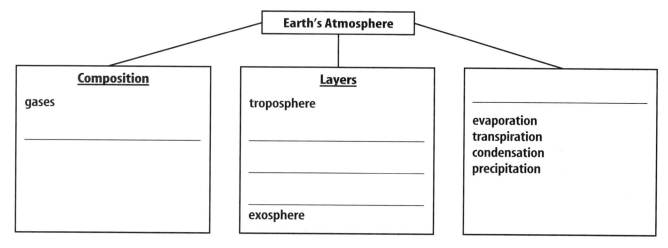

Earth's Atmosphere

Composition
gases
_____

Layers
troposphere
_____
_____
exosphere

_____
evaporation
transpiration
condensation
precipitation

3. You created quiz questions as you read this section. How many of the questions can you answer correctly? How did this strategy help you remember information about the atmosphere?

_____

_____

_____

 Visit **red.msscience.com** to access your textbook, interactive games, and projects to help you learn more about the atmosphere.

End of Section

The Atmosphere in Motion

section ❷ Earth's Weather

What You'll Learn

- how clouds form
- what causes precipitation
- what causes wind

Mapping Definitions As you read, make a definition map to describe and define vocabulary words. Your map should include questions about each word, such as, "What is it?" and "What are some examples?"

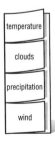

FOLDABLES

ⓒ Organize Information Make the following Foldable to help you organize information about Earth's weather.

temperature
clouds
precipitation
wind

● Before You Read

Hot, cold, windy, snowy, sunny, cloudy—these are all ways to describe weather. What is your favorite kind of weather? Describe it.

_____

_____

● Read to Learn

Weather

A weather bulletin has been issued for your area. Heavy snow is expected during the night. Will the schools be closed? Will people be able to get to work? How might this weather affect your family?

__Weather__ describes the current condition of the atmosphere, including temperature, cloud cover, wind speed, wind direction, humidity, and air pressure. A meteorologist (mee tee uh RAH luh jist) uses this information to forecast, or predict, the weather.

What is temperature?

Recall that the Sun's energy powers the water cycle. In fact, the Sun is the source of almost all of the energy on Earth. When the Sun's rays reach Earth, energy is absorbed. As gas molecules absorb more energy, they move faster and farther apart. Temperature is a measure of how fast air molecules are moving. The faster the molecules move, the higher the temperature. Temperature is measured with a thermometer. A thermometer has a scale divided into degrees. The two scales commonly used to measure temperature are the Celsius and Fahrenheit scales.

How does energy move through the atmosphere?

Fast-moving molecules transfer energy to slower-moving molecules when they bump into each other. This transfer of energy is called conduction. Conduction transfers heat from Earth's surface to nearby molecules in the air.

The heated air rises. As it rises, it starts to cool. When the rising air becomes cooler than the air around it, it sinks again. The process of warm air rising and cool air sinking is called convection. Convection is the main way heat is moved throughout the atmosphere. How conduction and convection transfer heat on Earth is shown in the illustration below.

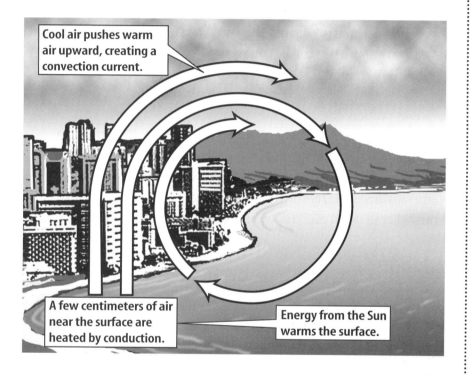

Cool air pushes warm air upward, creating a convection current.

A few centimeters of air near the surface are heated by conduction.

Energy from the Sun warms the surface.

Picture This

1. **Interpret Scientific Illustrations** Highlight the processes of conduction and convection on the diagram.

How is temperature related to air pressure?

The weight of air exerts pressure. Air pressure decreases as altitude increases. As you go higher, the weight of the atmosphere above you is less.

Temperature and air pressure are related. When air is heated, its molecules move faster, and the air expands. This makes the air less dense so it exerts less pressure on anything below it. The lighter, warmer air moves upward. Cooled air becomes more dense and sinks as the molecules slow down and move closer together. Sinking air produces more pressure. So, rising air usually means lower pressure and sinking air means higher pressure. Air pressure varies over Earth's surface.

Think it Over

2. **Infer** Is air pressure likely to be greater at the top or the base of a mountain? Why?

_____

_____

_____

What is humidity?

As air warms up, it can cause water that is touching it to evaporate and form water vapor. **Humidity** is the amount of water vapor in the atmosphere. Warm air causes evaporation to occur more quickly. Warm air also can hold more moisture. When air is holding as much water vapor as it can, it is said to be saturated and condensation may occur. The **dew point** is the temperature at which air becomes saturated and condensation can occur. ☑

What is relative humidity?

Suppose a mass of air is chilled. The amount of water vapor in the air does not change unless condensation occurs. However, less moisture can be evaporated into the chilled air. **Relative humidity** is a measure of the amount of water vapor in the air compared to the amount that could be held at that temperature. As air cools, relative humidity increases if the amount of water vapor in the air doesn't change. When the air holds all the water vapor it can hold at that temperature, the relative humidity is 100 percent.

Local TV weather reports sometimes give the dew point on summer days. If the dew point is close to the air temperature, relative humidity is high. If the dew point is much lower than the air temperature, relative humidity is low.

Clouds

One of the best signs that Earth's atmosphere is in motion is the presence of clouds. A cloud forms when air rises, cools to its dew point, and becomes saturated. Water vapor then condenses onto small particles in the air. If the temperature is warm, the clouds are made up of small drops of water. If the temperature is cold, the clouds are made up of small ice crystals. ☑

Clouds are classified according to the height above Earth's surface at which they form. The most common classification method separates clouds into low, middle, or high groups.

What are low clouds?

Clouds in the low-cloud group form at altitudes of 2,000 m or less. These include puffy cumulus (KYEW myuh lus) clouds that form when air currents rise, carrying moisture with them. Sometimes cumulus clouds are signs of fair weather. Other cumulus clouds can produce thunder, lightning, and heavy rain.

Stratus and Nimbostratus Clouds Another type of low cloud is layered stratus (STRA tus) clouds. Stratus clouds form as dull, gray sheets that can cover the entire sky. Nimbostratus (nihm boh STRA tus) clouds form low, dark, thick layers that block the Sun. Stratus and nimbostratus clouds produce precipitation.

What are middle clouds?

Clouds that form between about 2,000 m and 8,000 m are known as the middle-cloud group. Most of these clouds are of the layered variety. Their names often have the prefix *alto-* in front of them, such as altocumulus and altostratus. These clouds can hold enough moisture to produce light rain or snow. Sometimes they are made up of a mixture of liquid water and ice crystals.

How do high clouds form?

Some clouds form so high in the atmosphere that they are made up entirely of ice crystals. These are known as the high-cloud group. They include the high, wispy cirrus (SIHR us) clouds. They also include cirrostratus clouds, which are high, layered clouds that can cover the entire sky.

Some clouds extend from low levels to high levels of the atmosphere. These are clouds of vertical development. The most common type is cumulonimbus (kyew myuh loh NIHM bus) clouds. The term *nimbus* usually means the cloud creates precipitation. Cumulonimbus clouds produce the heaviest rains of all. Known as thunderstorm clouds, they start to form at heights of less than 1,000 m but can build to more than 16,000 m high. ☑

Precipitation

Rain, freezing rain, sleet, snow, and hail are all forms of precipitation. **Precipitation** forms when drops of water or crystals of ice become too large to be suspended in a cloud and fall to Earth. The type of precipitation that falls depends on temperature. For example, rain falls when the air temperature is above freezing. However, if the air at high altitudes is above freezing while the air near Earth's surface is below freezing, the result might be freezing rain.

☑ **Reading Check**

5. Draw Conclusions Which of these clouds means that a thunderstorm is on the way?

a. altocumulus
b. altostratus
c. cirrus
d. cumulonimbus

Think it Over

6. **Think Critically** Why do hailstones develop in cumulonimbus clouds?

_____

_____

Hail is balls of ice that form within a storm cloud. Strong winds inside the cloud toss ice crystals up and down. As the ice crystals move, droplets of water freeze around them. Hailstones keep growing until they are too heavy for the winds to keep up. Then they fall to the ground.

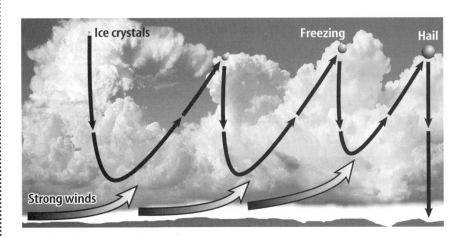

Wind

Warmer air is less dense and moves upward. This causes regions of low air pressure. When cooled, the molecules in air move closer together. The air becomes more dense and sinks. This forms regions of high air pressure. Air moves from areas of high pressure to low pressure. This movement is called wind. The greater the difference in temperature or pressure between two areas, the stronger the wind.

Think it Over

7. **Infer** If the wind is blowing from west to east, where is the area of high air pressure?

_____

_____

How does air circulate?

Look at the figure. You can see that the Sun's rays strike Earth at a higher angle near the equator than near the poles. This is why tropical areas heat up more than polar regions do. Warm air flows toward the poles from the tropics. Cold air flows from the poles toward the equator.

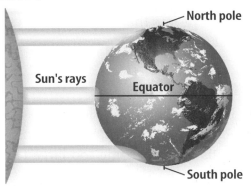

Picture This

8. **Compare and Contrast** Do areas near the equator heat up more or less than other regions? What about areas near the poles?

_____

_____

But the moving air doesn't flow in a straight line. Because Earth rotates, winds are pushed to their right in the northern hemisphere and to their left in the southern hemisphere. This is known as the Coriolis (kor ee OH lus) effect.

What are surface winds?

Air at the equator is heated by the rays of the Sun. This air expands, becomes less dense, and gets pushed upward. At about 30° latitude, the air is somewhat cooler. This air sinks and then flows toward the equator. As this air flows, it is turned by the Coriolis effect. The result is steady winds that blow from east to west. These steady winds are called the trade winds. Trade winds are also called tropical easterlies.

What are westerlies and easterlies?

Between 30° and 60° latitude north and south of the equator, winds usually blow from the west. These winds form between the cold air from the poles and warmer air closer to the equator. These winds are called the prevailing westerlies. These regions are known for frequent storms. Similar winds near the poles blow from the east and are known as the polar easterlies. The figure below shows Earth's major surface winds.

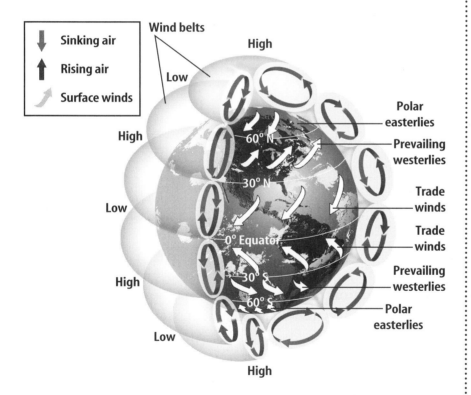

What are jet streams?

Jet streams are bands of strong winds that develop at higher altitudes within the zone of the prevailing westerlies. Jet streams are like giant rivers of air. They are important because weather systems move along their paths.

Copyright © Glencoe/McGraw-Hill, a division of The McGraw-Hill Companies, Inc.

Think it Over

9. **Infer** The tropical easterlies are called the trade winds. Why do you think they were given this name?

_____

_____

Picture This

10. **Interpret Scientific Illustrations** The city of Buenos Aires, Argentina is at about 34° latitude south of the equator. What type of winds affect the city's weather?

_____

● After You Read

Mini Glossary

dew point: the temperature at which air is saturated and condensation can occur

humidity: the amount of water vapor in the atmosphere

precipitation: occurs when drops of water or crystals of ice become too large to be suspended in a cloud and fall to Earth; rain, freezing rain, sleet, snow, or hail

relative humidity: a measure of the amount of water vapor in the air compared with the amount that could be held at a specific temperature

weather: the current condition of the atmosphere, including cloud cover, temperature, wind speed and direction, humidity, and air pressure

1. Review the terms and their definitions in the Mini Glossary. Choose a term and write a sentence in which you provide an example of that term.

_____

_____

2. Complete the concept map to show factors that affect Earth's weather.

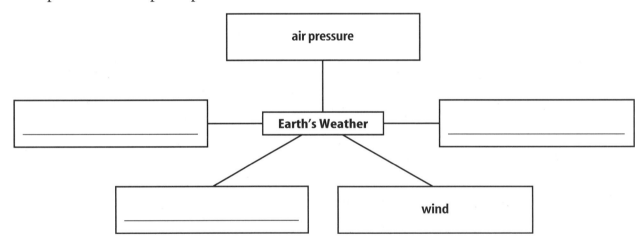

3. As you read this section, you made definition maps for the vocabulary words you learned. How did the mapping strategy help you? What is another strategy you could use to help you learn new vocabulary?

_____

_____

_____

End of Section

Science nline Visit **red.msscience.com** to access your textbook, interactive games, and projects to help you learn more about Earth's weather.

The Atmosphere in Motion

section ❸ **Air Masses and Fronts**

◉ Before You Read

Weather can change quickly from sunny to stormy and back again. What do you think causes the weather to change?

_____

_____

◉ Read to Learn

Air Masses

When you leave for school in the morning, it is raining. By lunchtime, it is sunny. Why did the weather change so quickly? A different air mass entered your area. An **air mass** is a large body of air that develops over a particular region of Earth's surface.

What types of air masses are there?

A mass of air that remains in one area for a few days picks up the characteristics of that area. For example, if the mass of air is over a desert, the air mass will become hot and dry. An air mass over tropical oceans becomes warm and moist.

Fronts

When two air masses meet, a front is formed. A **front** is a boundary between air masses of different temperatures. Air doesn't mix along a front. Because cold air is more dense, it sinks beneath warm air. The warm air is pushed upward and winds develop. Fronts usually bring a change in temperature as they pass, and they always bring a change in wind direction. There are four kinds of fronts—cold, warm, stationary, and occluded.

What You'll Learn

- how air masses and fronts form
- how storms develop
- about weather watches and warnings

▸ **Mark the Text**

Identify the Main Point
Highlight the main point in each paragraph. Use a different color to highlight a detail or an example that helps explain the main point.

FOLDABLES™

ⓓ **Describe** Make the following Foldable to help you describe how air masses, fronts, and pressure affect the weather.

Air Masses:

Fronts:

High-Low Pressure:

Severe Weather:

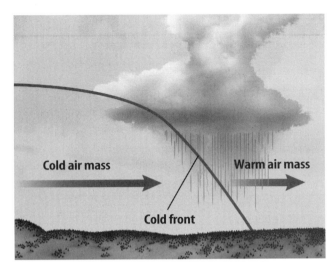

Cold Front

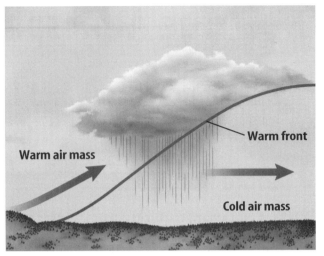

Warm Front

Picture This

1. **Identify** What moves out when a warm front moves in?

_____

_____

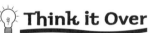

Think it Over

2. **List** What are the four kinds of fronts?

_____

_____

_____

Cold Front When a cold air mass moves toward a warm air mass, the cold air pushes under the warm air. The warm air is forced to rise. The place between the cold air mass and the warm air mass is called a cold front. Look at the figure above on the left. A cold front often produces short periods of storms with heavy precipitation. Cumulus and cumulonimbus clouds can develop. With a cold front, temperatures drop.

Warm Front When warm air approaches a region of colder air, a warm front is created. Look at the figure above on the right. Notice that warm air slides up and over a colder, denser air mass. Water vapor condenses. A warm front usually produces a long, steady period of precipitation over a wide area. The temperature rises. High cirrus clouds are one sign of an approaching warm front.

Stationary Front This type of front occurs where a warm air mass and a cold air mass meet but neither moves forward. A stationary front can stay in the same place for several days. Clouds occur along the front. There may be heavy precipitation because the front moves so little.

Occluded Front An occluded front occurs when a fast-moving cold front overtakes a warm front that is moving more slowly. These fronts also form in other ways. All occluded fronts produce cloudy weather with precipitation.

High- and Low-Pressure Centers

Where the air pressure is high, air sinks. Because the air is sinking, moisture cannot rise and condense. Air near a high-pressure center is usually dry with few clouds.

Where the air pressure is low, air flows in, rises, and cools. When the air reaches its dew point, water vapor condenses. Clouds and precipitation form. ☑

Severe Weather

Severe weather produces strong winds and heavy precipitation. People can be hurt by this weather, and property can be damaged. To prepare for severe weather, it helps to understand its causes.

What are thunderstorms?

Thunderstorms develop from cumulonimbus clouds. These clouds often form along cold fronts where air is pushed rapidly upward, causing water droplets to form. Falling droplets bump into other droplets and grow bigger. As these large droplets fall, they cool the air around them, creating strong winds. Hail can develop in these storms.

Cumulonimbus clouds also create lightning and thunder. Air rises quickly, which forms electric charges. Lightning is the energy flow that occurs between areas of opposite electrical charge. A bolt of lightning can be five times hotter than the surface of the Sun. Lightning heats the air nearby. The heated air expands faster than the speed of sound. The result is a sonic boom, which we call thunder. Close to the lightning, thunder sounds like a sharp bang. Further away, it sounds like a low rumble. The figure below shows how lightning forms.

Copyright © Glencoe/McGraw-Hill, a division of The McGraw-Hill Companies, Inc.

3. **Draw Conclusions** Is an area with very little rainfall likely to be a high- or low-pressure center?

_____

Picture This

4. **Describe** What types of electric charges are necessary for lightning to form?

_____

_____

What is a tornado?

Along some frontal bounderies, cumulonimbus clouds create severe weather. If conditions are right, rising air can start to spin. This forms a funnel cloud. If the funnel cloud reaches Earth's surface, it becomes a tornado. A **tornado** is a violent, whirling wind that moves in a narrow path over land. How a tornado develops is shown in the figures below.

Although tornadoes usually last less than 15 minutes, they can be very destructive. A tornado's winds can reach nearly 500 km/h. Powerful winds flow upward into the low pressure in the center of a tornado. These winds suck up anything in their path.

Picture This

5. Identify Color the arrows representing downdrafts blue. Color the arrows representing updrafts red.

Strong updrafts and downdrafts develop within cumulonimbus clouds when warm, moist air meets cool, dry air.

Winds within the clouds cause air to spin faster and faster.

A funnel of spinning air drops downward through the base of the cloud toward the ground.

What are hurricanes?

A <u>hurricane</u> is a large storm that begins as a low-pressure area over warm, tropical oceans. A hurricane has winds of at least 120 km/h. Hurricanes that affect the East Coast and Gulf Coast of the United States often begin over the Atlantic Ocean west of Africa. It can last for weeks and travel thousands of kilometers. A hurricane can be as much as 1,000 km across. The Coriolis effect causes the winds to flow around the storm's center. In the northern hemisphere, the winds move counterclockwise. When a hurricane passes over land, it produces high winds, tornadoes, heavy rains, and floods. ☑

What does the National Weather Service do?

In the United States, the National Weather Service keeps a careful eye on the weather. Radar, weather balloons, satellites, computers, and other instruments are used to measure the position and strength of storms. The National Weather Service uses the data to try to predict a storm's movements.

What is a weather watch?

If the National Weather Service believes conditions are right for severe weather to develop in a certain area, it issues a severe weather watch. If severe weather has already been seen in that area, a warning is issued. So, a tornado watch means that a tornado may occur in your area. A warning means a tornado has been seen in your area.

What are some weather safety measures?

Watches and warnings are issued for severe thunderstorms, tornadoes, tropical storms, hurricanes, blizzards, and floods. Radio and television stations announce watches and warnings. So does the National Weather Service's own radio network, called NOAA (NOH ah) Weather Radio.

To keep safe, learn how storms develop and what to do during watches and warnings. During a watch, stay tuned to a radio or television station. Have a plan of action in case a warning is issued. If the National Weather Service does issue a warning, act immediately to protect yourself.

✔ Reading Check

6. **Identify** What speed must the winds of a storm be for the storm to be considered a hurricane?

_____

_____

💡 Think it Over

7. **Plan** What should you do if a hurricane watch is issued for your area?

_____

_____

_____

● After You Read

Mini Glossary

air mass: a large body of air that develops over a particular region of Earth's surface

front: a boundary between air masses of different temperatures

hurricane: a large storm, up to 1,000 km in diameter, with winds of at least 120 km/h; produces heavy rains, tornadoes, and flooding

tornado: a violent, whirling wind that travels in a narrow path over land

1. Review the terms and their definitions in the Mini Glossary above. Then write a sentence using any two terms.

_____

_____

2. Complete the concept map to show the four different kinds of fronts.

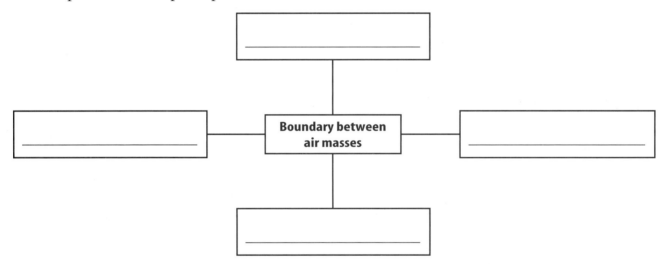

3. As you read, you used highlighting to find main points and supporting details. Did this strategy help you to understand the main ideas in this section? If it was helpful, describe how. If it was not helpful, tell why.

_____

_____

_____

End of Section

Science Online Visit **red.msscience.com** to access your textbook, interactive games, and projects to help you learn more about air masses and fronts.

202 The Atmosphere in Motion

 **Oceans**

section ❶ Ocean Water

● Before You Read

What is the first thing you notice when you look at a globe? Earth has been called "The Water Planet." Why do you suppose that is?

_____

_____

_____

What You'll Learn

- why Earth's oceans are important
- how Earth's oceans formed
- the composition of seawater
- how temperature and pressure change with depth

● Read to Learn

Importance of Oceans

Oceans cover almost three-fourths of Earth's surface. Oceans affect all living things and are important to life. They provide a place for many organisms to live. Oceans transport seeds and animals. Materials are shipped across the world on oceans. Oceans also provide humans with resources such as food, medicines and salt. For example, sea sponges are used in medicines for treating cancer and asthma. Fish and other sea creatures provide food. Salt is obtained by evaporating seawater. The water for most of Earth's rain and snow comes from evaporated ocean water. Just as important, 70 percent of the oxygen on Earth is given off by ocean organisms.

Formation of Oceans

When Earth was still a young planet, active volcanoes were everywhere. They erupted regularly, releasing lava, ash, and gases from deep within Earth. The volcanic gases entered Earth's atmosphere. One of the gases was water vapor. Scientists hypothesize that water vapor began gathering in the atmosphere about 4 billion years ago.

Mark the Text

Identify the Main Point
Highlight the main point in each paragraph. Use a different color to highlight a detail or example that helps explain the main point.

FOLDABLES

Ⓐ Organize Information
Make the following three-tab Foldable to help you organize information about oceans.

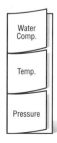

Copyright © Glencoe/McGraw-Hill, a division of The McGraw-Hill Companies, Inc.

How did water vapor help form oceans?

Over millions of years, the water vapor cooled enough to condense and form clouds. Heavy rains began to fall. With each rainfall, more water collected in the lowest parts of Earth's surface. As more rain fell, more land was covered. Eventually, much of the land was covered by water that formed oceans. Evidence suggests that Earth's oceans formed more than 3 billion years ago.

Composition of Ocean Water

Seawater does not taste like the water you drink. In fact, drinking seawater can make you sick. The salty taste is caused by dissolved substances. Rivers and groundwater dissolve elements like calcium and sodium and carry them to the ocean. Erupting volcanoes add elements like bromine and chlorine to ocean water.

The diagram shows that sodium and chlorine are the most common elements dissolved in seawater. When seawater evaporates, sodium and chloride ions combine to form halite. Halite is the salt used to flavor foods. ☑

Copyright © Glencoe/McGraw-Hill, a division of The McGraw-Hill Companies, Inc.

Composition of Ocean Water

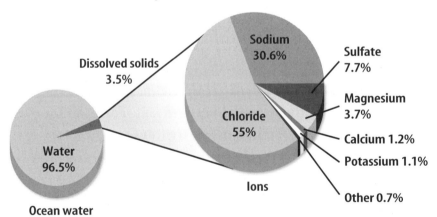

Dissolved solids 3.5%

Sodium 30.6%

Sulfate 7.7%

Magnesium 3.7%

Chloride 55%

Calcium 1.2%

Potassium 1.1%

Other 0.7%

Ions

Water 96.5%

Ocean water

What is salinity?

Salinity (say LIH nuh tee) is a measure of the amount of dissolved solids, or salts, in seawater. Salinity is measured in grams of dissolved salt in one kilogram of seawater. One kilogram of ocean water contains about 35 g of dissolved salts, or 3.5 percent salts. Remember that one kilogram is equal to 1,000 g.

☑ Reading Check

1. **Explain** How does seawater provide the salt used to flavor foods?

_____

_____

_____

Picture This

2. **Interpret Scientific Illustrations** What are the two most common solids dissolved in ocean water?

_____

_____

How does the ocean stay in balance?

Elements are removed from the ocean at the same rate that they are added to the ocean. This allows the composition of the ocean to stay in balance. Rivers, volcanoes, and the atmosphere constantly add substances to the ocean. Biological processes and chemical reactions remove many of these substances. For example, many marine organisms use calcium ions to make bones or shells. Calcium is also removed from ocean water through chemical reactions, forming sediments on the ocean floor.

What gases are found in seawater?

All of the gases in Earth's atmosphere dissolve in seawater. The three most important gases are carbon dioxide, oxygen, and nitrogen. ☑

Oxygen The greatest concentration of dissolved oxygen is near the surface of the ocean. There, oxygen enters seawater directly from the atmosphere. However, there is another reason so much oxygen is found near the surface. Organisms in the sea produce oxygen by photosynthesis. **Photosynthesis** is the process in which organisms use sunlight, water, and carbon dioxide to make food and oxygen.

Photosynthesis requires sunlight. Organisms that carry on photosynthesis are found only in the upper 200 m of the ocean, where sunlight reaches.

Below 200 m, dissolved oxygen levels drop. Here, many animals use oxygen for respiration and it is not replaced. However, dissolved oxygen is found in very deep water. This cold, deep water began as surface water in polar regions. It moves along the ocean floor to other regions.

Carbon Dioxide Most dissolved carbon dioxide found in seawater comes directly from the atmosphere. Some comes from carbon dioxide given off by ocean organisms during respiration. Carbon dioxide reacts with water molecules to form a weak acid called carbonic acid. Carbonic acid helps control the acidity in oceans.

Nitrogen There is more dissolved nitrogen in the ocean than any other gas. Some types of bacteria combine nitrogen and oxygen to form nitrates. Nitrates are important nutrients for plants. Nitrogen is also one of the important building blocks of plant and animal tissue.

Copyright © Glencoe/McGraw-Hill, a division of The McGraw-Hill Companies, Inc.

✔ **Reading Check**

3. Identify Name three important gases found dissolved in ocean water.

_____

_____

_____

💡 **Think it Over**

4. Draw Conclusions Kelp needs sunlight to photosynthesize. Would kelp be found above or below 200 m?

_____

_____

Water Temperature and Pressure

Oceans have three temperature layers—the surface layer, the thermocline layer, and the deep-water layer, as shown in the figure. The surface layer is the warmest because it is heated by solar energy. The warmest surface water is near the equator and the coolest surface water is near the poles.

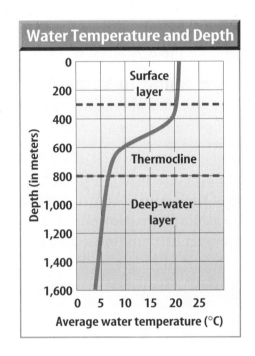

Water Temperature and Depth

The **thermocline** is the layer of ocean water that begins at a depth of about 200 m. In the thermocline, temperature drops quickly as depth increases. This occurs because solar energy does not reach this deep. Below the thermocline lies the deep-water layer, which contains extremely cold water.

Does pressure increase with ocean depth?

Pressure, or force per unit area, also changes with depth. At sea level, the pressure of the atmosphere pushing down on the ocean is referred to as 1 atmosphere (atm) of pressure. An atmosphere is the pressure placed on a surface at sea level by the column of air above it.

As you go deeper into the ocean, the pressure increases. At the surface, the only pressure is from air. But deeper, there is the added force of the water molecules pushing down. The pressure increases by about 1 atm for each 10 m of depth. For example, a scuba diver at 20 m would feel a pressure of 3 atm (1 atm of air + 2 atm of water).

Picture This

5. **Interpret Scientific Illustrations** At about what depth is the ocean's average temperature 15°C? What layer of the ocean is at this depth?

_____

_____

Applying Math

6. **Calculate** How much pressure would a scuba diver feel at 40 m?

_____

Oceans

Copyright © Glencoe/McGraw-Hill, a division of The McGraw-Hill Companies, Inc.

● After You Read

Mini Glossary

photosynthesis: process by which some organisms use sunlight, water, and carbon dioxide to make food and oxygen

salinity: measure of the amount of dissolved solids, or salts, in seawater

thermocline: layer of ocean water that begins at a depth of about 200 m and becomes colder with increasing depth

1. Review the terms and their definitions in the Mini Glossary above. Write a sentence describing one of the terms in your own words.

_____

_____

2. Number the boxes below in the correct order to describe the sequence of events that led to the formation of oceans.

Over millions of years, water vapor in the atmosphere condensed and formed clouds. _____	Volcanoes released lava, ash, and gases including water vapor. _____	Huge amounts of rain fell. _____

Water gathered in the lowest parts of Earth's surface. _____	Much of the land was covered by water that formed oceans. _____

3. As you read, you highlighted the main idea of each paragraph and other important details and examples that helped describe that idea. How did you decide what to highlight in each paragraph?

_____

_____

_____

Science Online Visit **red.msscience.com** to access your textbook, interactive games, and projects to help you learn more about ocean water.

End of Section

section 2 Ocean Currents and Climates

What You'll Learn

- how wind and Earth's rotation affect surface currents
- how ocean currents affect weather and climate
- the causes and effects of density currents
- how upwelling occurs

◀ Study Coach

Main Idea-Detail Notes
As you read about different types of currents, write notes in two columns. In the left column, write the type of current. In the right column, write details about that current.

FOLDABLES™

B Understand Cause and Effect Make the following Foldable to help you understand the cause-and-effect relationship of currents.

	cause	effect
currents		
waves		
tides		

● Before You Read

If you filled a bowl with water and gently dropped a scrap of paper onto the water surface, it would float. If you want to make the paper move without touching it or tilting the bowl, how could you do it? What are you creating when you make the paper move without touching it or tilting the bowl?

_____

_____

_____

● Read to Learn

Surface Currents

Ocean water never stands still. Currents move the water from place to place constantly. Ocean currents are like rivers that move within the ocean. They exist at both the ocean's surface and in deeper water.

What causes surface currents?

<u>Surface currents</u> are powered by wind and usually move only the upper few hundred meters of seawater. When the global winds blow on the ocean's surface, they set ocean water in motion. Because of Earth's rotation, the ocean currents that result do not move in straight lines. Earth's rotation causes surface ocean currents in the northern hemisphere to curve to their right. Surface ocean currents in the southern hemisphere curve to their left. You can see this on the map on the next page. The turning of ocean currents is an example of the Coriolis effect. Recall that the Coriolis effect also is observed on winds. Winds curve toward their right in the northern hemisphere and toward their left in the southern hemisphere.

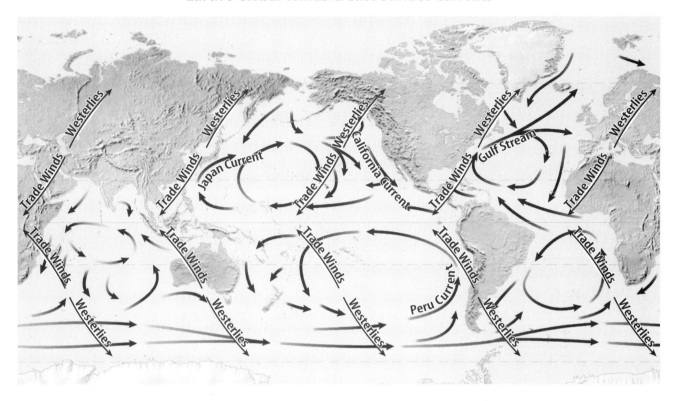

The Gulf Stream Much of what is known about surface currents comes from records kept by early sailors. Sailing ships depended on certain surface currents to carry them west and other currents to carry them east. One of the most important currents for sailing east across the North Atlantic Ocean is the Gulf Stream.

Find the Gulf Stream current on the map above. The Gulf Stream flows from Florida northeastward toward North Carolina. There it curves toward the east and becomes slower and broader.

The Gulf Stream is 100 km wide. It was discovered in the 1500s by Ponce de Leon. In 1770, Benjamin Franklin published a map of the Gulf Stream drawn by Captain Timothy Folger, a Nantucket whaler.

Can currents influence climates?

Since the Gulf Stream begins near the equator, it is a warm current. It carries heat from the equator to other parts of the ocean. Surface currents like the Gulf Stream, on the eastern coasts of continents, tend to be warm. They bring heat from the equator to other areas of Earth. Currents on the western coasts are usually cold. This can influence the climate of regions near these currents.

Picture This

1. **Explain** In the figure, follow a current with your pencil. Which way does your pencil turn, left or right? Why?

_____

_____

_____

Copyright © Glencoe/McGraw-Hill, a division of The McGraw-Hill Companies, Inc.

Reading Essentials **209**

How do surface currents affect the climates of Iceland and Southern California?

Based on its name, you might expect Iceland to have a cold climate. However, the warm water of the Gulf Stream helps keep Iceland's climate mild. The current's warm water flows past Iceland and heats the surrounding air. This warm air keeps Iceland's climate mild and its harbors ice-free all year.

Southern California is known for its warmth and sunshine. Look at the figure of surface currents on the previous page. Find the California Current. It carries cold water from polar regions toward the equator. Cold surface currents affect the climate of coastal cities. For example, San Francisco has cool summers and many foggy days because of the California Current. ✔

Density Currents

Wind has no effect on water deeper than a few hundred meters. However, currents may develop because of differences in the density of the water. Seawater becomes more dense as it gets colder or when it becomes more salty. Gravity causes dense seawater to sink beneath less dense seawater. As the mass falls, it spreads to less dense waters of the ocean. This creates a density current. A **density current** is a pattern in the ocean that forms when a mass of dense seawater sinks beneath less dense seawater. Changes in temperature and salinity work together to create density currents. A density current moves very slowly.

How does salinity affect density currents?

One important density current begins in the cold water north of Iceland. When water freezes, dissolved salts are left behind in the unfrozen water. The very salty water that is left behind is more dense and sinks. Slowly, it spreads along the ocean floor toward the equator and the southern Atlantic Ocean. As the water is sinking near Iceland, the warm surface water of the Gulf Stream moves up from the equator to replace it.

Another density current occurs in the Mediterranean Sea. Warm air in the Mediterranean region causes the seawater to evaporate. This leaves salt behind and increases the salinity of the water. The dense, salty water sinks and flows out to the Atlantic Ocean. At the surface, less dense water from the Atlantic Ocean flows into the Mediterranean Sea.

✔ **Reading Check**

2. **Describe** What affects the climate of coastal cities?

_____

_____

💡 **Think it Over**

3. **Sequence of Events** Number the events to show the order in which a density current forms near Iceland.

____ saltier water sinks and flows

____ warm water replaces the cold water

____ ocean water freezes

How do density currents affect climate?

What if the density currents near Iceland stopped forming? Some scientists hypothesize that this has happened in the past and could happen again. Pollution and population growth could lead to large amounts of carbon dioxide in the atmosphere. The carbon dioxide would trap more of the Sun's heat and raise Earth's temperature. If Earth's temperature rose enough, ice couldn't form easily near the polar regions. Glaciers on land would melt. The freshwater from the glaciers would reduce the salinity of the ocean water. The density currents would weaken or stop. If density currents stopped flowing southward, warm equatorial surface water would no longer flow northward. Earth could face drastic climate changes, including different rainfall patterns and temperatures.

Upwelling

An **upwelling** is a current in the ocean that brings deep, cold water to the ocean surface. The Coriolis effect pushes surface water away from some coastal regions. Cold water from deep in the ocean rises up to replace it. The illustration shows an upwelling of cold water. The cold water is full of nutrients from dead, decayed organisms. Tiny marine organisms thrive in these nutrient-rich areas, which, in turn, attract many fish. As a result, areas of upwelling are important fishing grounds because fish are attracted to the areas to eat the organisms.

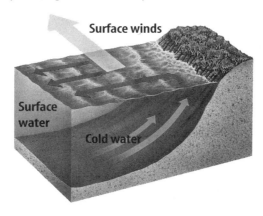

Surface winds

Surface water

Cold water

What happens during El Niño?

During an El Niño (el NEEN yoh) event, the winds blowing cold water from the coast of Peru slow down. The Eastern Pacific Ocean becomes warmer, and upwelling is reduced or stopped. Without nutrients provided by upwelling, fish and other organisms cannot find food. This disrupts the rich fishing grounds off Peru's coast.

Copyright © Glencoe/McGraw-Hill, a division of The McGraw-Hill Companies, Inc.

Think it Over

4. **Describe** What might be affected if density currents stopped?

_____

_____

Picture This

5. **Infer** Why does upwelling around Peru make Peru a rich fishing ground?

_____

_____

● After You Read

Mini Glossary

density current: current created by the circulation pattern in the ocean that forms when a mass of dense seawater sinks beneath less dense seawater

surface current: ocean current that usually moves only the upper few hundred meters of seawater

upwelling: ocean current that moves cold, deep water to the ocean surface

1. Review the terms and their definitions in the Mini Glossary above. Choose a term and write a sentence in which you provide an example of that term.

_____

_____

2. Complete the chart below to organize information from this section.

```
                        ┌──────────┐
                        │  Ocean   │
                        │ Currents │
                        └──────────┘
              ╱                              ╲
┌─────────────────────────────┐   ┌─────────────────────────────┐
│     Density Currents        │   │     Surface Currents        │
│                             │   │                             │
│ • travel in the ocean at a  │   │ • travel in the ocean at a  │
│   depth of                  │   │   depth of                  │
│                             │   │                             │
│ _____ .       │   │ _____ .       │
│                             │   │                             │
│ • caused by _____ water   │   │ • set in motion by global   │
│   sinking                   │   │   _____                   │
│                             │   │                             │
│   below less _____ water. │   │   blowing on Earth's        │
│                             │   │   surface.                  │
└─────────────────────────────┘   └─────────────────────────────┘
```

3. Earlier, you created two-column notes to help you learn about different types of currents. How did writing notes make learning about currents easier?

_____

_____

_____

End of Section

Science **O**nline Visit **red.msscience.com** to access your textbook, interactive games, and projects to help you learn more about ocean currents and climate.

Oceans

section ❸ Waves

⬤ Before You Read

Have you ever surfed? Maybe you have seen someone surf. How does a surfer who is out in the ocean return to shore?

_____

_____

_____

Copyright © Glencoe/McGraw-Hill, a division of The McGraw-Hill Companies, Inc.

⬤ Read to Learn

Waves Caused by Wind

Surfers catch and ride waves all the way back to the beach. A **wave** in water is a rhythmic movement that carries energy through the water. Waves that surfers ride could have started halfway around the world.

When wind blows across a body of water, friction pushes the water along with the wind. When wind speed is great enough, water will pile up into waves. Three things affect the height of a wave: the wind speed, the length of time the wind blows, and the distance over which the wind blows. As wind continues to blow, the waves become higher. When the wind stops, waves stop forming. But waves that have already formed will still continue to travel for long distances.

What are the parts of a wave?

Each wave has a crest, its highest point, and a trough, its lowest part. The wavelength is the horizontal distance between the crests or troughs of two waves. Wave height is the vertical distance from the trough of a wave to the crest. Most waves in the ocean are between 2 m and 5 m high. Some storms have been known to produce waves taller than a six-story building.

What You'll Learn

- how wind can form ocean waves
- how water molecules in a wave move
- how the Moon and Sun cause Earth's tides
- what forces cause shoreline erosion

◄ **Study Coach**

Authentic Questions
Before you begin reading, write down any questions you have about waves. Look for the answers as you read.

FOLDABLES™

Ⓑ Understand Cause and Effect Complete the sections for waves and tides on the Foldable you made earlier.

	cause	effect
currents		
waves		
tides		

How do waves move?

When you watch a wave, it looks as if the water is moving forward. But unless the wave is breaking onto the shore, the water is not moving forward. Each molecule of water returns to its original position when a wave passes. The molecule may be pushed forward by the next wave, but it will return to its original position when the wave passes. Water molecules move in circular patterns within a wave. ☑

What are breakers?

A breaker is a collapsing wave. As a wave approaches the shore, it changes shape. The bottom of a wave hits the shallow floor of the ocean and causes friction. This friction slows the bottom of the wave. However, the wave's crest keeps moving at the same speed. Eventually, the bottom of the wave moves too slowly to support the top of the wave. The crest outruns the trough, and the wave collapses. Water tumbles over on itself, and the wave breaks onto the shore. After a wave crashes, gravity pulls the water back to sea. The figure below shows how waves break.

Wave Motion

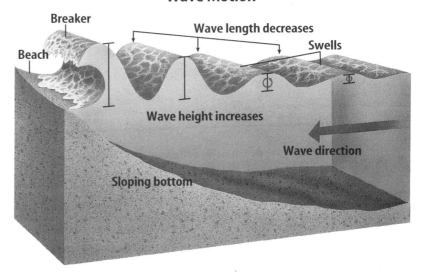

Breaker

Beach

Wave length decreases

Swells

Wave height increases

Wave direction

Sloping bottom

On coasts that slope gently, waves deposit eroded sediments on shore, forming beaches. Beaches extend inland as far as the tides and waves are able to deposit sediments.

Waves usually hit the shore at slight angles. This creates a longshore current. Longshore currents move sideways, parallel to the shore. As a result, beach sediments are moved sideways. Longshore currents carry many metric tons of loose sediment from one beach to another.

Tides

During the day, the water level at the ocean's edge changes. This rise and fall in sea level is called a **tide**. A tide is a wave that can be thousands of kilometers long but only 1 m to 2 m high in the open ocean. As the crest of this wave approaches the shore, the sea level rises to form high tide. Later in the day, the trough of the wave reaches the shore and the sea level drops to form low tide. The difference between sea level at high tide and low tide is the tidal range. ☑

How are tides created?

Tides are created by the gravitational attraction of Earth and the Moon and of Earth and the Sun. Because the Moon is much closer to Earth, it has a stronger pull. The Moon's gravity pulls at Earth, including its bodies of water. This forms two bulges of water. One is on the side of Earth closest to the Moon, caused by the water's attraction to the Moon's gravitational pull. The other is on the side farthest away, created because the Moon is pulling Earth away from the water. These two places will have high tide. As Earth rotates, the bulges follow the Moon. This results in high tide happening around the world at different times.

What are spring tides and neap tides?

The Sun's gravity can increase or decrease the Moon's pull. When the Moon, Earth, and Sun line up, spring tides are created. During spring tides, high tides are higher and low tides are lower than usual. When the Moon, Earth, and the Sun form a right angle, high tides are lower and low tides are higher than usual. These are called neap tides. The different positions of the Moon, Earth, and the Sun during spring tides and neap tides are illustrated below.

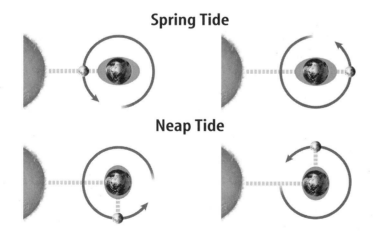

Spring Tide

Neap Tide

☑ **Reading Check**

3. Infer Is a tide always as high as it is long?

_____

_____

Picture This

4. Draw Conclusions There are more floods during a spring tide than there are during a neap tide. Why do you think that is?

_____

_____

● After You Read

Mini Glossary

tide: rhythmic rise and fall in sea level created by the gravitational attraction of Earth and the Moon, and Earth and the Sun

wave: in the ocean, the rhythmic movement that carries energy through water

1. Review the terms and their definitions in the Mini Glossary above. Then write a sentence using both vocabulary words.

   _____

   _____

2. Complete the cause-and-effect chart below to describe how the Moon's gravitational pull creates high and low tides.

CAUSE	EFFECT
The Moon is closer to Earth than the Sun.	The gravitational pull of the _____ is stronger than the pull of the _____ on Earth.
The Moon's gravity pulls at Earth.	Two _____ form in the ocean.
As Earth rotates, the bulges follow the Moon.	High _____ happens around _____ at different times.

3. You wrote down any questions you had about waves before you read. Were any of your questions answered in the text? If not, ask the class your questions.

   _____

   _____

   _____

End of Section

Science●**nline** Visit **red.msscience.com** to access your textbook, interactive games, and projects to help you learn more about waves and tides.

Oceans

section ❹ Life in the Oceans

● Before You Read

What do you know about life in the ocean? Name some marine organisms that you've seen or would like to learn more about.

_____

_____

What You'll Learn
- types of plankton, nekton, and bottom dwellers
- the differences between producers, consumers, and decomposers
- ocean food chains

● Read to Learn

Types of Ocean Life

Many different kinds of organisms live in the ocean. Where the organism lives and how it moves classifies it as plankton, nekton, or a bottom dweller.

What are plankton?

Plankton are tiny marine organisms that drift in the surface waters of every ocean. Most plankton are one-celled, microscopic organisms. Eggs of ocean animals, very young fish, and larval jellyfish are plankton. ☑

What are nekton?

Nekton are marine animals that actively swim in ocean waters. Fish, whales, shrimp, turtles, and squid are examples of nekton. Nekton are found in all temperatures and depths of the ocean.

What are bottom dwellers?

Bottom dwellers are animals that live on the ocean floor. Bottom dwellers include crabs, snails, and sea urchins. They can swim or move along the floor searching for food. Some bottom dwellers, such as sponges and anemones, are permanently attached to the ocean floor. They must obtain food by filtering out particles from the seawater.

◀ **Mark the Text**

Underline As you read, underline the definitions for nektons, planktons, and bottom dwellers.

☑ **Reading Check**

1. **Define** How many cells do most plankton have?

_____

Copyright © Glencoe/McGraw-Hill, a division of The McGraw-Hill Companies, Inc.

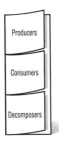
Think it Over

2. Draw Conclusions
Microscopic bacteria feed off decaying matter. Are they consumers or decomposers?

Ocean Ecosystems

No matter where an organism lives, it is part of an ecosystem. An **ecosystem** is a community of organisms, which includes producers, consumers, and decomposers, that interact with each other and their surroundings.

What are producers?

A **producer** is an organism that can make its own food. They are a food source for other organisms. Producers near the surface of the water contain chlorophyll and perform photosynthesis. These producers use sunlight and carbon dioxide to make food and oxygen.

Since sunlight cannot penetrate deep water, producers that live in deep water perform chemosynthesis. **Chemosynthesis** is a process in which bacteria make food from dissolved sulfur compounds. Chemosynthesis occurs most often along mid-ocean ridges. There, water is heated from gases, like sulfur, escaping through Earth's crust. Bacteria use the dissolved sulfur to produce food.

What are consumers and decomposers?

Consumers and decomposers depend on producers for survival. A **consumer** is an organism that gets its energy from eating other organisms. Consumers can use the energy stored in the cells of producers and other consumers. When producers and consumers die, decomposers digest them. **Decomposers** break down tissue and release nutrients and carbon dioxide back into the ecosystem. Bacteria are common decomposers.

What are food chains?

Throughout the ocean, energy is transferred from producers to consumers and decomposers through **food chains**. A food chain can start with microscopic algae. Microscopic animals eat the algae. These consumers are eaten by another consumer, the herring, which is eaten by a cod. Seals eventually feed on the cod. At each stage in the food chain, unused energy is passed from one organism to another. Most food chains are complicated. Usually, a species depends on more than one organism for food. Food chains that are complicated and interconnected are called food webs.

Ocean Nutrients

Nearly everything in an ecosystem is recycled. When organisms respire, or breathe, carbon dioxide is released back into the ecosystem. When organisms get rid of wastes, or die and decompose, nutrients are recycled. All organisms need certain nutrients to survive. Plants need nitrogen and phosphorous. Producer organisms need carbon dioxide to build tissue. These gases move through cycles through the ocean and between the ocean and the atmosphere. For example, carbon cycles through the ocean and between the ocean and the atmosphere. The illustration below shows this carbon cycle.

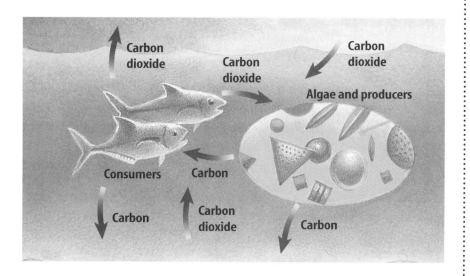

Picture This

3. Label the nekton you see in the illustration.

How are nutrients recycled in coral reefs?

Coral reefs are ecosystems that need clear, warm, sunlit water. Each coral animal builds a hard capsule around its body using calcium it removes from seawater. Each capsule then cements to another, and a large colony called a reef is formed. Bottom dwellers and nekton move to the reef. Nearly 25 percent of all marine species and 20 percent of all fish live on coral reefs. Coral reefs can usually be found in tropical regions in water no deeper than 30 m. ☑

A healthy reef is a delicate balance. Producers, consumers, and decomposers all share a reef. They form a complex food web. Energy, nutrients, and gases are cycled among them all.

✔ Reading Check

4. Define Where are coral reefs usually found?

_____

_____

_____

● After You Read

Mini Glossary

chemosynthesis: process that occurs in deep ocean water in which bacteria make food from dissolved sulfur compounds

consumer: organism that gets its energy from eating other organisms

decomposer: organism that breaks down tissue and releases nutrients and carbon dioxide back into the ecosystem

ecosystem: community of organisms—producers, consumers, and decomposers—that interact with each other and their surroundings

food chain: series of stages that shows the transfer of energy from producers to consumers and decomposers

nekton: marine animals, such as fish and turtles, that actively swim in ocean waters

plankton: tiny marine organisms, such as eggs of ocean animals, that drift in the surface waters of every ocean

producer: organism that can make its own food by photosynthesis or chemosynthesis

1. Review the terms and their definitions in the Mini Glossary above. Then choose a term and write a sentence that includes an example of that term.

_____

_____

2. Complete the main idea chart below.

Plankton	Nekton	Bottom dwellers
Definition: _____ _____ _____	Definition: _____ _____ _____	Definition: _____ _____ _____
Example: _____	Example: _____	Example: _____

3. Did underlining the definitions for plankton, nekton, and bottom dwellers help you read the text more carefully? Pick a term and try to define it in your own words without looking back at the text. Then reread the text and see how well you did.

_____

_____

End of Section

Science Online Visit **red.msscience.com** to access your textbook, interactive games, and projects to help you learn more about life in the oceans.

chapter 14 Exploring Space

section ❶ Radiation from Space

● Before You Read

How do we learn about objects in space? What are some of the tools astronomers use?

_____

_____

_____

Copyright © Glencoe/McGraw-Hill, a division of The McGraw-Hill Companies, Inc.

● Read to Learn

Electromagnetic Waves

With the help of telescopes, we can see objects in our solar system and far into space. For now, this is the only way to learn about distant parts of the universe. Even if we could travel at the speed of light, it would take many years to travel to the closest star.

What do you see when you look at a star?

When you look at a star, the light that you see left the star many years ago. Although light travels fast, distances between objects in space are so great that it sometimes takes millions of years for the light to reach Earth.

What is electromagnetic radiation?

The light and other energy leaving a star are forms of radiation. Radiation is energy that moves from one place to another by electromagnetic waves. Since the radiation has both electric and magnetic properties, it is called electromagnetic radiation. Electromagnetic waves carry energy through empty space as well as through matter. There are electromagnetic waves everywhere around you. When you turn on the radio, the TV, or the microwave, different types of electromagnetic waves surround you.

What You'll Learn

■ what the electromagnetic spectrum is
■ the differences between refracting and reflecting telescopes
■ the differences between optical and radio telescopes

Study Coach

Create a Quiz Strategy
As you read, create a five-question quiz about different kinds of telescopes in this section. Switch papers with a classmate and answer each other's questions.

FOLDABLES

Ⓐ Organize Information
Make quarter sheet Foldables to organize information from this section.

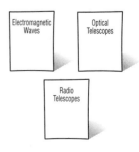

Where is electromagnetic radiation found?

Electromagnetic radiation is all around you. Two types of electromagnetic waves are radio waves that carry signals to your radio and the light that travels to Earth from the Sun. Other types of electromagnetic waves are gamma rays, X rays, ultraviolet waves, infrared waves, and microwaves. Each of these forms of electromagnetic radiation has a different wavelength.

What is the electromagnetic spectrum?

The different types of electromagnetic radiation are shown in the electromagnetic spectrum in the figure below. The **electromagnetic spectrum** is the arrangement of the different kinds of electromagnetic radiation according to their wavelengths. Forms of electromagnetic radiation also differ in their frequencies. Frequency is the number of wave crests that pass a given point per unit of time. The shorter the wavelength is, the higher the frequency. The figure below shows the wavelengths and frequencies of some types of electromagnetic radiation.

| Microwaves | Infrared | | radiation | Visible light | Ultraviolet radiation |

Frequency (hertz) 10^9 10^{10} 10^{11} 10^{12} 10^{13} 10^{14} 10^{15} 10^{16} 10^1

Wavelength (meters) 0^{-1} 10^{-2} 10^{-3} 10^{-4} 10^{-5} 10^{-6} 10^{-7} 10^{-8} 10

How fast do electromagnetic waves travel?

Even though electromagnetic waves have different wavelengths, they all travel at the same speed. All electromagnetic waves travel at the speed of light, or 300,000 km/s. Stars give off visible light and other electromagnetic waves. It can take millions of years for some stars' light waves to reach Earth because the universe is so large. The light you see when you look at a star left the star many years ago.

Scientists can learn about the source of the electromagnetic radiation by studying a star's light waves. One tool that scientists use to study electromagnetic radiation in space is a telescope. A telescope is an instrument that magnifies, or enlarges, images of distant objects. There are different kinds of telescopes.

Picture This

1. **Interpret Scientific Illustrations** Which type of electromagnetic radiation has a longer wavelength: infrared or ultraviolet?

_____

_____

Think it Over

2. **Identify** Which type of electromagnetic wave travels fastest?

_____

_____

_____

Optical Telescopes

An optical telescope collects visible light, which is a form of electromagnetic radiation, to produce magnified images of objects. The telescope collects light using either an objective lens or mirror. The objective lens or mirror then forms an image at the focal point of the telescope. The focal point is where light that is bent by the lens or reflected by the mirror comes together to form an image. The image is magnified by another lens, the eyepiece. There are two types of optical telescopes.

Refracting Telescope A <u>refracting telescope</u> collects light using convex lenses. Convex lenses curve outward, like the surface of a ball. Light from an object passes through the convex objective lens. The lens bends the light to form an image at the focal point. The eyepiece magnifies the image. The illustration below on the left shows how a refracting telescope works.

Reflecting Telescope A <u>reflecting telescope</u> collects light using a concave mirror. The concave mirror is curved inward, like the inside of a bowl. When light strikes the mirror, the mirror reflects, or bounces, light to the focal point where it forms an image. Sometimes a smaller mirror is used to reflect light into the eyepiece lens, where it is magnified for viewing. The illustration below on the right shows how a reflecting telescope works.

Picture This

3. Compare and Contrast Name one difference between a refracting telescope and a reflecting telescope.

_____

_____

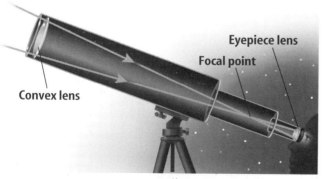

Refracting Telescope

Eyepiece lens

Focal point

Convex lens

In a refracting telescope, a convex lens focuses light to form an image at the focal point.

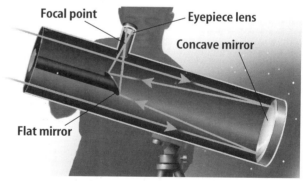

Reflecting Telescope

Focal point

Eyepiece lens

Concave mirror

Flat mirror

In a reflecting telescope, a concave mirror focuses light to form an image at the focal point.

How are optical telescopes used?

Most optical telescopes used by astronomers—scientists who study space—are housed in buildings called **observatories**. Observatories have dome-shaped roofs that open. This allows astronomers to view the night sky. ☑

What is the *Hubble Space Telescope*?

Not all optical telescopes are housed in observatories. The *Hubble Space Telescope* is a large reflecting telescope that orbits Earth. It was launched in 1990 by the space shuttle *Discovery*. Earth's atmosphere can absorb and distort energy received from space. Since *Hubble* was placed outside this atmosphere, scientists expected it to produce clear pictures. However, a mistake was made when the telescope's largest mirror was shaped. It did not produce clear images. In 1993, a set of small mirrors was installed to correct the faulty images. Two more missions to service *Hubble* happened in 1997 and 1999—as shown in the photograph. In 1999, *Hubble* sent back clear images of a large cluster of galaxies known as Abell 2218.

✔ Reading Check

4. Describe What is an observatory?

_____

_____

Picture This

5. Explain Why does the *Hubble Space Telescope* produce better images of space than telescopes on Earth?

_____

_____

How do reflecting telescopes work?

In the early 1600s, the Italian scientist Galileo Galilei aimed a small telescope at the stars. Since then, telescopes have been greatly improved. Today, large reflecting telescopes use mirrors to direct light and to magnify images. These mirrors are several meters wide and are extremely hard to build. Instead of constructing one large mirror, some telescopes have mirrors that are constructed out of many small mirrors that are pieced together. The mirrors of the twin Keck telescopes in Hawaii are 10 meters wide and were made in this way.

How do optical telescopes work?

The most recent advances in optical telescopes involve active and adaptive optics. Active optics use a computer to correct for changes in temperature, mirror distortions, and bad viewing conditions. Adaptive optics are even more advanced. Adaptive optics use lasers to probe the atmosphere for air turbulence and send back information to a computer. The computer then makes adjustments to the telescope's mirror. Telescope images are clearer when corrections for air turbulence, temperature changes, and mirror-shape changes are made.

Radio Telescopes

Stars and other objects in space give off different kinds of electromagnetic energy. One example of that energy is the radio wave. Radio waves are a kind of long-wavelength energy in the electromagnetic spectrum. A **radio telescope** is used to collect and record radio waves that travel through space. Unlike visible light, radio waves pass freely through Earth's atmosphere. Because of this, radio telescopes are useful 24 hours a day under most weather conditions. ☑

Radio waves reaching Earth's surface strike the large, concave dish of a radio telescope. This dish reflects the waves to a focal point where a receiver is located. The information gathered allows scientists to detect objects in space, to map the universe, and to search for signs of intelligent life on other planets.

💡 Think it Over

6. Think Critically Why should scientists continue to try to improve telescopes?

_____

_____

✔ Reading Check

7. Explain Why don't radio telescopes need to be above Earth's atmosphere in order to collect data from space?

_____

_____

_____

● After You Read

Mini Glossary

electromagnetic spectrum: arrangement of electromagnetic waves according to their wavelengths

observatory: building that can house an optical telescope; often has a dome-shaped roof that can open for viewing

radio telescope: telescope that collects and records radio waves that travel through space; can be used day or night and in most weather conditions

reflecting telescope: optical telescope that collects light using a concave mirror to reflect light and form an image at the focal point

refracting telescope: optical telescope that collects light using convex lenses to bend light and form an image at the focal point

1. Review the terms and their definitions above. Choose a term and write a sentence that shows you understand the meaning of that term.

_____

_____

_____

2. Fill in the missing information in the table.

	Optical Telescope	Radio Telescope
Type of electromagnetic radiation collected	_____	Radio Waves
Parts used to collect electromagnetic radiation	_____ and mirrors, eyepieces	Curved dish and _____
Affected by atmosphere?	_____	_____

3. Did you answer all the questions on the quiz you took? How did the *Create a Quiz* strategy help you remember what you read?

_____

_____

_____

End of Section

Science Online Visit **red.msscience.com** to access your textbook, interactive games, and projects to help you learn more about radiation from space.

chapter 14 · Exploring Space

section ❷ Early Space Missions

● Before You Read

What have humans sent into space? Why were those things sent into space?

_____

_____

What You'll Learn
- about natural and artificial satellites
- the difference between artificial satellites and space probes
- about the history of the race to the moon

● Read to Learn

The First Missions into Space

Astronomers have used telescopes to learn a lot about the Moon and the planets. However, astronomers want to gain more knowledge by sending humans to these places or by sending spacecraft where humans can't go.

How do spacecraft travel?

Spacecraft must travel faster than 11 km/s to break free of Earth's gravity and enter Earth's orbit. They can do this with special engines called rockets. **Rockets** are engines that carry their own fuel and have everything they need for the burning of fuel. They don't require air to carry out the process. Therefore, they can work in space, which has no air.

What are the different types of rockets?

The simplest rocket engine is made of a burning chamber and a nozzle. A more complicated rocket has more than one burning chamber. There are two types of rockets. The difference between them is what fuel, or propellant, they burn.

Solid-Propellant Rockets Solid-propellant rockets are simpler in design. However, they cannot be shut down and restarted after they are ignited.

Mark the Text

Identify the Main Point
Highlight the main point in each paragraph. Use a different color to highlight a detail or an example that helps explain the main point.

FOLDABLES™

Ⓑ Organizing Information Make a two-tab Foldable to help you organize information about satellites.

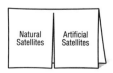

Natural Satellites | Artificial Satellites

Liquid-Propellant Rockets Liquid-propellant rockets can be shut down after they are ignited and restarted. For this reason, they are used for long-term space missions. Scientists on Earth send signals to stop and restart the spacecraft's engines in order to change the spacecraft's direction. Liquid propellant rockets powered many space probes, including the two *Voyagers* and *Galileo*. In the photograph below, a liquid-propellant rocket stands on the launchpad. ☑

✓ Reading Check

1. Identify What kind of rocket was used to power the two *Voyager* space probes?

_____

_____

Picture This

2. Describe What is the advantage of the liquid-propellant rocket in the photo over a solid-propellant rocket?

_____

_____

How are fuels used to launch rockets?

Solid-propellant rockets use a rubber-like fuel. The fuel contains its own oxidizer. The burning chamber of a rocket is a tube that has a nozzle at one end. As the solid propellant burns, hot gases exert pressure on all inner surfaces of the tube. The tube pushes back on the gas except at the nozzle where hot gases escape. Thrust builds up and pushes the rocket forward.

Liquid-propellant rockets use a liquid fuel and an oxidizer, such as liquid oxygen stored in separate tanks. To ignite the rocket, the oxidizer is mixed with the liquid fuel in the burning chamber. As the mixture burns, forces are exerted and the rocket is propelled forward.

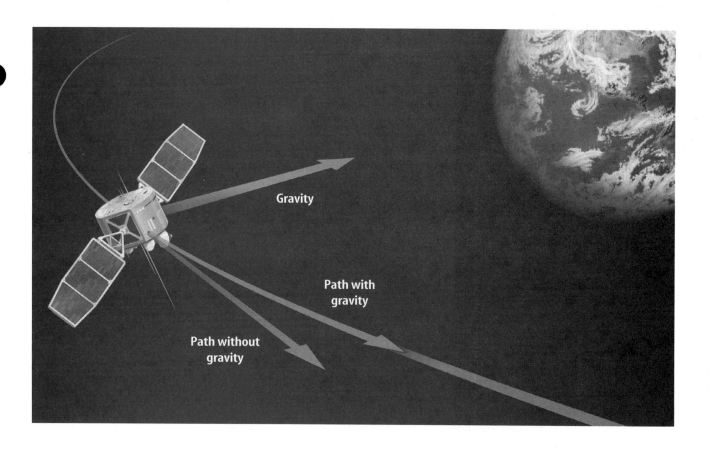

Gravity

Path with
gravity

Path without
gravity

What are satellites?

The space age began in 1957 when the former Soviet Union used a rocket to send *Sputnik I* into space. *Sputnik I* was the first artificial satellite. A **satellite** is any object that revolves around another object. The Moon, which circles Earth, is an example of a natural satellite.

When an object enters space, it travels in a straight line unless a force makes it change direction. Earth's gravity is such a force. Earth's gravity pulls a satellite toward Earth. The illustration above shows the effect of gravity on a satellite's path. The result of the satellite traveling forward while at the same time being pulled toward Earth is a curved path. This curved path is called an **orbit.** *Sputnik I* orbited Earth for 57 days before gravity pulled it back into Earth's atmosphere, where it burned up.

What are satellites used for?

Today, thousands of artificial satellites orbit Earth. They have many uses. Communications satellites transmit radio and television programs to locations around the world. Other satellites collect scientific data. Weather satellites constantly monitor Earth's global weather patterns.

Picture This

3. Interpret Scientific Illustrations Where would the satellite go if Earth's gravity did not exist?

_____

_____

_____

Space Probes

Rockets also carry instruments into space to collect data. A **space probe** is an instrument that gathers information and sends it back to Earth. Space probes travel into and beyond the solar system, carrying cameras and other equipment to collect data. They carry radio transmitters and receivers to communicate with scientists on Earth. The table shows some of the space probes launched by the National Aeronautics and Space Administration (NASA).

Copyright © Glencoe/McGraw-Hill, a division of The McGraw-Hill Companies, Inc.

Some Early Space Missions			
Mission Name	Date Launched	Destination	Data Obtained
Mariner 2	August 1962	Venus	verified high temperatures in Venus's atmosphere
Pioneer 10	March 1972	Jupiter	sent back photos of Jupiter—first probe to encounter an outer planet
Viking 1	August 1975	Mars	orbiter mapped the surface of Mars; lander searched for life on Mars
Magellan	May 1989	Venus	mapped Venus's surface and returned data on the composition of Venus's atmosphere

Where are other important space probes?

Voyager 1 and *Voyager 2* were launched in 1977. *Voyager I* flew past Jupiter and Saturn. *Voyager 2* flew past Jupiter, Saturn, Uranus, and Neptune. The objective of both probes is to explore beyond the solar system. Scientists expect both probes to send data back to Earth for at least 20 more years.

Galileo, launched in 1989, reached Jupiter in 1995. A smaller probe was released from *Galileo* into Jupiter's violent atmosphere. The small probe collected information about Jupiter's makeup, temperature, and pressure. *Galileo* also gathered information about Jupiter's moons, rings, and magnetic fields. The data from *Galileo* show that there may be an ocean of water under the surface of Europa, one of Jupiter's moons. *Galileo* also took photographs of a powerful volcanic vent on Io, another one of Jupiter's moons.

Think it Over

4. **Compare** What did the *Mariner 2* and *Magellan* space missions have in common?

_____

_____

Applying Math

5. **Calculate** How many years did it take the probe *Galileo* to reach Jupiter?

_____

Moon Quest

Sputnik I only sent out a beeping sound as it orbited Earth. But people soon realized that sending a human into space was not far off.

The former Soviet Union sent the first human into space in 1961. Cosmonaut Yuri A. Gagarin orbited Earth and returned safely. President John F. Kennedy called for the United States to send humans to the Moon and return them safely to Earth. He wanted to do this by the end of the 1960s. The race for space had begun.

The U.S. program to reach the Moon began with **Project Mercury.** The goal of *Project Mercury* was to orbit a piloted spacecraft and to bring it back safely. On May 5, 1961, Alan B. Shepard became the first U.S. citizen in space. In 1962, John Glenn became the first U.S. citizen to orbit Earth. ☑

What was Project Gemini?

The next step in reaching the Moon was **Project Gemini.** There were two astronauts on every *Gemini* mission. *Gemini* spacecraft were larger than *Mercury* spacecraft. On one mission, astronauts met and connected with another spacecraft that was in orbit. The *Gemini* program also studied the effects of space travel on the human body.

Scientists also sent robotic probes to learn about the Moon. These probes did not carry humans. The probe *Ranger* proved that a spacecraft could be sent to the Moon. In 1966, *Surveyor* landed on the Moon's surface, proving that the surface could support spacecraft and humans. *Lunar Orbiter* took pictures of the Moon's surface to help choose future landing sites.

When did humans first walk on the Moon?

The final stage of the U.S. program to reach the Moon was **Project Apollo.** On July 20, 1969, the spacecraft *Apollo 11* landed on the Moon's surface. Neil Armstrong was the first human to set foot on the Moon. Edwin Aldrin walked on the Moon with Armstrong while Michael Collins remained in the Command Module. There were a total of six *Apollo* landings. Astronauts brought more than 2,000 samples of Moon rock and soil back to Earth before the program ended in 1972.

Copyright © Glencoe/McGraw-Hill, a division of The McGraw-Hill Companies, Inc.

✔ **Reading Check**

6. Summarize What was the goal of *Project Mercury*?

_____

_____

_____

💡 **Think it Over**

7. Sequence Write the year in which each event occurred.

_____ The first human is sent into space.

_____ The first human orbits Earth.

_____ The first human walks on the Moon.

● After You Read

Mini Glossary

orbit: a curved path around a star or planet

Project Apollo: the final stage in the U.S. program to reach the Moon; the first person walked on the Moon on July 20, 1969

Project Gemini: the second stage in the U.S. program to reach the Moon in which an astronaut team connected with another spacecraft that was in orbit

Project Mercury: the first stage in the U.S. program to reach the Moon, in which a spacecraft with an astronaut orbited Earth and returned safely

rocket: engine that can work in space and burns liquid or solid fuel

satellite: any object that revolves around another object

space probe: an instrument that is carried into space, collects data, and sends the data back to Earth

1. Review the terms and their definitions in the Mini Glossary. Use the term *orbit* to describe a satellite.

_____

2. Complete the following diagram to describe early U.S. space missions. Use the terms: *Earth, Gemini, Apollo, Mercury,* and *the Moon.*

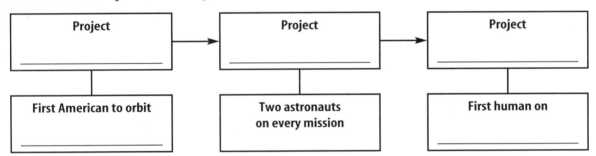

Project		Project		Project
_____	→	_____	→	_____
First American to orbit _____		**Two astronauts on every mission**		**First human on** _____

3. Choose one of the question headings in the Read to Learn section. Write the question in the box. Then answer it in your own words.

> **Write your question here.**

_____

_____

End of Section

Science Online   Visit **red.msscience.com** to access your textbook, interactive games, and projects to help you learn more about early space missions.

 **Exploring Space**

section ❸ Current and Future Space Missions

● Before You Read

Do you have questions about the other planets? Write three questions about the planets on the lines below.

_____

_____

_____

● Read to Learn

The Space Shuttle

NASA's early rockets cost millions of dollars and could be used only once. They were used to launch a small capsule holding astronauts into orbit.

NASA realized it would be less expensive and less wasteful to reuse resources. The space shuttle was created. The **space shuttle** is a reusable spacecraft that carries astronauts, satellites, and other materials to and from space.

At launch, the space shuttle stands on end and is connected to an external liquid-fuel tank and two solid-fuel booster rockets. When the shuttle reaches an altitude of about 45 km, the emptied, solid-fuel booster rockets drop off and parachute back to Earth. The rockets are recovered and reused. The liquid-fuel tank also separates and falls to Earth but is not recovered.

What happens on the space shuttle?

In space, the shuttle orbits Earth. Astronauts conduct scientific experiments, such as how space flight affects the human body. They also launch, repair, and retrieve satellites. When the mission is complete, the shuttle glides back to Earth and lands like an airplane.

What You'll Learn

- about the space shuttle
- about orbital space stations
- about plans for future space missions
- about the application of space technology to everyday life

Study Coach

Outline Outline the facts you learn about current and future space missions. For each mission, include a question that scientists hope to answer.

FOLDABLES

C Find Main Ideas Create a six-tab Foldable to summarize the main ideas from the section.

Space Stations

Astronauts can spend only a short time living in the space shuttle. Its living area is small, and the crew needs more room to live, exercise, and work. A **space station** has living quarters, work and exercise areas, and all the equipment and life support systems that humans need in order to live and work in space.

In 1973, the United States launched the space station *Skylab*. Crews of astronauts spent up to 84 days there. They performed scientific experiments and collected data on the effects on humans of living in space. In 1979, the empty *Skylab* fell out of orbit and burned up as it entered Earth's atmosphere.

The former Soviet Union launched the space station *Mir*. Crews from the former Soviet Union spent more time on board *Mir* than crews from any other country.

Cooperation in Space

In 1995, the United States and Russia began an era of cooperation and trust in exploring space. One American and two Russians were launched into space together on a Russian spacecraft. Then a Russian traveled into space on an American shuttle. There were many missions involving space shuttles docking at *Mir*. Each was an important step toward building and operating the new *International Space Station*.

What is the *International Space Station*?

The *International Space Station (ISS)* will be a permanent laboratory in space designed for long-term research projects. Some of the research will be used to improve medicines and the treatment of many diseases. Sixteen nations are working together to build sections of the *ISS*. The sections will then be carried into space where the *ISS* will be constructed. The space shuttle and Russian rockets will transport the sections. The illustration below shows the proposed design for the *ISS*. ☑

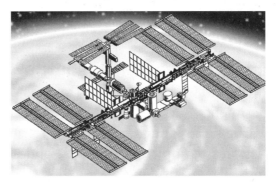

Proposed *International Space Station*

Think it Over

1. **Infer** Why can't long-term projects be done on the space shuttle?

_____

_____

✔ **Reading Check**

2. **Identify** What are some ways that the *ISS* will be used?

_____

_____

_____

How is the *ISS* being constructed?

The *ISS* is being built in phases. Phase One involved the space shuttle *Mir* docking missions. Phase Two began in 1998 when the first *ISS* module, or unit, was put into orbit. Another unit was attached, and the first crew of three people went to live and work on the station. Phase Two ended in 2001 when a U.S. laboratory was added. Labs from Japan, Europe, and Russia will follow. It will take 47 launches to finish the *ISS* by 2006, its scheduled completion date. NASA plans to station seven-person crews onboard for several months at a time.

Exploring Mars

In 1996, two Mars missions were launched, *Mars Global Surveyor* and *Mars Pathfinder*. *Surveyor* orbited Mars. It took high-quality photos of the planet's surface. *Pathfinder* landed on Mars. Rockets and a parachute slowed its fall. *Pathfinder* carried scientific instruments to study the surface, including a remote-controlled robot rover called *Sojourner*. ✔

In 2002, the spacecraft *Mars Odyssey* began to map Mars. The information it gathered proved that soil contained frozen water on one part of Mars. In 2003, the twin robot rovers *Spirit* and *Opportunity* were launched from Earth to explore the surface of Mars. They will study the rocks, soils, and water on Mars. In 2008, a rover called *Phoenix* will be sent to dig over a meter into the surface.

New Millennium Program

NASA has plans for future space missions. The New Millennium Program (NMP) will develop equipment to be sent into the solar system.

Exploring the Moon

The *Lunar Prospector* spacecraft was launched in 1998. For one year it orbited the Moon, mapped it, and collected data. The data showed that there might be ice in craters at the Moon's poles. At the end of the mission, *Prospector* was crashed, on purpose, into a lunar crater. Scientists used special telescopes to look for water vapor that might have been tossed up when the spacecraft hit. They didn't find any water. But they believe that water ice is there. This water would be useful if a colony is ever built on the Moon.

✔ Reading Check

3. Identify What was the name of the probe launched in 1996 that landed on Mars?

_____

_____

💡 Think it Over

4. Infer How could digging in Martian soil help scientists learn about Mars?

_____

_____

_____

Cassini

In October 1997, NASA launched the space probe *Cassini*. This probe's destination is Saturn. When it lands, the space probe will explore Saturn and surrounding areas for four years. One part of its mission is to deliver the European Space Agency's *Huygens* probe to Saturn's largest moon, Titan. Some scientists theorize that Titan's atmosphere may be similar to the atmosphere of early Earth. ☑

What will the new space telescopes be like?

Not all missions involve sending astronauts or probes into space. Plans are being made to launch a new space telescope that is capable of observing the first stars and galaxies in the universe. The *James Webb Space Telescope*, shown in the figure below, will be the successor to the *Hubble Space Telescope*. As part of the Origins project, it will provide scientists with the chance to study how galaxies evolved, how stars produce elements, and how stars and planets are formed. To accomplish these tasks, the telescope will have to see objects that are 400 times fainter than any objects seen by telescopes on Earth. NASA hopes to launch the *James Webb Space Telescope* as early as 2010.

5. Describe What do scientists hope to learn about Saturn's moon Titan from *Huygens*?

_____

_____

Picture This

6. Think Critically Why might scientists want to learn how galaxies evolved?

_____

_____

_____

What are some benefits of space technology?

Research done for the space programs is also used to solve problems on Earth. It has led to better ways to detect and treat heart disease. It has helped doctors create a way to find eye problems in infants. Knowledge gained from shuttle research has helped scientists develop cochlear implants. These tiny ear devices have helped thousands of deaf people hear.

Space technology can even help catch criminals and prevent accidents. Scientists developed a way to sharpen images they got from space. Now police use this same method to read blurry photos of license plates, as shown in the picture below.

Police cars and ambulances use an instrument developed in space research. As an emergency vehicle approaches a traffic light, the instrument changes the signal so other cars have time to stop safely. Global Positioning System (GPS) technology uses satellites to determine location on Earth's surface.

Think it Over

7. Think Critically What are some ways space technology benefits people on Earth?

_____

_____

_____

Picture This

8. Draw Conclusions How might the use of space technology help police enforce the law?

_____

_____

_____

● After You Read

Mini Glossary

space shuttle: reusable spacecraft that carries astronauts, satellites, and other materials to and from space

space station: a structure with living quarters, work and exercise areas, and equipment and life support systems for humans to live and work in space

1. Review the terms and their definitions in the Mini Glossary. Write a sentence to explain how the space shuttle is used to build the space station.

_____

_____

2. Complete the diagram to review what you learned about the *International Space Station.*

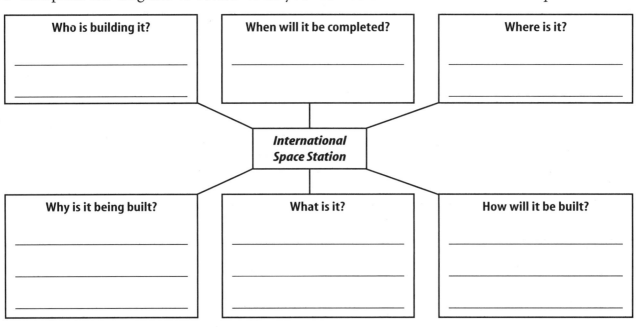

Who is building it?	When will it be completed?	Where is it?

International Space Station

Why is it being built?	What is it?	How will it be built?

3. Describe two ways that space research has helped people on Earth.

_____

_____

End of Section

Science Online Visit **red.msscience.com** to access your textbook, interactive games, and projects to help you learn more about current and future space missions.

The Solar System and Beyond

section ❶ **Earth's Place in Space**

⬤ Before You Read

What is different about daytime and nighttime? Write what you have noticed.

_____

_____

What You'll Learn

■ movements of Earth
■ movements of the Moon
■ the cause of Earth's seasons

⬤ Read to Learn

Earth Moves

Each morning the Sun seems to rise in the east. Throughout the day, it seems to move higher up in the sky. Around noon it reaches its highest point. Then it appears to fall toward the west until it disappears below the horizon. Is the Sun moving? It is Earth that is moving, with you on it.

What is Earth's rotation?

Earth spins like a top. The imaginary center line that Earth spins around is called Earth's axis. Earth spinning around its axis is Earth's **rotation** (roh TAY shun).

Earth's rotation causes day and night. As Earth rotates, the Sun appears to move across the sky. Earth rotates one time each day. That takes about 24 hours. It is the rotation of Earth that makes the Sun appear to be moving across the sky. Because the Sun only appears to move across the sky, this movement is called apparent motion.

What is Earth's revolution?

Earth's rotation causes day and night. Earth moves around the Sun in a regular, curved path called an **orbit**. The movement of Earth around the Sun is known as Earth's **revolution** (reh vuh LEW shun). Earth revolves around the Sun one time each year.

Mark the Text

Underline As you read, underline the answer to the question in each heading to help you focus on the main ideas.

FOLDABLES

Ⓐ **Compare and Contrast** Make the following two-tab Foldable to show how the movements of Earth and the movements of the Moon are similar and different.

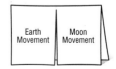

What causes Earth's seasons?

Flowers bloom as the days get warmer. The Sun appears higher in the sky, and daylight lasts longer. Spring seems like a fresh, new beginning. What causes these changes? Earth's axis is not straight up and down—it is slightly tilted. Earth's tilted axis combined with Earth's revolution around the Sun causes seasons. ☑

In the northern hemisphere summer begins in June and ends in September. This is when the northern hemisphere is tilted toward the Sun. During summer, there are more hours of daylight. Longer days are one reason summer is warmer than winter, but not the only reason. During summer, the Sun's rays strike at a higher angle. The angle of the sunlight causes summer to be warmer than winter. More hours of daylight and more intense sunlight during summer are both caused by Earth's tilt.

Earth's Moon

The Moon's surface has many depressions called craters. It has mountainous regions, too. The mountainous areas of the Moon are called **lunar highlands.** The Moon also has dark and flat regions called **maria** (MAHR ee uh). Maria is the Latin word for seas. The maria formed when lava erupted from the Moon's interior and cooled in low areas on its surface.

What orbits Earth?

While Earth revolves around the Sun, the Moon orbits Earth. Human-made objects also orbit Earth. These include the *International Space Station,* other satellites, and debris. The debris is sometimes called space junk. Space junk can include parts from old rockets, old tools, and old equipment.

How does the Moon move?

The Moon's movements are similar to Earth's movements. Earth rotates on an axis, and so does the Moon. Earth revolves around the Sun. The Moon revolves around Earth. It takes the Moon 27.3 days to rotate once. This is the same amount of time it takes the Moon to revolve one time around Earth. Because the Moon rotates and revolves at the same rate, the same side of the Moon always faces Earth. The side of the Moon that faces Earth is called the near side. The opposite side of the Moon is called the far side.

What lights the Moon?

The Moon does not have its own source of light. It reflects the light of the Sun. Just as half of Earth experiences day while the other half experiences night, half of the Moon is lighted while the other half is dark. The appearance of the Moon changes slightly each night. As the Moon revolves around Earth, you see different amounts of its lighted side. These changes are called phases of the Moon.

What is the lunar cycle?

The phase of the Moon that you see depends on the relative positions of the Moon, the Sun, and Earth. It takes one month for the Moon to go through its phases. That time is called a lunar cycle.

New Moon The lunar cycle begins with the new moon. During the new moon, the Moon is between Earth and the Sun. The lighted half of the Moon is facing the Sun and the dark side faces Earth.

Waxing After a new moon, the phases get larger. The phases are waxing because more of the lighted half of the Moon can be seen each night.

Full Moon The middle of the lunar cycle is full moon. Earth is between the Moon and the Sun. The lighted half of the Moon faces Earth.

Waning After full moon, the phases begin waning. During waning phases, less of the lighted half of the Moon can be seen each night. The Moon appears smaller and smaller until it can't be seen at all. Then the cycle begins again.

What is a solar eclipse?

When the Moon is directly between the Sun and Earth, it blocks sunlight from reaching Earth. This event is called a solar **eclipse** (ih KLIHPS). Solar eclipses happen rarely. They always take place during the new moon phase.

Only a few people can witness a total solar eclipse. The Moon is small compared to Earth. Therefore, the darkest part of the Moon's shadow falls on only a small area of Earth during a solar eclipse. Even a partial solar eclipse is unusual. **WARNING:** *Never look directly at the Sun, even during an eclipse. The light can permanently damage your eyes.*

Picture This

3. Label Earth, the Sun, and the Moon during a full moon in the figure below.

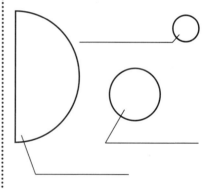

Think it Over

4. Draw Conclusions Why do you think a solar eclipse always occurs during a new moon phase?

_____

_____

_____

Think it Over

5. Draw Conclusions
Why do you think a lunar eclipse always occurs during a full moon phase?

_____

_____

Picture This

6. Identify Look at the figure. Label an area where low tides would occur.

7. Recognize Cause and Effect List the two objects that cause tides on Earth.

_____

_____

What is a lunar eclipse?

When Earth is directly between the Sun and the Moon, its shadow falls on the Moon. This is called a lunar eclipse. A lunar eclipse is unusual because the Moon's orbit is not in the same plane as Earth's orbit around the Sun. When lunar eclipses do occur, it is always the full moon phase. The full moon then becomes dim and sometimes turns deep red.

What causes Earth's tides?

The Moon's gravity pulls on Earth and causes Earth's tides. **Tides** are the regular rise and fall in sea level. When the Moon is closer to a particular place on Earth, the Moon's gravity pulls harder on that place. The figure shows the effect of the Moon's gravity on Earth. Two bulges form in Earth's oceans. One bulge is on the side of Earth close to the Moon. The other bulge is on the side of Earth on the opposite side, away from the Moon. These two bulges of water are the high tides. Because Earth rotates, different places on Earth experience high or low tides.

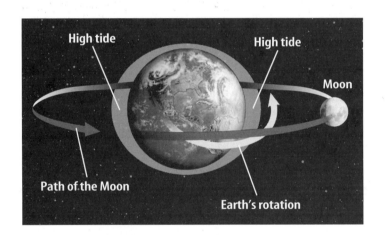

Does the Sun affect tides?

The Sun also affects tides on Earth. Because the Sun is much farther from Earth, the Sun does not affect tides as much as the Moon. When the Sun, Earth, and the Moon are lined up, high tides are higher and low tides are lower. This is called spring tide. Spring tides occur because the force of the Moon's gravity and force of the Sun's gravity combine. Together they produce a greater effect. When the Sun, Earth, and the Moon form a 90-degree angle, high tides are not as high as usual, and low tides are not as low as usual. This is called a neap tide. During neap tide, the Sun's gravity reduces the effect of the Moon's gravity. ✔

● After You Read

Mini Glossary

eclipse (ih KLIHPS): event that occurs when the Moon moves between the Sun and Earth (solar eclipse), or when Earth moves between the Sun and the Moon (lunar eclipse), and casts a shadow

lunar highlands: mountainous areas on the Moon that are about 4.5 billion years old

maria: smooth, dark regions on the Moon that formed when lava flowed onto the Moon's surface

orbit: regular, curved path around the Sun

revolution (rev uh LEW shun): movement of Earth around the Sun, which takes a year to complete

rotation (roh TAY shun): spinning of Earth on its axis, which occurs once every 24 hours, produces day and night, and causes the planets and stars to appear to rise and set

tides: the alternate rise and fall of sea level caused by the gravitational attractions of the Moon and Sun

1. Review the terms above and their definitions in the Mini Glossary. In your own words, explain the cause of tides.

_____

_____

2. *Circle the word or phrase that best answers the question.*

   a. What is the event called when Earth's shadow falls on the Moon or when the Moon's shadow falls on Earth?
      A. lunar highlands   **B.** eclipse   **C.** tides   **D.** maria

   b. What is caused by the tilt of Earth's axis and its revolution?
      A. eclipses   **B.** phases   **C.** tides   **D.** seasons

   c. How much time does it take for Earth to rotate one time?
      A. 24 hours   **B.** 27.3 hours   **C.** 24 days   **D.** 365 days

3. Reread the topic sentences you underlined in the text. How did this strategy help you remember the main ideas about Earth's seasons, Earth's moon, and the cause of tides?

_____

_____

 **Science Online** Visit **red.msscience.com** to access your textbook, interactive games, and projects to help you learn more about Earth's place in space.

End of Section

Copyright © Glencoe/McGraw-Hill, a division of The McGraw-Hill Companies, Inc.

The Solar System and Beyond

section 2 The Solar System

What You'll Learn

- distances in space
- the planets and moons in the solar system
- how Earth is a unique planet

Create a Quiz After you have read this section, create a five-question quiz. Exchange quizzes with a partner. Review your answers together.

FOLDABLES™

B Build Vocabulary Make quarter-sheet Foldables as shown below. Write the vocabulary terms and the definitions from this section.

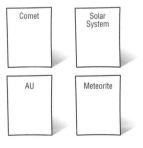

● Before You Read

On the lines below, write three facts that you know about the solar system. As you read the section, check your facts to see if you were correct.

_____

_____

● Read to Learn

Distances in Space

The **solar system** is made up of the nine planets and many other objects that orbit the Sun. Objects in the solar system are held in their orbits by the Sun's strong gravity.

The planets in the solar system revolve around the Sun in elliptical, or oval-shaped, orbits. The orbits of most of the planets are only slightly elliptical, almost circular. Pluto and Mercury have orbits that are shaped more like flattened circles.

How are distances measured?

Distances in space are hard to imagine because space is so vast. Suppose you had to measure the hallway outside your classroom or the distance from your home to school. You probably would measure the hallway using meters and the distance home using kilometers. Larger units are used to measure greater distances.

What is an astronomical unit?

Units bigger than kilometers are needed to measure the enormous distances between planets. One such measure is the astronomical (as truh NAH mih kul) unit. An **astronomical unit** equals 150 million km, the average distance from Earth to the Sun. The abbreviation for astronomical unit is *AU*.

Touring the Solar System

Now you know a little bit more about how to measure distance in the solar system. Next, you can travel outward from the Sun and take a look at the objects in the solar system. What will you see first?

Inner Planets

Traveling away from the Sun, the first group of planets is the inner planets. They are mostly solid, with minerals similar to those on Earth. Much of what is known about these planets comes from spacecraft that send data back to Earth.

Mercury Mercury is the planet closest to the Sun and the second smallest planet. Like Earth's moon, it has a lot of craters. Craters form when meteorites strike a planet's surface. Mercury has no true atmosphere. Mercury's small size and low gravity allow gases that could form an atmosphere to escape into space. Because it has no atmosphere and it is so close to the Sun, Mercury has extreme temperatures. The surface can reach temperatures as high as 425°C during the day and fall to −170°C at night. Mercury is unfit for life.

Venus Venus is the second planet from the Sun. Venus is sometimes called Earth's twin. Its size and mass are similar to Earth's. The surface of Venus is surrounded by thick clouds. The clouds trap solar energy, causing surface temperatures to average around 472°C.

Earth Earth has an atmosphere that allows life to exist on its surface. As far as scientists know, Earth is the only planet that supports life. Earth's surface temperatures allow water to exist as a solid, a liquid, and a gas. Also, ozone in Earth's atmosphere works like a screen to limit the harmful rays from the Sun that reach Earth's surface.

Mars Mars is the fourth planet from the Sun. It is sometimes called the red planet. The red color of Mars is caused by iron oxide in the soil. Several spacecraft have made missions to Mars, and some of their robots have been left behind on the surface of the planet. From these missions scientists have learned that there might once have been flowing water on Mars. There is some water there today. Polar ice caps on Mars are made of frozen water and frozen carbon dioxide. Like Earth, Mars also has seasons. Mars has two small moons, Phobos and Deimos. ☑

Think it Over

1. **Recognize Cause and Effect** What are two reasons that gases from the planet Mercury escape into space?

_____

_____

_____

☑ Reading Check

2. **Explain** What causes the surface of Mars to appear red?

_____

_____

_____

What is the asteroid belt?

The asteroid belt is an area between Mars and Jupiter in which many asteroids travel around the Sun. Asteroids are pieces of rock made of minerals similar to those that formed the rocky planets and moons. In fact, these asteroids might have become a planet if it weren't for the giant planet, Jupiter. Jupiter's huge gravitational force might have prevented a small planet from forming in the area of the asteroid belt. The asteroid belt might be parts of larger objects that collided in space. The asteroid belt separates the solar system's planets into two groups—the inner planets and the outer planets. ☑

Outer Planets

The outer planets orbit beyond the asteroid belt. The outer planets are Jupiter, Saturn, Uranus, Neptune, and Pluto. All the outer planets, except Pluto, are huge balls of gas called gas giants. Each might have a solid core, but none of them has a solid surface. The gas giants have many moons orbiting them. They have rings made of dust and ice surrounding them. Pluto is different. It is made up of ice and rock.

Jupiter Jupiter is the fifth planet from the Sun. It is the largest planet in the solar system. Jupiter has the shortest day—less than 10 hours long. This means that Jupiter rotates faster than any other planet. A huge, red storm near the equator is called the Great Red Spot. Jupiter has 61 moons. One, called Ganymede (GA nih meed), is larger than the planet Mercury. Ganymede, along with two other moons, Europa and Callisto, might have liquid water under their icy crusts. Another of Jupiter's moons, Io, has more active volcanoes than any other object in the solar system.

Saturn Saturn is the sixth planet from the Sun. Saturn has several broad rings made up of hundreds of smaller rings. All the rings are made up of pieces of ice and rock. Some of these pieces are as small as specks of dust. Other pieces are large, even many meters across. Saturn has at least 31 moons. The largest moon is Titan. Titan has an atmosphere that is similar to the atmosphere on Earth long ago. Some scientists hypothesize that Titan's atmosphere might provide clues about how life began on Earth.

✔ **Reading Check**

3. Identify What separates the inner planets from the outer planets?

_____

_____

☼ **Think it Over**

4. Infer How might scientists learn more about Titan's atmosphere?

_____

_____

_____

Uranus Uranus is the seventh planet from the Sun. You can use the table below to find the distance between Uranus and the Sun. The axis of most planets is tilted just a little, somewhat like the handle of a broom that is leaning against a wall. The axis of Uranus is tilted almost even with the plane of its orbit, like a broomstick lying on the floor. Uranus's atmosphere is made mostly of hydrogen with smaller amounts of helium and methane. The methane gives Uranus a bluish-green color. Uranus has rings and at least 21 moons. ☑

Neptune Neptune is the eighth planet from the Sun. It's atmosphere is made up of hydrogen, helium, and methane. Like Uranus, methane gives Neptune a blue color. In 1989, *Voyager 2* sent pictures of Neptune to Earth. These pictures showed a Great Dark Spot in it's atmosphere. By 1994, the spot was gone. Neptune is the last of the big, gas planets with rings around it. It has 11 moons. Triton, the largest, has geysers that shoot gaseous nitrogen into space. Triton does not have many craters. Lava still is flowing onto its surface.

Pluto Pluto is the ninth planet from the Sun. Pluto was discovered in 1930. It is the last planet in the solar system, and it is also the smallest planet. Pluto is smaller than Earth's moon. Pluto is a rocky planet with a frozen crust. It is the only planet in the solar system that has never been visited by a spacecraft. Pluto has one moon, called Charon. Charon is about half the size of Pluto.

Solar System Data			
Planet	**Distance from the Sun (AU)**	**Planet**	**Distance from the Sun (AU)**
Mercury	0.39	Jupiter	5.20
Venus	0.72	Saturn	9.54
Earth	1.00	Uranus	19.19
Mars	1.52	Neptune	30.07
Asteroid belt	2–4	Pluto	39.48

How can you model the solar system?

The table above shows the distances of the planets and the asteroid belt from the Sun. Notice that the inner planets are fairly close together, and the outer planets are far apart. The distances from the Sun can be used to make a scale model of the solar system.

Copyright © Glencoe/McGraw-Hill, a division of The McGraw-Hill Companies, Inc.

✔ **Reading Check**

5. **Explain** What is unique about the axis of Uranus?

_____

_____

_____

Applying Math

6. **Interpret Data** Imagine that you are making a scale model of the solar system. On your model, 1 cm equals 1 AU. How far from the Sun will Saturn be on your model?

_____

Comets

A **comet** is a large body of ice and rock that orbits the Sun. It can be as large as fifty kilometers across. Comets might come from the Oort cloud, an area far beyond the orbit of Pluto. The Oort cloud is about 50,000 AU from the Sun. Other comets come from an area called the Kuiper Belt, which lies just past the orbit of Neptune.

When a comet gets closer to the Sun, solar radiation changes some of its ice into gas. Solar winds blow gas and dust away from the comet. From Earth, the gas and dust that follow the comet appear as a bright tail. The figure below shows a comet in the night sky. ☑

What is a meteorite?

Sometimes, chunks of rock and metal from outer space fall to Earth's surface. **Meteorites** are any fragments from space that land on Earth. Small meteorites can be the size of pebbles. A large meteorite can have a mass as large as 14.5 metric tons. Hundreds of meteorites fall to Earth each year. Only a few of the meteorites that fall are ever found.

Scientists are interested in meteorites because they help them understand more about space. For example, many meteorites seem to be about 4.5 billion years old. This gives an estimate of the age of the solar system.

There are three types of meteorites—irons, stones, and stoney-irons. Irons are made almost all of iron, with some nickel mixed in. Stones are rocky. Stoney-irons, a mixture of metal and rock, are the rarest meteorites. ☑

☑ **Reading Check**

7. Why does a comet appear to have a tail?

_____

_____

_____

☑ **Reading Check**

8. Recall What are the three types of meteorites?

_____

_____

_____

● After You Read

Mini Glossary

astronomical (as truh NAH mih kul) unit: a unit of measure equal to the distance from Earth to the Sun, or about 150 million km

comet: large body of ice and rock that orbits the Sun; a comet develops a bright, glowing tail as it nears the Sun

meteorite: any rock from space that survives its plunge through the atmosphere and lands on Earth's surface

solar system: the nine planets and numerous other objects that orbit the Sun, all held in place by the Sun's gravity

1. Review the terms above and their definitions in the Mini Glossary. Use two of the vocabulary words in sentences that show you understand the words.

_____

_____

_____

2. Complete the chart below to review the main ideas and details about the solar system.

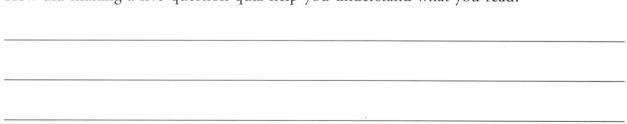

INNER PLANETS	OUTER PLANETS	OTHER OBJECTS
_____	_____	MOONS
VENUS	_____	_____
_____	_____	_____
_____	_____	_____
_____	PLUTO	_____

3. How did making a five-question quiz help you understand what you read?

_____

_____

_____

 **Science** Online Visit **red.msscience.com** to access your textbook, interactive games, and projects to help you learn more about the solar system.

End of Section

The Solar System and Beyond

section ❸ Stars and Galaxies

What You'll Learn

- why stars appear to move across the sky
- about constellations
- how stars change over time

Study Coach

KWL Chart Create a three-column chart to help you organize the information in this section. Before you read, write what you already know about stars and galaxies. Then write what you want to know. As you read, write what you have learned about stars and galaxies.

● Before You Read

What are some different ways that scientists have learned about stars and galaxies? Write your ideas on the lines below.

_____

_____

_____

● Read to Learn

Stars

Stars are always in the sky. You can't see them during the day because the Sun's light makes Earth's atmosphere so bright that it hides them. Earth's rotation makes it look like the stars move across the night sky, just like another star, the Sun, seems to move across the sky during the day. Earth's revolution around the Sun also causes the stars to appear as if they changed location.

What is a constellation?

Constellations (kahn stuh LAY shuns) are groups of stars that form patterns in the sky. Around the world, different people throughout history have given different names to the constellations. Ursa Major, Ursa Minor, Orion, and Taurus are some of the names in use today.

What makes one star different from another?

They may look about the same from Earth, but stars are actually different colors. They are different colors because they are different temperatures. Red stars are the coolest visible stars. Yellow stars have medium temperatures, and blue stars are the hottest. Stars are different sizes, too. Most stars are small. The Sun is a medium-sized, yellow star.

Can a star's brightness be classified?

Some stars are brighter than others. You can see this on a clear night. Scientists classify a star's brightness by a system called apparent magnitude. From Earth, stars that appear the dimmest have an apparent magnitude of 6. Brighter stars have smaller numbers, even numbers below zero. The Sun is the brightest with an apparent magnitude of −26.7. It looks bright because it is so close to Earth, not because it is so much brighter than other stars. The Sun is really a medium-bright star compared to other stars.

The Lives of Stars

Scientists hypothesize that stars begin as huge clouds of gas and dust. Gravity pulls together the dust and gases. Then temperatures begin to rise. When the dust and gas draw very close and the temperature gets very hot, atoms begin to merge, or join, together. This merging process is called fusion. Fusion changes matter into the energy that powers the star.

After a medium-sized star has formed and used up some of the gas at its center, it expands. The star becomes a giant. Giants are large, cool, reddish stars. The Sun will become a giant in about five billion years. It will remain a giant for about a billion years. Then the Sun will lose its outer shell, the core will shrink, and the Sun will become a white dwarf—a hot, small star. Finally, the Sun will cool and stop shining. It will become a black dwarf.

How long a star lives depends on how massive it is. Larger stars have shorter lives. Smaller stars have longer lives.

What is the life cycle of a supergiant?

When a large star begins to use up the fuel in its core, it expands to become a supergiant. Eventually, the core of the supergiant collapses. This sends an explosion through the star and the star becomes bright. The exploding star is called a **supernova**. Gas and dust are released and might become part of a new star.

The core of the supergiant may become a neutron star if it isn't too large. If the core is more than three times as massive as the Sun, it collapses to form a black hole. No light can escape from a black hole. ✔

Copyright © Glencoe/McGraw-Hill, a division of The McGraw-Hill Companies, Inc.

FOLDABLES

Ⓖ Find Main Ideas Make the following half-sheet Foldables to help you identify the main ideas about stars and galaxies.

Lives of Stars:

Types of Galaxies:

✔ Reading Check

1. **Identify** What is the end of the life of a massive supergiant?

_____

_____

Galaxies

A **galaxy** is a group of stars, gas, and dust held together by gravity. Galaxies look like dim clumps of stars in the sky.

Are all galaxies the same?

There are different shapes and sizes of galaxies. The three major types of galaxies are elliptical, spiral, and irregular. Elliptical galaxies are shaped like huge basketballs or footballs. Spiral galaxies can be shaped like huge pinwheels. Some spiral galaxies have bars at the center. Irregular galaxies come in all sorts of shapes. They are smaller than other galaxies. ☑

What is the Milky Way galaxy?

We live in a giant spiral galaxy called the Milky Way. Hundreds of billions of stars are in the Milky Way, including the Sun. Just as Earth revolves around the Sun, stars revolve around the centers of galaxies. The Sun revolves around the center of the Milky Way about once every 225 million years.

You can see part of the Milky Way from Earth as a band of light across the night sky. The band of light is made up of the light of stars in the galaxy's disk. The Milky Way is bigger and brighter than most other galaxies in the universe. Every star you see in the night sky is part of the Milky Way Galaxy.

✔ Reading Check

2. Classify What are the three major types of galaxies?

_____

_____

_____

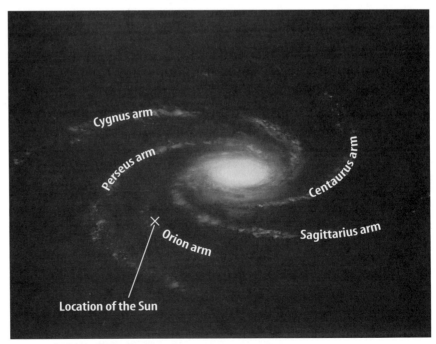

The Sun is located toward the edge of the Milky Way.

Picture This

3. Interpret Scientific Illustrations How many arms does the Milky Way Galaxy have.

_____

Why is the speed of light unique?

The speed of light is about 300,000 km/s. Light could go around Earth seven times in one second. Nothing travels faster. Light always travels at the same speed, no matter what. The speed of light is a constant that scientists use to talk about the large distances in the universe. The figure shows how scientists can calculate distances in space.

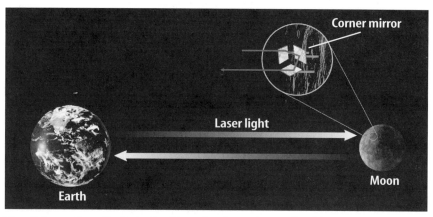

The distance from Earth to the Moon has been determined by bouncing a laser beam off mirrors left by *Apollo 11* astronauts.

Picture This

4. Draw Conclusions
When scientists measured the distance between Earth and the Moon, they used a laser beam and mirrors. What did they measure?

_____

_____

_____

What is a light-year?

One light-year is a unit of measurement that is even larger than one astronomical unit. A **light-year** is the distance light travels in one year. A light-year is about 9.5 trillion km.

Galaxies are so big that they are measured in light-years. Small galaxies are a few thousand light-years across. Large galaxies may be 100,000 light-years across. The distance between galaxies is also measured in light-years. When light from some stars reaches Earth, that light has been traveling for millions of years. ✓

The Universe

Each galaxy contains billions of stars. As many as 100 billion galaxies might exist. All these galaxies with all their billions of stars make up the universe. The universe is the great vastness of space dotted with exploding stars, black holes, and star-filled galaxies. In all this space is one small planet called Earth. In relation to the vastness of the universe, Earth is smaller than one speck of dust. Earth looks even smaller when you consider that the universe seems to be expanding. Could it be the only place where life exists?

✔ **Reading Check**

5. Explain What is measured in light-years?

_____

_____

● After You Read

Mini Glossary

constellation (kahn stuh LAY shun): group of stars that forms a pattern in the sky

galaxy: group of stars, gas, and dust held together by gravity

light-year: about 9.5 trillion km—the distance that light travels in one year—which is used to measure large distances between stars or galaxies

supernova: very bright explosion of a supergiant that takes place after its core collapses

1. Review the terms and their definitions in the Mini Glossary. Use two or more terms in a short poem about the universe. Your poem doesn't have to rhyme.

_____

_____

_____

2. Fill in the summary chart with information you have learned in this section.

Stars	_____ are made up of stars that form patterns in the sky. Stars begin as _____.
Galaxies	Earth is in the _____ arm of the _____ Galaxy.
The Universe	The universe has billions of _____ made up of billions of _____.

3. Reread the Know column of your K-W-L chart. Did you find out what you wanted to know by reading the section? Make sure you filled in the column labeled *Learned.* What other resources could help you find out what you want to know about stars and galaxies?

_____

_____

_____

End of Section

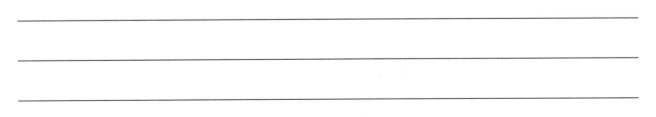

Science Online Visit **red.msscience.com** to access your textbook, interactive games, and projects to help you learn more about stars and galaxies.

Copyright © Glencoe/McGraw-Hill, a division of The McGraw-Hill Companies, Inc.

Cells—The Units of Life

section ❶ The World of Cells

⬤ Before You Read

What did you use as a small child to build with? What did you make? In this section, you will learn about cells, the building blocks of life.

_____

_____

_____

_____

What You'll Learn

- what the cell theory is
- the parts of animal and plant cells
- the functions of different cell parts

⬤ Read to Learn

Importance of Cells

The cell is the smallest unit of life in all living things. Cells are organized structures that help living things carry on the activities of life. They help living things move, grow, reproduce, and break down food. Different cells have different jobs. In the human body, for example, white blood cells help fight disease. Red blood cells carry oxygen to different parts of the body. Even though different cells have different jobs, all cells are alike in many ways.

What is the cell theory?

Cells were not observed until microscopes were invented. In 1665, scientist Robert Hooke made a microscope and used it to observe tiny, boxlike objects in a slice of cork. He called the objects cells because they reminded him of small rooms, called cells, where monks lived.

Throughout the 17th and 18th centuries, scientists continued to observe many living things under microscopes. Their observations led to the development of the cell theory.

Study Coach

Identify the Main Point
Read each subhead. Then work with a partner to write questions about the information in each subhead. Take turns asking and answering the questions. Use the questions as a study guide about cells.

FOLDABLES

Ⓐ List Make a layered-look Foldable, as shown below. List the three main ideas of the cell theory on the tabs.

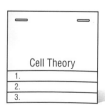

Cell Theory
1.
2.
3.

Ideas of the Cell Theory There are three main ideas of the cell theory.

- All living things are made of one or more cells.

- The cell is the basic unit of life. All the activities of life take place inside cells.

- All cells come from cells that already exist.

How many cells do living things have?

The smallest organisms on Earth are **bacteria**. Bacteria are one-celled organisms, meaning they are made up of only one cell. Larger organisms are made of many cells. The human body, for example, is made up of more than 10 trillion (10,000,000,000,000) cells.

How do microscopes help scientists?

Scientists have used microscopes to study cells for more than 300 years. In recent years, better microscopes have helped scientists learn more about the differences between cells and observe the small parts that are inside cells.

Most science classrooms use a microscope called a compound light microscope. In a compound microscope, light passes through the object that you are looking at and then through two or more lenses before it reaches your eye. The lenses make the image of the object look larger.

What are cells made of?

Even though cells are small, they are made of even smaller parts. Each cell part has its own job. Just as every building has walls, every cell has a boundary. All of the cell's activities take place inside this boundary. Some parts of the cell are used as storage areas. Other parts use oxygen, water, minerals, and other nutrients to make substances the cell needs. Still other parts release the energy needed for maintaining life.

What makes up the outside of a cell?

The **cell membrane** is the outer boundary of the cell. It helps hold the cell together, like walls hold a building together. The cell membrane forms a flexible boundary between the cell and its environment. It helps to control what goes into and comes out of the cell. Some kinds of cells, including plant cells, have a rigid **cell wall** that surrounds the cell membrane. The cell wall helps support and protect the cell. Animal cells do not have cell walls. ☑

Reading Check

1. **Explain** one of the roles of the cell membrane.

_____

_____

_____

What makes up the inside of a cell?

The inside of a cell contains a gelatinlike substance called **cytoplasm** (SI tuh pla zum). Water makes up most of the cytoplasm. The cytoplasm also contains many chemicals that are needed by the cell. Most of the cell's activities happen in the cytoplasm.

What are organelles?

Except for bacterial cells, all cells have **organelles** (or guh NELZ). Organelles are specialized cell parts that move around in the cytoplasm. They perform jobs that are necessary for life. Each kind of organelle does a different job. In the figure of the animal cell below, the nucleus, the vacuole, and the mitochondrion are organelles.

What makes up the nucleus?

Every cell contains hereditary material that directs most of the cell's activities. The hereditary material is a chemical called DNA. DNA is contained in the chromosomes (KROH muh zohmz). In the cells of all organisms except bacteria, the chromosomes are contained in an organelle called the **nucleus** (NEW klee us).

Where are substances stored in cells?

Food, water, and other substances are stored in balloonlike organelles called **vacuoles** (VA kyuh wohlz). Some vacuoles store wastes. In plants, most cells contain a large vacuole that stores water and other substances.

Copyright © Glencoe/McGraw-Hill, a division of The McGraw-Hill Companies, Inc.

💡 Think it Over

2. Explain why cells have many different kinds of organelles.

_____

_____

_____

Picture This

3. Identify Highlight the name of the cell part that is a storage area. Circle two organelles.

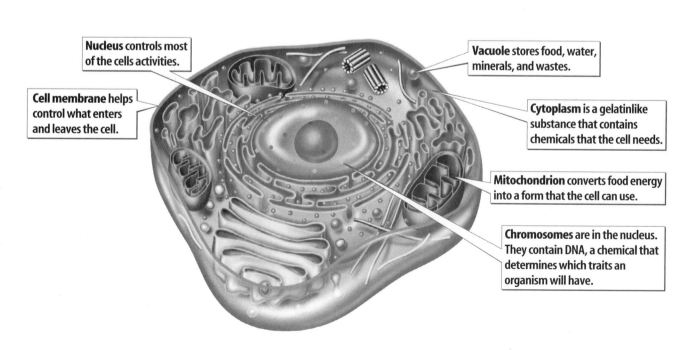

Nucleus controls most of the cells activities.

Cell membrane helps control what enters and leaves the cell.

Vacuole stores food, water, minerals, and wastes.

Cytoplasm is a gelatinlike substance that contains chemicals that the cell needs.

Mitochondrion converts food energy into a form that the cell can use.

Chromosomes are in the nucleus. They contain DNA, a chemical that determines which traits an organism will have.

Energy and the Cell

All cells need energy. Except for bacteria, all cells have organelles called **mitochondria** (mi tuh KAHN dree uh) (singular, *mitochondrion*) that supply the energy the cell needs. Inside the mitochondria, a process called cellular respiration (SEL yuh lur • res puh RAY shun) takes place as shown in the figure below.

Picture This

4. **Identify** Highlight the names of the two materials needed by the mitochondrion to produce energy.

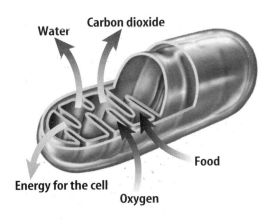

Water

Carbon dioxide

Energy for the cell

Oxygen

Food

Cellular respiration involves chemical reactions that change the energy stored in food into a form of energy the cell can use. This energy is released as food and oxygen combine. The waste products of cellular respiration are carbon dioxide and water. Cells that have mitochondria use energy from cellular respiration to do all of their work.

What happens during photosynthesis?

Plants, algae, and many types of bacteria use a process called **photosynthesis** (foh toh SIHN thuh sus) to make their food. In plants, most photosynthesis happens in leaf cells. Inside the leaf cells are green organelles called **chloroplasts** (KLOR uh plasts). Most leaves are green because of chloroplasts. During plant photosynthesis, chloroplasts take in light energy and use it to combine carbon dioxide from the air with water to make food. Energy is stored in food. As the plant needs energy, its mitochondria release the food's energy. The energy is passed to other organisms when they eat the plants. ☑

☑ Reading Check

5. **Recall** What plant organelle is used in photosynthesis?

_____

● After You Read

Mini Glossary

bacteria: the smallest organisms on Earth; made of single cells

cell membrane: a flexible structure that holds the cell together

cell wall: rigid structure that surrounds the cell membrane; helps support and protect the cell

chloroplasts: green organelles located in leaf cells

cytoplasm: the inside part of a cell in which most of the cell's activities take place

mitochondria: an organelle in which the process of respiration takes place

nucleus: an organelle that contains hereditary material

organelles: specialized cell parts that move around in the cytoplasm and perform activities that are necessary for life

photosynthesis: the process through which plants, algae, and many types of bacteria make food

vacuoles: balloonlike organelles in the cytoplasm in which food, water, and other substances are stored

1. Review the terms and their definitions in the Mini Glossary. Choose two terms and write a sentence that explains how plants make their own food.

_____

_____

2. Complete the chart below to identify the job of each of the listed cell parts.

Part of Cell	Part's Job
cell membrane	
	helps support and protect cells of plants
cytoplasm	
nucleus	
	contains DNA

3. How is asking and answering questions with a partner helpful in remembering what you have read?

_____

_____

 Visit **red.msscience.com** to access your textbook, interactive games, and projects to help you learn more about the world of cells.

End of Section

Cells—The Units of Life

section ❷ The Different Jobs of Cells

What You'll Learn
- how different cells have different jobs
- the differences among tissues, organs, and organ systems

⦿ Before You Read

A poster in a store window reads: "We specialize in repairing DVD players." What does the word *specialize* in the poster mean?

_____

_____

Mark the Text

Identify the Main Point Underline the main point of each paragraph as you read the section.

⦿ Read to Learn

Special Cells for Special Jobs

Cells in many-celled organisms are specialized. A specialized cell does a specific job. Specialized cells work together to perform all the life activities of a many-celled organism.

What types of cells do animals have?

The human body and the bodies of other animals are made up of many types of specialized cells. These cells come in various sizes and shapes. The figure below shows examples of the shapes and sizes of human cells.

Picture This

1. **Identify** Highlight the part of the description for nerve, muscle, and skin cells that describes their shape. Circle the part of the description that explains what the cells do.

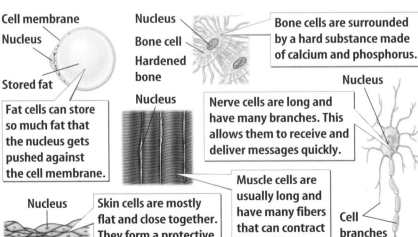

Cell membrane
Nucleus
Stored fat

Fat cells can store so much fat that the nucleus gets pushed against the cell membrane.

Nucleus
Bone cell
Hardened bone

Bone cells are surrounded by a hard substance made of calcium and phosphorus.

Nucleus

Nerve cells are long and have many branches. This allows them to receive and deliver messages quickly.

Cell branches

Nucleus

Muscle cells are usually long and have many fibers that can contract and relax.

Nucleus

Skin cells are mostly flat and close together. They form a protective layer for your body.

What types of cells make up plants?

Plants also are made up of many types of specialized cells. Plants have different types of cells in their leaves, roots, and stems. Each type of cell has a certain job. Some plant cells, such as those in plant stems, are long and tubelike. They form a system through which water, food, and other substances move from one part of the plant to another. Other cells, like those on the outside of a plant stem, are shorter and thicker. They help to make the stem strong. ☑

Cell Organization

The cells of many-celled organisms are not just mixed together in any kind of way. Cells are organized into systems that work together to perform jobs that keep the organism healthy and alive.

How are tissues and organs different?

Cells that are alike are organized into tissues (TIH shewz). **Tissues** are groups of similar cells that all do the same sort of work. For example, bone tissue is made up of bone cells that are organized to form the bones in your body.

Different types of tissues working together can form an **organ** (OR gun). For example, the stomach is an organ that includes muscle tissue, nerve tissue, and blood tissue. The tissues in the stomach work together to help the stomach digest food. The heart and the kidneys are other organs in the human body.

What are organ systems?

A group of organs that work together to do a certain job is called an **organ system**. For example, the mouth, stomach, and intestines are used in digestion. These and other organs make up the digestive system. Other organ systems in the human body include the respiratory system, the circulatory system, the reproductive system, and the nervous system.

Organ systems also work with each other. For example, your muscular system works with your skeletal system to make your body move. Your muscular system is made up of hundreds of muscles that are attached to your bones. The bones make up your skeletal system. The muscles help bones move.

✔ **Reading Check**

2. Compare What is the purpose of a plant's inner and outer stem cells?

_____

_____

_____

FOLDABLES

ⓒ Organize Make a four-tab Foldable using notebook paper, as shown below. Inside each tab, list facts about each level of cell organization.

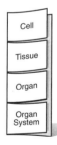

Cell

Tissue

Organ

Organ System

● After You Read

Mini Glossary

organ: structure formed by different types of tissues working together

organ system: a group of organs that work together to do a certain job

tissue: group of similar cells that all do the same sort of work

1. Review the terms and their definitions in the Mini Glossary. Write a sentence that explains how the three terms are related.

_____

_____

_____

2. Choose one of the question headings in the Read to Learn section. Write the question in the space below. Then write your answer to that question on the lines that follow.

> **Write your question here.**

_____

_____

_____

End of Section

 Science nline Visit **red.msscience.com** to access your textbook, interactive games, and projects to help you learn more about the different jobs of cells.

chapter 17 Invertebrate Animals

section ❶ What is an animal?

◉ Before You Read

List the names of five animals on the lines below. Then write one thing that these animals have in common.

_____

_____

_____

What You'll Learn
■ the characteristics of animals
■ the differences between vertebrates and invertebrates

◉ Read to Learn

Animal Characteristics

If you asked ten people what all animals have in common, you would get many different answers. Animals come in many different shapes and sizes. All animals, however, have five common characteristics.

1. All animals are many-celled organisms that are made of different kinds of cells.
2. Most animal cells have a nucleus and organelles. The nucleus and many of the organelles are surrounded by a membrane. A cell that contains a nucleus and organelles surrounded by membranes is called a eukaryotic (yew ker ee AH tihk) cell.
3. Animals cannot make their own food.
4. Animals digest their food.
5. Most animals can move from place to place.

What is symmetry?

As you study different groups of animals, you will look at their symmetry (SIH muh tree). **Symmetry** refers to the way parts of an object are arranged. If the parts are arranged in a way that allows the object to be divided into similar halves, it is symmetrical.

◀ **Study Coach**

Quiz Yourself As you read the section, write a question for each paragraph. Answer the question with information from the paragraph. Use the questions and answers to study the section.

💡 **Think it Over**

1. **Analyze** Name one reason animals need to move from place to place.

_____

_____

_____

What kind of symmetry do most animals have?

Most animals have either radial symmetry or bilateral symmetry. An animal with body parts arranged in a circle around a central point has radial symmetry. As you can see in the figure below, a sea anemone has radial symmetry. An animal with radial symmetry can find food and gather information from all directions. Other animals that have radial symmetry are jellyfish and sea urchins. ☑

An animal with bilateral symmetry has parts that are nearly mirror images of each other. You can draw a line down the center of its body to divide it into two similar parts. The figure below shows that a lobster has bilateral symmetry. A human also has bilateral symmetry.

Sea anemones have radial symmetry.

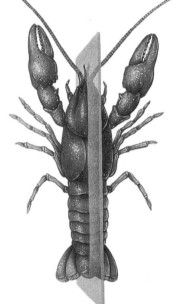

Lobsters have bilateral symmetry.

Many sponges are asymmetrical.

Picture This

3. Classify Draw a simple human figure beside the type of symmetry that humans have.

What is an asymmetrical animal like?

An animal with an uneven shape is called asymmetrical (AY suh meh trih kul). Its body cannot be divided into halves that are similar. Look at the sponge in the figure above. Notice that you cannot draw a line down the center of its body to divide it into two halves that are similar. As you learn more about invertebrates, think about their body symmetry. Notice how body symmetry affects the way they gather food and do other things.

Animal Classification

Animals have many characteristics in common. But when you think about the variety of animals you can name, you know that there are many different kinds of animals. Some animals have legs, others have wings. Some live on land, others live in water. Scientists use a classification system to place all animals into related groups.

Scientists separate animals into two groups—vertebrates (VUR tuh bruts) and invertebrates (ihn VUR tuh bruts). These two groups are shown in the figure below. Vertebrates are animals that have a backbone. **Invertebrates** are animals that do not have a backbone. About 97 percent of all animals are invertebrates.

Animal Kingdom

Invertebrates   Vertebrates

Scientists further classify the invertebrates into smaller groups, as shown in the figure below. The animals in each group share similar characteristics. These characteristics show that the animals within the group may have had a common ancestor.

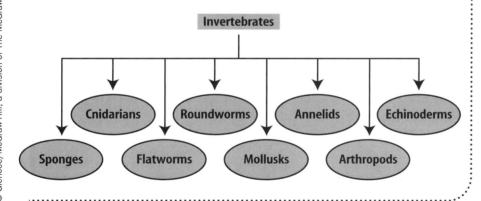

Applying Math

4. Create a Circle Graph
In the circle below, draw a circle graph showing the percent of invertebrates and the percent of vertebrates.

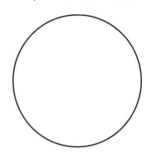

Picture This

5. Identify Circle any words in the diagram that you do not know. When you have finished reading this chapter, review the words you circled and state a characteristic of each one.

● After You Read

Mini Glossary

invertebrates (ihn VUR tuh bruts): animals that do not have a backbone

symmetry (SIH muh tree): the way parts of an object are arranged

1. Review the terms and their definitions in the Mini Glossary. Write a sentence that explains the difference between an animal that has symmetry and one that is asymmetrical.

_____

_____

_____

2. Fill in the table below to describe the common characteristics of all animals.

Common Characteristics of All Animals
1.
2.
3.
4.
5.

3. How did writing and answering quiz questions help you remember what you have read about animal characteristics and classification?

_____

_____

_____

End of Section

 Science Online Visit **red.msscience.com** to access your textbook, interactive games, and projects to help you learn more about the characteristics of animals.

Invertebrate Animals

section ❷ Sponges, Cnidarians, Flatworms, and Roundworms

Copyright © Glencoe/McGraw-Hill, a division of The McGraw-Hill Companies, Inc.

● Before You Read

On the lines below, list a difference between the way plants and animals get food.

_____

_____

What You'll Learn
- the structures of sponges and cnidarians
- how sponges and cnidarians get food and reproduce
- about flatworms and roundworms

● Read to Learn

Sponges

Sponges are classified as animals because they cannot make their own food. A sponge's body is made of two layers of cells. Adult sponges remain attached to one place for their lifetime. There are about 15,000 species of sponges.

How does a sponge eat?

All sponges are filter feeders. Sponges filter tiny food particles from the water that flows through their bodies. The inner part of a sponge's body is lined with collar cells. Thin, whiplike structures, called flagella (flah JEH luh), are attached to the collar cells. The whiplike movements of the flagella keep water moving through the sponge. Other cells digest the food, carry nutrients to all parts of the sponge, and remove wastes.

How does a sponge protect itself?

Many sponges have soft bodies that are supported by sharp, glass-like structures called spicules (SPIHK yewlz). Other sponges contain a substance called spongin, which is like foam rubber. Spongin makes sponges soft and stretchable. Some sponges have both spicules and spongin to protect their soft bodies.

Study Coach

Sticky-Note Discussions
As you read the section, use sticky-note paper to mark paragraphs you find interesting. Share the interesting information with a partner.

FOLDABLES

Ⓐ Explain Make a four-tab book Foldable, as shown below. Take notes on what you read about each classification of animal.

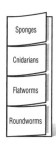

How do sponges reproduce?

Sponges can reproduce asexually and sexually. A sponge reproduces asexually when a bud on the side of the parent sponge develops into a small sponge. The small sponge breaks off, floats away, and attaches itself to a new surface. New sponges also can grow from pieces of a sponge.

Most sponges that reproduce sexually are hermaphrodites (hur MA fruh dites). This means they produce both eggs and sperm. The figure below shows sexual reproduction in sponges. Sponges release sperm into the water. The sperm float until they are drawn into another sponge. The sperm fertilizes an egg. A larva develops in the sponge. The larva leaves the sponge and settles to the bottom. It attaches to the surface on which it lands and grows into a new sponge.

Picture This

1. **Identify** Circle the names of two structures needed for sexual reproduction.

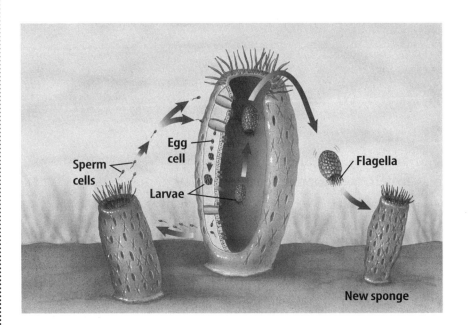

Sperm cells

Egg cell

Larvae

Flagella

New sponge

Cnidarians

Jellyfish, sea anemones, hydra, and corals are cnidarians. **Cnidarians** (nih DAR ee unz) are hollowed-bodied animals with two cell layers that are organized into tissues. Cnidarians have tentacles surrounding their mouths. The tentacles shoot out harpoon-like stinging cells to capture prey. Cnidarians have radial symmetry, so they can locate food that floats by from any direction. The inner cell layer digests the food. Nerve cells work together as a nerve net throughout the whole body. ☑

2. **Explain** Why does a cnidarian use stinging cells?

_____

_____

What kinds of body forms do cnidarians have?

Cnidarians have two different body forms. The vase-shaped body form is called a **polyp** (PAH lup). Sea anemones and hydras are polyps. Polyps usually remain attached to a surface. A jellyfish has a free-swimming, bell-shaped body that is called a **medusa** (mih DEW suh). Jellyfish are not strong swimmers. Instead they drift with the ocean currents. Some cnidarians go through both a polyp stage and a medusa stage during their life cycles. ☑

How do cnidarians reproduce?

Cnidarians reproduce both sexually and asexually. The polyp form of a cnidarian reproduces asexually by budding. The bud falls off the parent and develops into a new polyp. Some polyps also can reproduce sexually by releasing eggs or sperm into the water. Eggs that are fertilized by the sperm develop into new polyps.

The medusa form of a cnidarian has a two-stage life cycle, as shown in the figure below. A medusa reproduces sexually to produce polyps. Then each polyp reproduces asexually to form new medusae.

☑ **Reading Check**

3. **Identify** the two body forms of cnidarians.

_____

_____

Picture This

4. **Apply** Draw a circle around the three pictures of the medusae in the diagram.

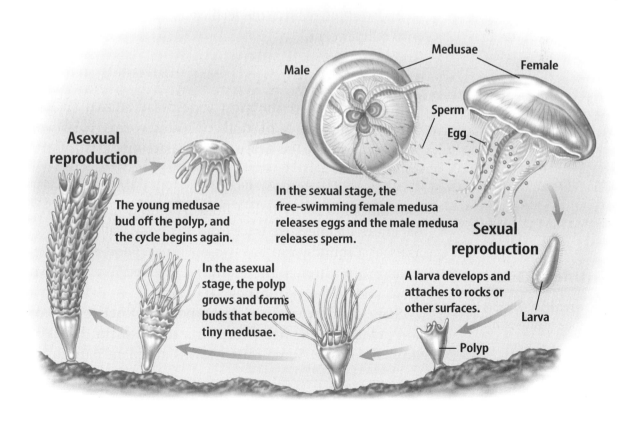

Asexual reproduction

The young medusae bud off the polyp, and the cycle begins again.

In the asexual stage, the polyp grows and forms buds that become tiny medusae.

Male

Medusae

Female

Sperm

Egg

In the sexual stage, the free-swimming female medusa releases eggs and the male medusa releases sperm.

Sexual reproduction

A larva develops and attaches to rocks or other surfaces.

Larva

Polyp

Flatworms

Unlike sponges and cnidarians, flatworms search for food. Flatworms are invertebrates with long, flattened bodies and bilateral symmetry. A flatworm's body is soft and has three layers of tissue organized into organs and organ systems. Some kinds of flatworms can move around and search for food. These flatworms have a digestive system with one opening. Most flatworms are parasites that live in or on their hosts. A parasite gets its food and shelter from its host.

What are tapeworms?

Tapeworms are flatworms that live in the intestines of their hosts. A tapeworm does not have a digestive system. It gets its nutrients from digested food in the host's intestine. A tapeworm's head has hooks and suckers that attach to the host's intestine. A human can be a host for a tapeworm. ✔

How do tapeworms reproduce?

The body of a tapeworm is made up of segments. A tapeworm grows by adding segments directly behind its head. Each body section has both male and female reproductive organs. Eggs and sperm are released inside the segment. After it is filled with fertilized eggs, the segment breaks off. The segment passes with wastes out of the host's body. If it is eaten by another host, the fertilized egg hatches and develops into a tapeworm.

Roundworms

Roundworms are the most widespread animal on Earth. There are thousands of kinds of roundworms. Heartworms, which can infect the hearts of dogs, are one kind of roundworm.

A roundworm's body is a tube inside a tube. Between the two tubes is a cavity full of fluid. The fluid-filled cavity separates the digestive tract from the body wall. The digestive tract of a roundworm has two openings. Food enters the roundworm through the mouth, is digested in a digestive tract, and wastes exit through the anus.

Some roundworms are decomposers. Other roundworms are predators. The heartworm is a roundworm that is an animal parasite. Some roundworms are plant parasites.

Copyright © Glencoe/McGraw-Hill, a division of The McGraw-Hill Companies, Inc.

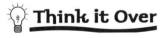

● After You Read

Mini Glossary

cnidarian (nih DAR ee un): a hollow-bodied animal with tentacles for catching food and two cell layers that are organized into tissues

medusa (mih DEW suh): a free-swimming, bell-shaped body of a cnidarian

polyp (PAH lup): a vase-shaped body of a cnidarian

1. Review the terms and their definitions in the Mini Glossary. Choose the term that names an invertebrate. Write a sentence describing the animal.

_____

_____

_____

2. Complete the Venn diagram below to help you compare flatworms and roundworms.

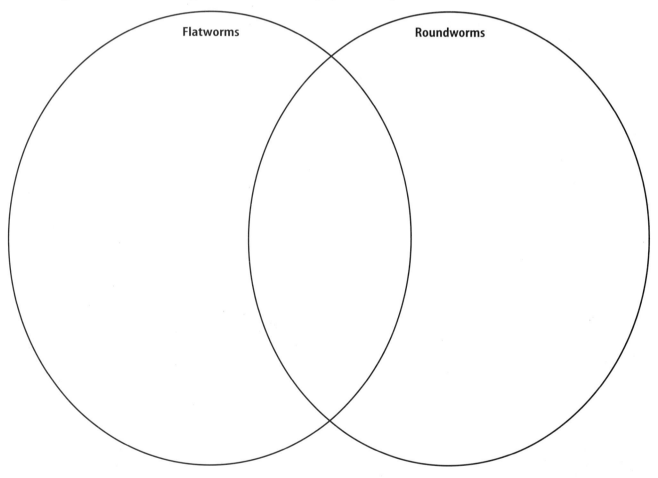

Flatworms   Roundworms

Science Online Visit **red.msscience.com** to access your textbook, interactive games, and projects to help you learn more about sponges, cnidarians, flatworms, and roundworms.

End of Section

Invertebrate Animals

section ❸ Mollusks and Segmented Worms

What You'll Learn

- the characteristics of mollusks
- differences between an open and a closed circulatory system
- the characteristics of segmented worms
- the digestive process of an earthworm

Identify Main Ideas
Highlight the main idea in each paragraph. Review the main ideas after you have finished reading.

✔ **Reading Check**

1. Define What is a radula?

_____

_____

● Before You Read

On the lines below, describe some characteristics of an earthworm.

_____

_____

_____

● Read to Learn

Mollusks

A **mollusk** is a soft-bodied invertebrate that usually has a shell. A mollusk also has a mantle and a large, muscular foot. The **mantle** is a thin layer of tissue that covers the mollusk's soft body. The foot is used for moving or for holding the animal in one place. Snails, mussels, and octopuses are mollusks. Mollusks that live in water have gills. **Gills** are organs in which carbon dioxide from the animal is exchanged for oxygen from the water. Mollusks that live on land have lungs in which carbon dioxide from the animal is exchanged for oxygen from the air.

What body systems does a mollusk have?

A mollusk has a digestive system with two openings. Many mollusks have a scratchy tonguelike organ called the **radula** (RA juh luh). The radula has rows of tiny, sharp teeth that the mollusk uses to scrape small bits of food off rocks and other surfaces. Some mollusks have an **open circulatory system**, which means they do not have blood vessels. Instead, the blood washes over the organs, which are grouped together in a fluid-filled cavity inside the animal's body. ✔

Types of Mollusks

Scientists use three characteristics to classify a mollusk.

1. Does the mollusk have a shell?
2. If the mollusk has a shell, what kind of shell is it?
3. What type of foot does the mollusk have?

What are gastropods?

Gastropods are the largest group of mollusks. Most gastropods have one shell. Snails and conchs are examples of single-shelled gastropods. A slug is a gastropod that has no shell. Some gastropods live in water and others live on land. A gastropod uses its large, muscular foot to move about. Gastropods secrete mucus, which helps them glide across surfaces.

What are bivalves?

Bivalves are mollusks with two shell halves joined by a hinge. Scallops and clams are bivalves. Large, powerful muscles open and close the shell halves. Bivalves are water animals. A bivalve filters food from water that enters into and is filtered through the gills.

What are cephalopods?

Squid and octopuses are cephalopods (SE fah lah pawdz). Most cephalopods have a stiff plate inside their bodies instead of a shell on the outside. They have a well-developed head and a "foot" that is made up of tentacles with suckers. The mouth is at the base of the tentacles. A cephalopod has a **closed circulatory system** in which blood is carried through blood vessels.

Cephalopods can move quickly through the water. The figure below compares the movement of a squid as it releases water to the movement of a balloon as it releases air.

Copyright © Glencoe/McGraw-Hill, a division of The McGraw-Hill Companies, Inc.

FOLDABLES

B Describe Make a six-tab book Foldable, as shown below. Write the main ideas as you read about each type of mollusk or segmented worm.

Gastropods
Bivalves
Cephalopods
Earthworms
Leeches
Marine Worms

Picture This

2. **Explain** Use the figure to explain to a partner how a squid moves.

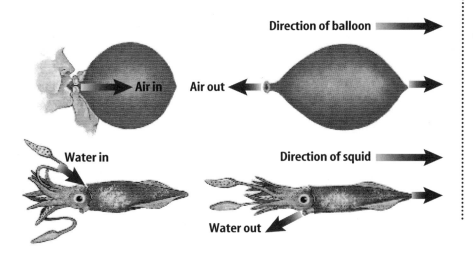

Direction of balloon

Air in   Air out

Water in   Direction of squid

Water out

How does a cephalopod move?

A muscular envelope, called the mantle, surrounds a cephalopod's internal organs. Water enters the space between the mantle and the body organs. When the mantle closes, water is squeezed through a funnel-like structure called a siphon. This squeezing creates a force that causes the animal to move in the opposite direction of the stream of water.

Segmented Worms

Earthworms, leeches, and marine worms are segmented worms. Segmented worms are also called annelids (A nul idz). A segmented worm's body is made up of repeating rings that make the worm flexible. Each ring or segment has nerve cells, blood vessels, part of the digestive tract, and the coelom (SEE lum). The coelom is a body cavity that separates the internal organs from the inside of the body wall. A segmented worm has a closed circulatory system and a complete digestive system with two body openings. ✔

How does an earthworm move and eat?

An earthworm has more than 100 rings or segments. Each segment has bristles, or setae (SEE tee), on the outside. Setae are used to grip the soil while two sets of muscles move them through the soil. As the earthworm moves, it takes soil into its mouth. The earthworm gets its food from the soil. The soil moves from the mouth, to the crop, to the gizzard. In the gizzard, the food and the soil are ground. In the intestine, the food is broken down and absorbed by the blood. Waste materials and undigested soil leave the earthworm through the anus. All of these structures are shown in the figure below.

Copyright © Glencoe/McGraw-Hill, a division of The McGraw-Hill Companies, Inc.

Picture This

4. **Identify** Circle the parts of an earthworm that are also found in humans.

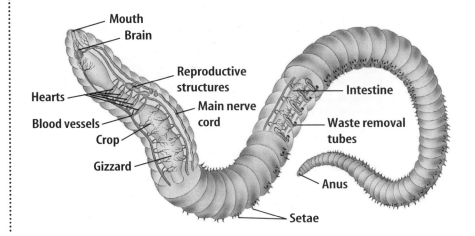

Mouth
Brain
Reproductive structures
Hearts
Blood vessels
Crop
Gizzard
Main nerve cord
Intestine
Waste removal tubes
Anus
Setae

How does an earthworm breathe?

An earthworm does not have lungs or gills. An earthworm breathes through its mucous-covered skin. Carbon dioxide moves out of the body and oxygen moves into the body through the skin. If the mucus covering the skin is removed, the earthworm may die of suffocation. ☑

How does a leech get its food?

Leeches can be found in freshwater, salt or marine water, and on land. A leech is a segmented worm with a flat body. It has suckers on both ends that it uses to attach itself to an animal to remove blood.

A leech can store large amounts of blood that it slowly releases into its digestive system when it needs food. Some leeches can store as much as ten times their own weight in blood, and the blood can be stored for months. Although leeches like a diet of blood, most can eat small water animals.

What are the characteristics of a marine worm?

There are more than 8,000 kinds of marine worms. Marine worms are the most varied group of annelids. The word **polychaete** means "many bristles." A marine worm has bristles, or setae, along the sides of its body. Because of these bristles, marine worms are sometimes called bristle worms. Marine worms can use these setae to walk, swim, or dig. ☑

Some marine worms are filter feeders. They either dig down into the mud or build hollow tubes. Then they use their bristles to filter food from the water. Others eat plants or decaying materials. Some marine worms are predators and some are parasites. The many ways that marine worms get food explains why they are so varied.

✔ **Reading Check**

5. **Explain** how an earthworm breathes.

_____

_____

_____

✔ **Reading Check**

6. **Apply** How do marine worms use setae?

_____

_____

_____

● After You Read

Mini Glossary

closed circulatory system: a circulatory system in which blood is carried through blood vessels

gill: an organ in which carbon dioxide from an animal is exchanged for oxygen from the water

mantle: a thin layer of tissue that covers a mollusk's soft body

mollusk: a soft-bodied invertebrate that has a mantle and a large muscular foot; usually has a shell

open circulatory system: a circulatory system without blood vessels in which blood washes over the organs

radula (RA juh luh): a tonguelike organ in mollusks

1. Review the terms and their definitions in the Mini Glossary. Write two sentences that explain the difference between an open circulatory system and a closed circulatory system.

_____

_____

_____

2. Fill in the table below to identify the main characteristics of mollusks and segmented worms.

	Main Characteristics
Mollusks	1. 2. 3. 4. 5. 6.
Segmented Worms	1. 2. 3. 4.

End of Section

**Science** **nline** Visit **red.msscience.com** to access your textbook, interactive games, and projects to help you learn more about mollusks and segmented worms.

Invertebrate Animals

section ❹ Arthropods and Echinoderms

● Before You Read

On the lines below, list three kinds of insects. Next to the name of each insect, write a short description of the insect.

_____

_____

_____

Copyright © Glencoe/McGraw-Hill, a division of The McGraw-Hill Companies, Inc.

What You'll Learn

- the features used to classify arthropods
- the structure and function of the exoskeleton
- the features of echinoderms

● Read to Learn

Arthropods

An **arthropod** (AR thruh pahd) is an invertebrate animal with jointed appendages (uh PEN dih juz). **Appendages** are structures such as claws, legs, or antennae that grow from the body. Arthropods have bilateral symmetry and segmented bodies.

How does an arthropod protect itself?

Arthropods have hard body coverings called **exoskeletons.** The exoskeleton protects and supports the animal's body and reduces water loss. As the animal grows, the old exoskeleton must be shed because it does not grow with the animal. The process of shedding the exoskeleton is called molting.

What are the characteristics of insects?

Insects make up the largest group of arthropods. Scientists have classified more than 700,000 species of insects. Insects have three body regions—head, thorax, and abdomen. Insects have an open circulatory system. Many insects, such as butterflies, completely change their body form as they grow. This change in body form is called **metamorphosis** (met uh MOR fuh sus).

> **Study Coach**
>
> **Summarize** As you read this section, stop after every paragraph and summarize what you have just read in your own words.

> **FOLDABLES**
>
> **❻ Compare** Make a two-tab book Foldable, as shown below. Write statements or phrases about Arthropods and Echinoderms as you read. Use the statements to compare these animals.
>
>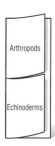
>
> Arthropods
>
> Echinoderms

What are two kinds of metamorphosis?

There are two kinds of insect metamorphosis—complete and incomplete. Complete metamorphosis is shown on the left in the figure below. It has four stages—egg, larva, pupa (PYEW puh), and adult. Notice that each stage is different from the others. The three stages of incomplete metamorphosis—egg, nymph, and adult—are shown on the right in the figure below. A nymph looks like a small adult.

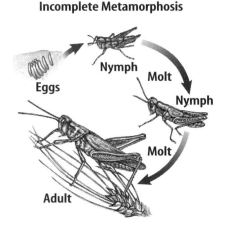

Complete Metamorphosis

Adult
Egg
Pupa
Larva

Incomplete Metamorphosis

Eggs
Nymph
Molt
Nymph
Molt
Adult

What is an arachnid?

Arachnids (uh RAK nudz) are arthropods that have only two body regions—a cephalothorax (sef uh luh THOR aks) and an abdomen. The cephalothorax is a body region made up of a head and a thorax. An arachnid has four pairs of legs attached to its cephalothorax. Spiders, ticks, mites, and scorpions are arachnids.

How do spiders catch their food?

Spiders are predators that use a pair of appendages near their mouths to inject venom, or poison, into their prey. The venom makes the prey unable to move. After the prey has been injected with venom, spiders inject another substance that turns the prey's body into a liquid, which spiders drink. Some spiders weave webs to trap their prey. Other spiders chase and catch their prey.

What are centipedes and millipedes?

Centipedes and millipedes are long, thin segmented animals. Centipedes have one pair of jointed legs attached to each segment. They are predators that use poison to catch prey. Millipedes have two pairs of jointed legs attached to each segment. They eat plants.

Picture This

1. **Identify** Circle the names of the stages that are the same for complete and incomplete metamorphosis.

Applying Math

2. **Calculate** Complete the following sentence by filling in the correct numbers. A centipede with 30 segments has _____ legs. A millipede with 30 segments has _____ legs.

What are the characteristics of crustaceans?

Crustaceans include some of the largest arthropods, such as crabs and lobsters. Most crustaceans are small marine animals called zooplankton. Zooplankton are tiny free-floating animals that serve as food for other marine animals.

Most crustaceans have two pairs of antennae attached to the head, three types of chewing appendages, and five pairs of legs. Many crustaceans that live in water also have appendages called swimmerets on the abdomen. Swimmerets help exchange carbon dioxide from the animal for oxygen in the water. ☑

Echinoderms

Echinoderms (ih KI nuh durmz) are animals that have radial symmetry. Sea stars and sand dollars are echinoderms. Echinoderms have spines of different lengths that cover the outside of their bodies. Most echinoderms have an internal skeleton made up of bonelike plates that supports and protects the animal. Echinoderms have a simple nervous system, but no head or brain. Some echinoderms are predators, some are filter feeders, and some feed on decaying matter.

What is a water-vascular system?

An echinoderm has a water-vascular system, which is a network of water-filled canals and thousands of tube feet. The tube feet work like suction cups to help the animal move and capture prey. The figure below shows the parts of a sea star. A sea star eats by pushing its stomach out of its mouth and into the opened shell of its prey. After the prey's body is digested, the sea star pulls in its stomach. Like some other invertebrates, sea stars can regrow lost or damaged parts.

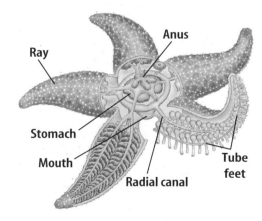

Copyright © Glencoe/McGraw-Hill, a division of The McGraw-Hill Companies, Inc.

✔ **Reading Check**

3. **Determine** What is the purpose of swimmerets?

_____

_____

_____

Picture This

4. **Explain** Use the diagram to explain to a partner how the sea star eats.

● After You Read

Mini Glossary

appendage (uh PEN dihj): a structure such as a claw, leg, or antennae that grows from the body

arthropod (AR thruh pahd): an invertebrate animal with jointed appendages and an exoskeleton

exoskeleton: a hard body covering that protects and supports the body and reduces water loss

metamorphosis (met uh MOR fuh sus): a change in body form

1. Review the terms and their definitions in the Mini Glossary. Write a sentence that describes how an arthropod might use an appendage.

   _____

   _____

   _____

2. Complete the concept map below about arthropod classification.

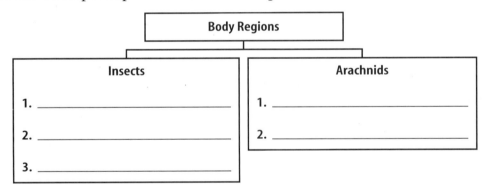

Body Regions	
Insects	**Arachnids**
1. _____	1. _____
2. _____	2. _____
3. _____	

3. Complete the flowcharts to compare complete and incomplete metamorphosis.

Complete Metamorphosis

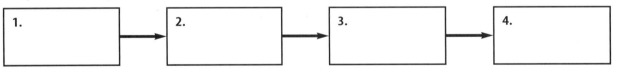

1.	→	2.	→	3.	→	4.

Incomplete Metamorphosis

1.	→	2.	→	3.

End of Section

Science Online Visit **red.msscience.com** to access your textbook, interactive games, and projects to help you learn more about arthropods and echinoderms.

Vertebrate Animals

section ❶ Chordate Animals

● Before You Read

List three animals on the lines below. Then write one thing that all these animals have in common with humans.

_____

_____

_____

Copyright © Glencoe/McGraw-Hill, a division of The McGraw-Hill Companies, Inc.

What You'll Learn

- the characteristics of chordates
- the characteristics of all vertebrates
- the difference between ectotherms and endotherms
- the three classes of fish

● Read to Learn

What is a chordate?

Chordates (KOR dayts) are animals that have the following three characteristics—a notochord (NOH tuh cord), a nerve cord, and pharyngeal (fur RIN jee uhl) pouches at some time during their development.

The notochord is a flexible rod that runs the length of the developing organism. The nerve cord is made of nerve tissue. In most chordates, one end of the nerve cord develops into the organism's brain.

Pharyngeal pouches are slitlike openings between the inside of the body and the outside of the body. They are present only in the early stages of the organism's development. In some chordates, like the lancelet in the figure below, the pharyngeal pouches develop into gill slits.

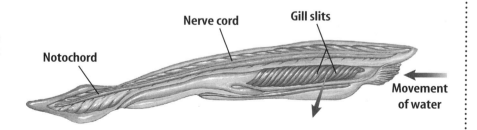

Notochord   Nerve cord   Gill slits   Movement of water

Study Coach

Create a Quiz Write a question about the main idea under each heading. Exchange quizzes with another student. Together discuss the answers to the quiz questions.

FOLDABLES

Ⓐ Define Use a quarter sheet of notebook paper, as shown below, to define the key words in this section—chordate, ectotherm, endotherm, and cartilage.

Chordate
Ectotherm
Endotherm
Cartilage

What are the characteristics of vertebrates?

Chordates are classified into several smaller groups. The largest group of chordates is made up of the vertebrates, which include humans. All vertebrates have an internal system of bones called an endoskeleton. The endoskeleton supports and protects the body's internal organs. For example, the skull is the part of the endoskeleton that surrounds and protects the brain.

How do vertebrates control body temperature?

Vertebrates are either ectotherms or endotherms. **Ectotherms** (EK tuh thurmz) are cold-blooded animals. Their body temperature changes as the temperature of their surroundings changes. Fish are ectotherms.

Endotherms (EN duh thurmz) are warm-blooded animals. Their body temperature does not change with the surrounding temperature. Humans are endotherms. Your body temperature is usually about 37°C.

Fish

Fish are the largest group of vertebrates. All fish are ectotherms and live in water. Some species of fish are adapted to live in freshwater and other species are adapted to live in salt water.

Fish have gills. Gills are fleshy filaments where carbon dioxide and oxygen are exchanged. Water that contains oxygen passes over the gills. When blood is pumped into the gills, the oxygen in the water moves into the blood. At the same time, carbon dioxide moves out of the blood in the gills and into the water. ☑

Most fish have pairs of fanlike fins. Fish use fins to steer, balance, and move. The motion of the tail fin pushes the fish through the water.

Most fish have scales. Scales are thin structures made of a bony material that overlap to cover the skin.

Types of Fish

Scientists classify fish into three groups—bony, jawless, and cartilaginous (kar tuh LA juh nuhs). Bony fish have endoskeletons made of bone. Jawless fish and cartilaginous fish have endoskeletons made of cartilage. **Cartilage** (KAR tuh lihj) is a tough, flexible tissue that is similar to bone but is not as hard or as easily broken.

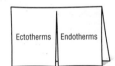
✔ **Reading Check**

1. **Explain** the purpose of fish gills.

_____

_____

_____

What are the characteristics of bony fish?

About 95 percent of all fish species are bony fish. Goldfish, trout, and marlins are examples. The body structure of a bony fish is shown in the figure below. Bony fish swim easily in water because their scales are covered with slimy mucus.

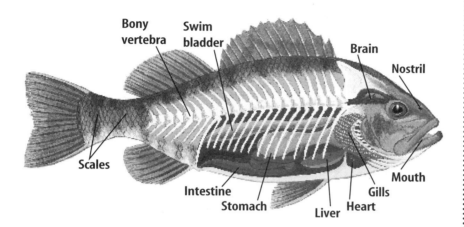

Bony vertebra | Swim bladder | Brain | Nostril | Scales | Intestine | Stomach | Liver | Heart | Gills | Mouth

Most bony fish have a swim bladder. A swim bladder is an air sac that helps control the depth at which the fish swims. Gases move between the swim bladder and the fish's blood. When gases move into the swim bladder, the fish rises in the water. When gases leave the swim bladder, the fish sinks lower in the water.

How do bony fish reproduce?

Most bony fish reproduce using external fertilization (fur tuh luh ZAY shun). External fertilization takes place when egg and sperm cells join outside the female's body. First, a female releases large numbers of eggs into the water. Then, a male swims over the eggs, releasing sperm into the water. Many eggs are fertilized by the sperm. ☑

What are jawless and cartilaginous fish?

Jawless fish have long, tubelike bodies with no scales. They have round, muscular mouths with no jaw. Their mouths have sharp toothlike structures. Their endoskeleton is made of cartilage. Lampreys are jawless fish that attach to another fish with their strong mouths. Lampreys feed by removing blood and other body fluids from the host fish.

Cartilaginous fish also have endoskeletons made of cartilage. They have movable jaws that usually have well-developed teeth. Their bodies are covered with sandpaperlike scales. Sharks, skates, and rays are cartilaginous fish. Most cartilaginous fish are predators.

Picture This

2. **Highlight** In the drawing of a bony fish, color the skeleton of the fish and label it *Skeleton*.

☑ **Reading Check**

3. **Determine** How does external fertilization take place?

_____

_____

_____

● After You Read

Mini Glossary

cartilage (KAR tuh lihj): a tough, flexible tissue that is similar to bone, but not as hard or as easily broken

chordate (KOR dayt): an animal that has three characteristics present at some time during its development—a notochord, nerve cord, and pharyngeal pouches

ectotherm (EK tuh thurm): a cold-blooded animal whose body temperature changes as the temperature of its surroundings changes

endotherm (EN duh thurm): a warm-blooded animal whose body temperature does not change with the temperature of its surroundings

1. Review the terms and their definitions in the Mini Glossary. Write a sentence that explains the difference between an ectotherm and an endotherm.

_____

_____

_____

2. Complete the concept map below to show the three classes of fish.

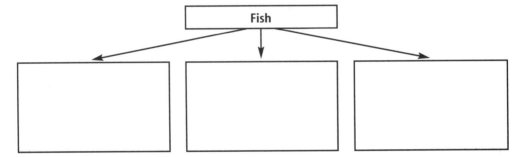

Fish

3. How does working with a partner to ask and answer quiz questions prepare you for a test that covers the material you have read?

_____

_____

_____

End of Section

 **Science** nline Visit **red.msscience.com** to access your textbook, interactive games, and projects to help you learn more about chordate animals.

Vertebrate Animals

section ❷ Amphibians and Reptiles

● Before You Read

On the lines below, write four characteristics of frogs and lizards.

_____

_____

_____

● Read to Learn

Amphibians

Amphibians (am FIH bee unz) are animals that spend part of their lives in water and part on land. They have many adaptations that allow for life both on land and in the water. Amphibians include frogs, toads, salamanders, and newts.

How do amphibians adjust when the temperature changes?

Amphibians are ectotherms. Their body temperature changes along with changes in the temperature of their environment. In cold weather, amphibians become inactive. They bury themselves in mud or leaves until the temperature warms. This time of inactivity during cold weather is called **hibernation**. Amphibians that live in hot, dry climates become inactive and hide in the ground when the temperature becomes too hot. This time of inactivity during hot temperatures is called **estivation** (es tuh VAY shun).

What is the body structure of amphibians?

Amphibians are vertebrates with a strong endoskeleton made of bones. The skeleton helps support their body while on land. Adult frogs and toads have strong hind legs that they use for swimming and jumping.

Copyright © Glencoe/McGraw-Hill, a division of The McGraw-Hill Companies, Inc.

What You'll Learn

■ how amphibians have adapted to live in water and on land
■ what happens during frog metamorphosis
■ the adaptations that allow reptiles to live on land

Study Coach

K-W-L Chart Fold a sheet of paper into three columns. In the first column, write what you know about amphibians and reptiles. In the second column, write what you want to know about amphibians and reptiles. Then read the section. In the third column, write what you learned about amphibians and reptiles from reading the section.

FOLDABLES

❻ Define Use a quarter-sheet of notebook paper, as shown below, to define the key words in this section—hibernation, estivation, and amniotic egg.

Hibernation
Estivation
Amniotic egg

1. Describe two characteristics that allow amphibians to live on land.

_____

_____

_____

Picture This

2. Compare Circle the stage of metamorphosis in which frogs are most like fish.

How do amphibians live on land?

Adult amphibians use lungs instead of gills to exchange oxygen and carbon dioxide. Lungs are an important adaptation for living on land. Amphibians have three-chambered hearts, in which blood carrying oxygen mixes with blood carrying carbon dioxide. This mixing makes less oxygen available to the amphibian. Adult amphibians also exchange oxygen and carbon dioxide through their moist skin, which increases their oxygen supply. Amphibians can live on land, but they must stay moist for the exchange of oxygen and carbon dioxide to occur.

Amphibian hearing and vision also are adapted to life on land. Amphibians have tympanums (TIHM puh nuhmz), or eardrums, that vibrate in response to sound waves. Large eyes help some amphibians catch their prey. Land environments provide many insects as food for adult amphibians. They have long, sticky tongues used to capture the insects.

How do amphibians develop?

Most amphibians go through a series of body changes called metamorphosis (me tuh MOR fuh sus). Eggs are most often laid in water and hatch into larvae. Young larval forms of amphibians live in water. They have no legs and breathe through gills. Over time, they develop the body structures needed for life on land, including legs and lungs. The rate of metamorphosis depends on the species, the water temperature, and the amount of available food. The figure below shows the stages of development for one amphibian—the frog.

Stage 2: Fertilized frog eggs are hatched into tadpoles. Tadpoles live in water. They use their gills for gas exchange.

Stage 4: The adult frog can live and move about on land.

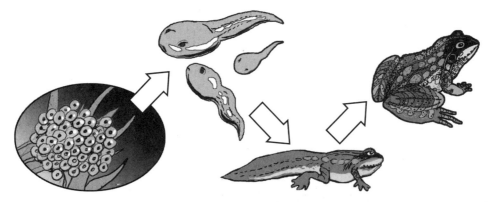

Stage 1: Frog eggs are laid and fertilized.

Stage 3: Tadpoles begin to grow into adults. They develop legs and lungs.

How do amphibians reproduce?

Most amphibians have external fertilization and require water for reproduction. Most female amphibians lay eggs in a pond or lake. However, some amphibians reproduce away from large bodies of water. For example, some tree frogs that live in the rain forest lay eggs in rainwater that collects in leaves.

Reptiles

Snakes, lizards, turtles, and crocodiles are reptiles. Reptiles are vertebrates and ectotherms. Most reptiles live their entire lives on land and do not depend on water for reproduction.

What are some types of reptiles?

Turtles have bodies covered with a hard shell. Most turtles can bring their heads and legs into the shell for protection. Alligators and crocodiles are large reptiles that live in or near water. Alligators and crocodiles are predators that live in warmer climates.

Lizards and snakes make up the largest group of reptiles. These reptiles have a highly developed sense of smell. An organ in the roof of the mouth senses molecules collected by the tongue. The constant in-and-out motion of the tongue allows a snake or lizard to smell its surroundings. Lizards have movable eyelids and external ears. Most lizards have legs with clawed toes on each foot. Snakes move without legs. They don't have eyelids or ears. Snakes feel vibrations in the ground instead of hearing sounds. ☑

What are some reptile adaptations?

A thick, dry waterproof skin is an adaptation that allows reptiles to live on land. Reptile skin is covered with scales to reduce water loss and help prevent injury. Reptiles breathe with lungs. Reptiles that live in water, like sea turtles, must come to the surface to breathe.

Two adaptations allow reptiles to reproduce on land—internal fertilization and laying shell-covered eggs. Sperm are deposited directly into the female's body. Female reptiles lay fertilized eggs that are covered by tough shells. These eggs are called amniotic (am nee AH tihk) eggs. An **amniotic egg** supplies the embryo with everything it needs to develop. A leathery shell protects the embryo and yolk. The yolk gives the embryo a food supply. When it hatches, a reptile is fully developed. ☑

✔ **Reading Check**

3. Identify the largest group of reptiles.

_____

_____

_____

✔ **Reading Check**

4. Determine What is the purpose of the yolk in the amniotic egg?

_____

_____

_____

Copyright © Glencoe/McGraw-Hill, a division of The McGraw-Hill Companies, Inc.

● After You Read

Mini Glossary

amniotic egg: the environment for the development of a reptile embryo

estivation (es tuh VAY shun): a time of inactivity during hot temperatures

hibernation: a time of inactivity during cold weather

1. Review the terms and their definitions in the Mini Glossary. Choose one term that describes an adaptation of an amphibian to its environment. Explain this adaptation in one or two sentences.

_____

_____

_____

2. Complete the concept web below to show the adaptations of reptiles for life on land.

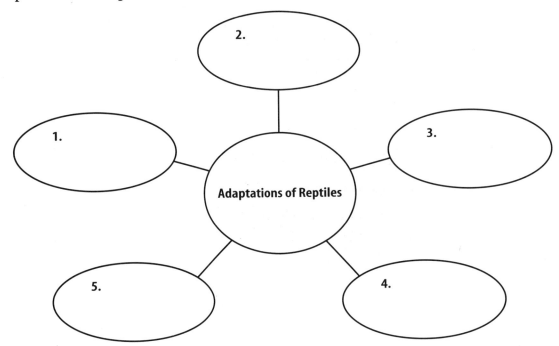

Science nline Visit **red.msscience.com** to access your textbook, interactive games, and projects to help you learn more about amphibians and reptiles.

 **Vertebrate Animals**

section ⊜ **Birds**

● Before You Read

Think of the wide variety of birds. On the lines below, list three things all birds have in common.

_____

_____

_____

What You'll Learn
- the characteristics of birds
- the adaptations birds have for flight
- the function of feathers

● Read to Learn

Characteristics of Birds

Birds are vertebrates that have two wings, two legs, and a bill or beak. Birds are covered mostly with feathers. They lay eggs with hard shells and sit on their eggs to keep them warm until they hatch. All birds are endotherms. There are more than 8,600 species of birds. Different species have different adaptations. For example, ostriches have strong legs for running. Penguins can't fly, but they are excellent swimmers. Wrens have feet that allow them to perch on branches.

Adaptations for Flight

The bodies of most birds are designed for flight. They are streamlined and have light, strong skeletons. The inside of a bird's bones is almost hollow. Special structures make the bones strong, but lightweight. A bird's tail is designed to provide the stiffness, strength, and stability needed for flight. Birds use their tail to steer.

Birds need a lot of energy and oxygen to fly. They eat high-energy foods like nectar, insects, and meat. They have a large, efficient heart. A bird's lungs connect to air sacs that provide a constant supply of oxygen to the blood and make the bird more lightweight.

Study Coach

Summarize the Main Ideas Read the section. Recall and write down the main ideas. Go back and check the main ideas to make sure they are accurate.

Think it Over

1. Infer What features do airplanes have that are similar to birds?

_____

_____

_____

Copyright © Glencoe/McGraw-Hill, a division of The McGraw-Hill Companies, Inc.

How do birds fly?

Birds beat their wings up and down as well as forward and backward. As wind passes above and below the wing, it creates lift. Lift is what allows birds to stay in flight.

Functions of Feathers

Birds are the only animals with feathers. They have two main types of feathers—contour feathers and down feathers. **Contour feathers** are strong and lightweight. They give adult birds their streamlined shape and coloring. Contour feathers have parallel strands, called barbs, that extend from the main shaft. Outer contour feathers on the wings and tail help a bird move, steer, and keep from spinning out of control. Feather color and patterns help attract mates. The color patterns also protect birds from predators by helping the birds blend into their surroundings.

Have you ever noticed that the hair on your arm stands up on a cold day? This response is one way your body works to trap and keep warm air close to your skin. Birds have **down feathers,** such as the one below, that trap and keep warm air next to their bodies. In adult birds, down feathers provide a layer of insulation under the contour feathers. Down feathers cover the bodies of some young birds.

How do birds care for their feathers?

Feathers need to be cared for to keep birds dry, warm, and able to fly. Birds preen, or use their bills, to clean and rearrange their feathers. During preening, birds also spread oil over their bodies and feathers. This oil comes from a gland found on the bird's back near its tail. The oil keeps the bird's skin soft and keeps feathers and scales from becoming brittle. ☑

Copyright © Glencoe/McGraw-Hill, a division of The McGraw-Hill Companies, Inc.

FOLDABLES™

Ⓓ Define Use a quarter-sheet of notebook paper, as shown below, to define the key words in this section—contour feathers and down feathers.

Contour feathers
Down feathers

☑ **Reading Check**

2. Identify What term is used to describe birds cleaning and rearranging their feathers?

_____

_____

_____

● After You Read

Mini Glossary

contour feathers: strong, lightweight feathers that give adult birds their stream-lined shape and coloring

down feathers: feathers that trap and keep warm air next to birds' bodies

1. Review the terms and their definitions in the Mini Glossary. Write two sentences that compare and contrast contour feathers and down feathers.

_____

_____

_____

2. Complete the concept web below. List any six adaptations birds have for flight.

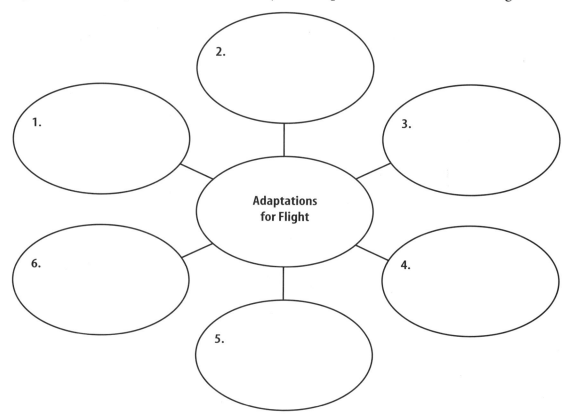

Science Online Visit **red.msscience.com** to access your textbook, interactive games, and projects to help you learn more about birds.

End of Section

chapter 18

Vertebrate Animals

section ❹ Mammals

What You'll Learn

- the characteristics of mammals
- how mammals are adapted to different environments
- the differences among monotremes, marsupials, and placentals

---

Mark the Text

Define Words Skim the section before reading it. Highlight words that you do not know. As you read the section, underline the portion of the text that helps you understand the meaning of these words.

FOLDABLES

E Define Use two quarter-sheets of notebook paper, as shown below, to define the key words in this section—herbivore, carnivore, omnivore, monotreme, marsupial, and placental.

Herbivore	Monotreme
Carnivore	Marsupial
Omnivore	Placental

● Before You Read

Make a list of five mammals. Describe one feature that they have in common.

_____

_____

_____

● Read to Learn

Mammal Characteristics

Moles, dogs, bats, and humans are some examples of mammals. Mammals are vertebrates and endotherms. They live in water and in many different climates on land. They burrow through the ground and fly through the air. Mammals have mammary glands in their skin.

A mammal's skin usually is covered with hair that keeps the body from being too hot or too cold. The hair also protects mammals from wind and water. Some mammals, like bears, have thick fur. Other mammals, like humans, have a few patches of thick hair while the rest of the body has little hair. Dolphins have little hair. Porcupines have quills, which are a kind of modified hair.

Why do mammals have mammary glands?

In females, the mammary glands produce and release milk for the young. For the first few weeks or months of life, the milk provides all the nutrients the young mammal needs.

What kinds of teeth do mammals have?

Plant-eating animals are called **herbivores**. Animals that eat meat are called **carnivores**. Animals that eat plants and meat are called **omnivores**.

Mammals have teeth that are specialized for the type of food they eat. The four types of teeth are incisors, canines, premolars, and molars. As you can see in the figure below, you usually can tell from the kind of teeth a mammal has whether it eats plants, meat, or both.

Mountain lions are carnivores. They have sharp canines that are used to rip and tear flesh.

Humans are omnivores. They have incisors that cut vegetables, premolars that are sharp enough to chew meat, and molars that grind food.

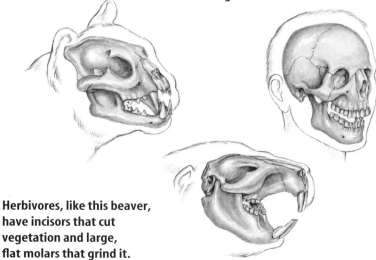

Herbivores, like this beaver, have incisors that cut vegetation and large, flat molars that grind it.

Picture This
1. **Identify** Circle the teeth that carnivores use to rip and tear flesh. Highlight the teeth that omnivores and herbivores use to cut vegetables.

What body systems do mammals have?

Mammals have well-developed lungs. Mammal lungs are made of millions of small sacs called alveoli. Alveoli allow the exchange of carbon dioxide and oxygen during breathing. Mammals also have a complex nervous system that lets them learn and remember more than many other animals. Mammals have larger brains than other animals of similar size.

All mammals have internal fertilization. After an egg is fertilized, the developing mammal is called an embryo. Most mammal embryos develop inside the female in an organ called the uterus. ☑

✔ **Reading Check**
2. **Apply** What kind of fertilization do all mammals have in common?
_____
_____
_____

Mammal Types

Mammals are divided into three groups based on where their embryos develop. The three groups of mammals are monotremes, marsupials, and placentals.

How do monotreme embryos develop?

Unlike other mammals, **monotremes** lay eggs with tough, leathery shells instead of having live births. This small group of mammals includes duck-billed platypuses and spiny anteaters. The female monotreme sits on the eggs for about ten days before they hatch. Monotremes also differ from other mammals because their mammary glands do not have nipples. The milk seeps through the skin onto their fur. The young monotremes lick the milk off the fur. Monotremes live in New Guinea and Australia. ☑

How do young marsupials develop?

Most **marsupials** carry their young in a pouch. A marsupial embryo develops for only a few weeks within the uterus. When a marsupial is born, it is not fully formed. It has no hair and is blind. The young marsupial uses its sense of smell to find its way to a nipple usually within the mother's pouch. It attaches to the nipple to feed and finishes developing in the pouch. Most marsupials, such as kangaroos and koalas, live in Australia. The opossum is the only marsupial native to North America.

How do placental embryos develop?

Most mammals belong to a group called placentals. **Placentals** are named for the placenta, which is a saclike organ that develops from tissues of the embryo and uterus. An umbilical cord connects the embryo to the placenta. A human embryo is shown in the figure below.

Human Embryo at Two Months

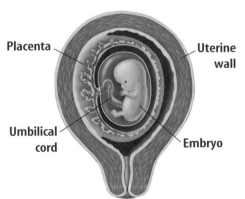

Placenta

Uterine wall

Umbilical cord

Embryo

Picture This

4. Determine What connects the embryo to the placenta?

_____

_____

_____

How does the embryo obtain food and oxygen?

In the placenta, food, oxygen, and wastes are exchanged between the mother's blood and the embryo's blood, but their bloods do not mix. The umbilical cord connects the embryo to the placenta. Food and oxygen are absorbed from the mother's blood. Blood vessels in the umbilical cord carry food and oxygen to the developing young. The blood vessels also take away wastes. In the placenta, the mother's blood absorbs wastes from the developing young.

The time of development from fertilization to birth is called the gestation period. Gestation periods vary widely, from about 21 days in rats to about 616 days in elephants. Human gestation lasts about 280 days. ☑

Mammals Today

There are more than 4,000 species of mammals on Earth today. Mammals can be found on every continent, from cold arctic regions to hot deserts. Each kind of mammal has adaptations that enable it to live successfully within its environment.

What roles do mammals have?

Mammals, like all other groups of animals, have an important role in maintaining a balance in the environment. Large carnivores, such as wolves, prey on herbivores, such as deer. This helps prevent overcrowding and overgrazing. Bats and other small mammals help pollinate flowers. Other mammals spread seeds that stick to their fur.

What are some mammals in danger?

Some species of mammals are in danger of becoming extinct because their habitats are being destroyed. They are left without enough food, shelter, and space to survive because their habitats are damaged by pollution or developed for human needs. The grizzly bear of North America and Europe is a threatened species. A threatened species is one that is likely to become endangered in the near future. Grizzly bears were once found all over the western half of the United States. Today, they are found only in Alaska, Montana, Wyoming, Idaho, and Washington. Habitat loss due to human settlement has greatly reduced the grizzly bear population. If the grizzly bear population continues to decline and becomes endangered, the species will be in danger of becoming extinct. ☑

Copyright © Glencoe/McGraw-Hill, a division of The McGraw-Hill Companies, Inc.

✔ Reading Check

5. Define What is the gestation period?

_____

_____

_____

✔ Reading Check

6. Explain Why has the grizzly bear population in the United States been greatly reduced?

_____

_____

_____

● After You Read

Mini Glossary

carnivore: an animal that eats meat

herbivore: a plant-eating animal

marsupial: a mammal that carries its young in a pouch where it continues to develop after birth

monotreme: a mammal that lays eggs with tough, leathery shells

omnivore: an animal that eats plants and meat

placental: a mammal whose embryos depend on the mother's placenta for food and oxygen

1. Review the terms and their definitions in the Mini Glossary. Write one or more sentences to explain how herbivores, carnivores, and omnivores are different.

_____

_____

_____

2. Complete the diagram below to identify the three types of mammals.

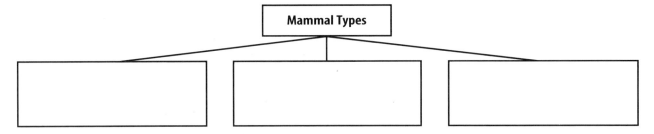

3. Complete the table below to list the common characteristics of mammals.

Common Characteristics of Mammals
1.
2.
3.
4.
5.
6.

End of Section

Science ●nline Visit **red.msscience.com** to access your textbook, interactive games, and projects to help you learn more about mammals.

The Human Body

section ❶ Body Systems

◉ Before You Read

Why do you think communities often have blood drives? On the lines below write a slogan that urges people to donate blood.

_____

_____

_____

◉ Read to Learn

Structure and Movement

Have you ever seen a building under construction? First, a framework of steel or wood is built. Then the framework is covered by walls. The bones are the framework of your body. Bones are covered by skin and muscle.

What does the skeletal system do?

All the bones in your body make up your **skeletal system**. It gives your body its shape and support. The skeletal system also protects the internal organs. For example, your skull protects your brain.

Bones are made of living cells. The cells need nutrients and use energy. The calcium and phosphorus in bones make bones hard. ☑

What do joints do?

Your bones can move. Joints make the movements possible. The place where two or more bones come together is called a joint. The shoulder joint is shown to the right. Muscles can move your bones by moving your joints.

What You'll Learn

- how the skeletal and muscular systems provide structure and allow movement
- the functions of the digestive, respiratory, and circulatory systems
- the differences between the nervous and endocrine system

▸ **Study Coach**

Create a Quiz As you study the information in this section, create questions about the information you read. Be sure to answer the questions.

✔ **Reading Check**

1. **Explain** What do calcium and phosphorus do?

_____

_____

_____

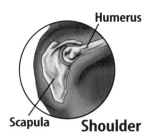

Humerus

Scapula **Shoulder**

What purpose does the skin serve?

The skin is the largest human body organ. The skin has several purposes. Skin forms a protective covering for your body. It can protect your body from disease-causing organisms. The pigment, or coloring, in the skin protects it from damage by ultraviolet light. The pigment is called **melanin** (MEH luh nun). The skin is a sense organ. The skin has special nerve cells that help you sense heat or cold. They can help you feel a sharp object. The skin helps control your body temperature. Sweat is made by sweat glands in your skin. Sweat helps to cool down the body. ☑

The skin also helps provide vitamin D, a nutrient your body needs for good health. Vitamin D is formed when your skin receives ultraviolet light from the Sun. This vitamin helps the body absorb calcium from food in the digestive tract.

What does the muscular system do?

Muscles attach to bones and help them move. A **muscle** is an organ that can relax, contract, and provide force to move you and your body parts. Some muscles are voluntary muscles. You can choose to move them. Other muscles, such as your heart, are not controlled consciously. They are called involuntary muscles.

Voluntary muscles work in pairs. One muscle contracts, or gets shorter, while another muscle relaxes or returns to its original length, as shown in the figure below.

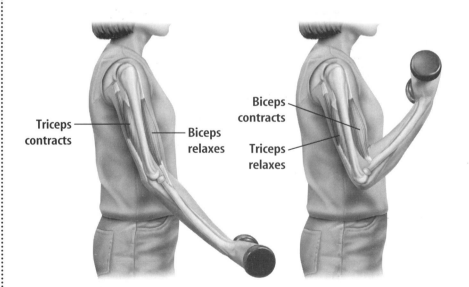

Triceps contracts

Biceps relaxes

Biceps contracts

Triceps relaxes

Digestion and Excretion

Your body gets the energy it needs through the food you eat. Food enters the body's digestive system through your mouth. As the food moves through the organs of the digestive system, it is broken down into smaller molecules. These molecules are absorbed from the digestive system and enter the blood. Then the food molecules move into the cells. Food that is undigested is eliminated from the digestive system.

What are the organs of the digestive system?

Food is moistened in the mouth by saliva. The teeth break the food down into smaller particles. Food enters the esophagus (ih SAH fuh gus) and moves to the stomach. Chemicals in the stomach break down the food, which then moves into the small intestine. Most of the food is absorbed in the small intestine. Food particles in the small intestine move from the digestive tract into the blood. The blood carries the food particles to the body's cells. The remaining food moves into the large intestine where water is absorbed. The undigested food is excreted from the body. ✔

Why are nutrients important?

Your body needs certain foods to stay healthy. **Nutrients** (NEW tree unts) are the substances in food that provide for cell development, growth, and repair. There are six kinds of nutrients—proteins, carbohydrates (kar boh HI drayts), lipids, vitamins, minerals, and water. Proteins, carbohydrates, lipids, and vitamins contain the element carbon. So they are called organic nutrients. Minerals and water do not contain carbon. So they are called inorganic nutrients.

The chart below shows why organic nutrients are important and what foods provide them.

Organic Nutrient	What It Does	Where It Is Found
Proteins	replace and repair cells; cell growth	meats, poultry, eggs, fish, beans, nuts
Carbohydrates	main energy source	sugar, honey, fruits, vegetables, grains, breads, cereals
Lipids (fats)	provide energy; help body absorb vitamins; cushion internal organs	meats, butter, oils
Vitamins	help growth; regulate body functions; prevent some diseases	fruits, vegetables, beans, cereals

Copyright © Glencoe/McGraw-Hill, a division of The McGraw-Hill Companies, Inc.

✔ **Reading Check**

4. **Explain** What happens in the small intestine?

_____

_____

_____

Picture This

5. **Identify** Highlight the two nutrients that meat provides.

6. List What are two minerals that the body needs to keep bones healthy?

_____

_____

_____

<u>Picture This</u>

7. Explain Draw arrows showing how urine moves from the kidneys to the bladder.

How do vitamins help the body?

Vitamins are nutrients that are needed in small amounts. Vitamins do many things. They regulate body functions and prevent some diseases. No single food supplies all the vitamins your body needs. There are two kinds of vitamins. Water-soluble vitamins dissolve easily in water. They are not stored in the body. Fat-soluble vitamins dissolve only in fat and can be stored by the body.

What are inorganic nutrients?

Minerals control many chemical reactions. Minerals, like vitamins, are needed in small amounts. Calcium and phosphorus are two minerals that the body uses in the largest amounts. These two minerals are important for making and keeping bones healthy. ☑

People cannot live for more than a few days without water. The body cannot use most of the other nutrients unless they are carried in water. Cells need water to carry out the chemical reactions that are needed to live.

What is the purpose of the urinary system?

The digestive system gets rid of some body wastes. However, wastes that are made by cells are removed by the blood through the urinary system. The main organs in the urinary system, as shown in the figure to the right, are the kidneys. The kidneys get rid of excess water, salts, and other wastes from the blood. The wastewater, called urine, passes through tubes called ureters (YOO ruh turz) into the bladder. The bladder holds the urine until it is ready to leave the body. Urine leaves the bladder through the body by the urethra (yoo REE thruh).

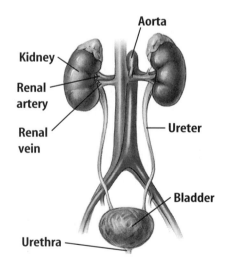

Aorta
Kidney
Renal artery
Renal vein
Ureter
Bladder
Urethra

What are the other organs of the excretory system?

Wastes are also removed in other ways. The respiratory system removes waste gases, such as carbon dioxide. Salt and other wastes are lost through the skin.

Respiration and Circulation

The cells in the body need oxygen, a gas that is found in the air. The body's cells make carbon dioxide. This is a waste gas that must be removed from the body.

What is the purpose of the respiratory system?

The <u>respiratory system</u> is made up of structures and organs that help move oxygen into the body and waste gases out of the body. When you breathe in, air enters through the mouth or nose and travels through a series of passageways. Bronchi (BRAHN ki) then carry air into your lungs. In the lungs, bronchi branch into smaller tubes called bronchioles (BRAHN kee ohlz). As you can see in the figure below, grapelike clusters of air sacs called <u>alveoli</u> (al VEE uh li) are at the end of each bronchiole. Tiny blood vessels called <u>capillaries</u> (KAP uh ler eez) surround each alveolus (singular of *alveoli*). Air moves through bronchioles and reaches the alveoli.

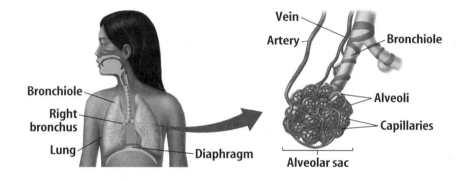

Bronchiole
Right bronchus
Lung
Diaphragm
Vein
Artery
Bronchiole
Alveoli
Capillaries
Alveolar sac

Oxygen leaves alveoli and enters capillaries. Blood carries the oxygen to every cell in the body. The body's waste gases, such as carbon dioxide, are carried to the lungs through the blood. The gases are removed when you exhale.

What does the circulatory system do?

The job of the circulatory system is to get nutrients and oxygen to the cells and to remove wastes. The circulatory system is made up of the heart, blood vessels, and blood.

The heart pumps blood to all the cells. Blood that is pumped out of the heart travels through blood vessles— arteries (AR tuh reez), capillaries, and then veins. Arteries carry blood away from the heart. Veins carry blood back to the heart. Capillaries connect arteries and veins. Because capillaries are very thin, nutrients can move easily from capillaries into the cells. Waste materials can leave body cells and enter the capillaries. ☑

Picture This

8. Identify Highlight the name of the blood vessels that surround the alveoli.

✔ Reading Check

9. Explain Which part of the circulatory system carries blood away from the heart?

Why is blood important?

Blood is important to your body's cells. They would die without blood because they could not get the oxygen and nutrients needed for life. Blood also removes wastes from the cells. Blood is made up of liquid and cells. Oxygen is carried by red blood cells. White blood cells fight infections and heal wounds.

When you cut yourself, special cell fragments called platelets (PLAYT luts) in the blood form a clot. This clot plugs the wounded blood vessels and acts like a bandage. Blood clots stop bleeding in minor wounds.

If a person loses a lot of blood because of a serious wound, he or she might need a blood transfusion. A person who receives a blood transfusion receives donated human blood. All humans have similar blood. However, blood must be classified or typed. A person has to receive the correct blood type, or the person may die.

What are the different blood types?

People inherit one of four major blood types. Each type is different because of chemical identification tags, or antigens (AN tih junz), on red blood cells. Type A blood has A antigen, type B has B antigen, type AB has A and B antigens, and type O has no antigens. Each blood type has specific antibodies in the liquid part of the blood. Antibodies destroy substances that are not part of your body. Because of antibodies, certain types of blood types cannot be mixed when receiving blood transfusions. The table to the right shows blood transfusion possibilities.

Blood Transfusion Possibilities		
Type	Can Receive	Can Donate To
A	O, A	A, AB
B	O, B	B, AB
AB	All	AB
O	O	All

Rh factor is another identification tag of red blood cells. If a person's red blood cells have an Rh factor, that person has Rh-positive (RH+) blood. If the factor is not there, the person has Rh-negative (Rh−) blood. An Rh− person cannot receive Rh+ blood in a blood transfusion.

How are extra tissue fluids collected?

Water and other dissolved substances become part of tissue fluid, which is found between cells. The fluid is collected and returned to the blood through the lymphatic (lihm FA tihk) system.

Copyright © Glencoe/McGraw-Hill, a division of The McGraw-Hill Companies, Inc.

Think it Over

10. Analyze What would happen if a blood clot did not form?

_____

_____

_____

Picture This

11. Analyze Circle the blood type that hospitals would like to have in large supply. Explain your choice on the lines below.

_____

_____

_____

What is the purpose of the lymphatic system?

The lymphatic system has vessels like the circulatory system. But it does not have an organ like the heart to pump the fluid. The fluid moves because of the contraction of muscles in the walls of the lymph vessel and skeletal muscles. The lymphatic vessels also have cells called lymphocytes. These cells help defend the body against disease-causing organisms.

How does the body protect itself from disease?

The body has many ways to defend itself against disease-causing organisms. Disease-causing organisms cannot get through unbroken skin. Certain parts of the respiratory system trap disease organisms. The circulatory system has white blood cells that destroy invading disease-causing organisms. These are first-line defenses.

A second-line of defense, called specific immunity, attacks disease-causing organisms that get past the first-line defenses. In specific immunity, the body makes antibodies that can destroy disease-causing organisms. For example, when you get a cold, your body makes antibodies that attack that cold virus. This helps the body fight off the infection.

You also can develop antibodies to fight off diseases when you receive vaccinations. You received vaccinations against many diseases, such as mumps and polio, before you started school. Your body formed antibodies against these diseases after you received the vaccinations.

Control and Coordination

The nervous and endocrine systems help make all the body systems work together. They are the control systems of the body, and they coordinate your body functions.

What does the nervous system do?

The nervous system is made up of the brain, spinal cord, nerves, and nerve receptors. The neuron (NOO rahn), or nerve cell, is the basic unit of the nervous system. Neurons are made up of a cell body and branches called dendrites and axons (AK sahns). Messages travel from one neuron to another. Dendrites receive messages from other neurons and send them to the cell body. Axons carry messages away from the cell body. For example, a prick from a pin can move from a skin nerve receptor to a neuron, then from one neuron to the next until the message reaches the brain. The brain coordinates all the body's activities. ☑

FOLDABLES

A Explain Make a two-tab Foldable, as shown below. As you read, list the ways your body defends itself from disease. Organize your notes into first-line defenses and second-line defenses.

First-Line Defenses | Second-Line Defenses

☑ Reading Check

12. **Identify** What is the basic unit of the nervous system?

_____

What is a reflex?

When you touch something very hot and pull your hand away quickly, you are experiencing a reflex. A **reflex** is an involuntary, automatic response to a stimulus. You cannot control a reflex. Reflexes help protect your body by allowing your body to respond without having to think about what to do.

What is the purpose of the endocrine system?

The endocrine (EN duh krun) system is the other control system in the body. In the nervous system, messages travel quickly through nerves to and from all parts of your body. In the endocrine system, chemicals called hormones (HOR mohnz) carry messages throughout the body. Hormones are released by endocrine glands directly into the bloodstream. The hormones travel through the blood to reach certain tissues. ☑

Some endocrine glands are found in the brain. The pineal gland makes a hormone that regulates sleeping and waking. The pituitary (pih TEW uh ter ee) gland makes several hormones that regulate many body activities, such as growth and reproduction. The thyroid gland, shown in the figure below, secretes a hormone that controls the rate of chemical reactions in your body.

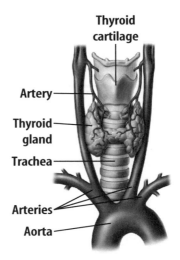

Some endocrine glands are found in the abdomen area. The pancreas is a gland that makes a hormone that controls the amount of sugar that is in the bloodstream. The adrenal glands make several hormones. They include hormones that help the body respond in times of stress.

Copyright © Glencoe/McGraw-Hill, a division of The McGraw-Hill Companies, Inc.

✔ **Reading Check**

13. Identify What part of the endocrine system carries messages throughout the body?

_____

_____

Picture This

14. Conclude Examine the other structures around the thyroid gland. Where in the body is this gland located?

_____

_____

● After You Read

Mini Glossary

alveoli (al VEE uh li): grapelike clusters of air sacs at the end of the bronchiole

capillary (KAP uh ler ee): small blood vessel that connects arteries and veins

melanin (MEH luh nun): the pigment in the skin that protects it from damage by ultraviolet light

muscle: an organ that can relax, contract, and provide force to move a person and to move body parts

nutrient (NEW tree unt): the substance in food that provides for cell development, growth, and repair

reflex: an involuntary, automatic response to a stimulus

respiratory system: the structures and organs that help move oxygen into the body and waste gases out of the body

skeletal system: the bones in the body that provide the body's framework

1. Review the terms and their definitions in the Mini Glossary. Choose one of the terms and write a sentence that explains its purpose in the body.

_____

_____

2. In the chart below, explain the function of the body systems listed and identify the parts of the system.

Body Systems	Function of System	Parts of System
Skeletal system		
Digestive system		
Respiratory system		
Circulatory system		
Nervous system		

 Visit **red.msscience.com** to access your textbook, interactive games, and projects to help you learn more about body systems.

End of Section

The Human Body

section ❷ Human Reproduction

What You'll Learn
- the organs of the male and female reproductive systems
- the stages in the menstrual cycle
- the stages of development before birth
- the life stages of humans

Study Coach

Summarize Read each section—"Male Reproductive System," "Female Reproductive System," and "Life Stages." After you finish reading write a sentence or two that summarizes the main idea of each section.

Picture This
1. **Identify** Draw arrows on the figure to indicate how semen moves through the male reproductive system.

● Before You Read

Think about a time you observed a baby. What kinds of skills did the baby have? What skills did the baby still need to learn?

_____

_____

_____

● Read to Learn

Male Reproductive System

The reproductive system, unlike other systems, is different in males and females. The male reproductive system, shown in the figure below, is made up of several organs and structures. The scrotum has two testes (TES teez) that make the male hormone testosterone and **sperm,** the male reproductive cells. Testosterone and sperm are made in sexually mature males.

After sperm are made in the testes, they travel through the sperm ducts. Fluid from the seminal vesicles, which are organs behind the bladder, is mixed with the sperm. This mixture is called **semen** (SEE mun). Semen leaves the body through the urethra. This is the same tube that carries urine from the body. However, a muscle in the bladder does not allow urine to enter the urethra when sperm leave the body.

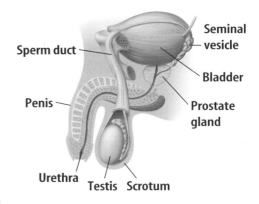

Sperm duct — Seminal vesicle

Penis — Bladder

Prostate gland

Urethra — Testis — Scrotum

Female Reproductive System

The female's reproductive organs are inside a female's body. Ovaries are the female sex organs that produce eggs and the female sex hormones, estrogen (ES truh jun) and progesterone (proh JES tuh rohn). These hormones are produced when a female matures sexually. The hormones help prepare the female body for having a baby. ☑

Egg Production The female sex hormones control the development and release of eggs from the ovaries. About every 28 days, one of the ovaries releases an egg. This process is called **ovulation** (ahv yuh LAY shun). The ovaries usually take turns releasing eggs.

The released egg moves into the oviduct. The egg moves along the oviduct to the uterus, a muscular, pear-shaped organ. If the egg is fertilized by a sperm while it is in the oviduct, the egg can grow and develop in the uterus. The lower part of the uterus, as shown in the figure to the right, is the cervix. It connects the uterus to the vagina. The vagina is a muscular tube that is known as the birth canal. When a baby is being born, the baby moves from the uterus through the vagina to outside the mother's body.

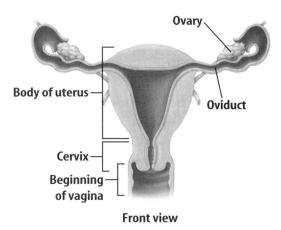

Front view

What is the menstrual cycle?

The **menstrual cycle** is the monthly cycle of changes to the female reproductive system. The average length of the menstrual cycle is 28 days. However, the cycle can range from 20 to 40 days.

The menstrual cycle is divided into three parts, or phases. The first phase is the menstrual flow, or menstruation (men STRAY shun). The flow is made of tissue cells from the thickened lining of the uterus and blood. This flow usually lasts from four to six days.

In phase two of the menstrual cycle, an egg develops in the ovary and the lining of the uterus thickens. Ovulation occurs about 14 days before the menstrual flow begins.

☑ **Reading Check**

2. **List** the two female sex hormones.

_____

_____

Picture This

3. **Identify** Draw arrows on the figure to indicate how an egg would move from an ovary to the uterus.

Phase three Phase three is the phase between ovulation and menstruation. The lining of the uterus continues to thicken. If the egg is fertilized, it can attach to the uterus wall and start to develop while hormones continue to be produced. If the egg is not fertilized, the hormone levels decrease. Decreased hormone levels cause the lining of the uterus to break down, and menstruation begins.

Life Stages

Humans begin to develop when an egg from the female is united with a sperm from the male. This is called fertilization. It usually happens in the oviduct. The nucleus of the egg and the nucleus of the sperm join together to make a fertilized cell called a zygote. As this cell moves through the oviduct, it divides many times. If the zygote attaches to the uterus, it will develop into a baby in about nine months. The time of development from fertilized egg to birth is called **pregnancy**.

How does the body develop before birth?

After the zygote attaches to the uterine wall, it is called an **embryo**. During the first two months of pregnancy, the embryo period, the organs develop and the heart begins to beat. A placenta (pluh SEN tuh) develops from tissues of the uterus and tissues of the embryo, as shown in the figure below. The umbilical cord connects the embryo to the placenta. The placenta brings nutrients and oxygen from the mother and takes away wastes from the embryo.

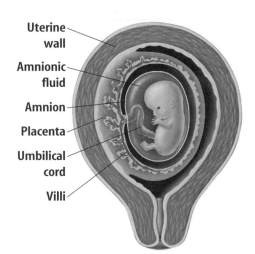

Uterine wall
Amnionic fluid
Amnion
Placenta
Umbilical cord
Villi

After two months, the embryo is called a **fetus**. It continues to grow and develop during the pregnancy. At nine months the fetus is usually in a head-down position in the uterus.

Copyright © Glencoe/McGraw-Hill, a division of The McGraw-Hill Companies, Inc.

FOLDABLES™

B **Explain** Make a three-tab Foldable, as shown below. As you read, use the Venn diagram to explain fertilization.

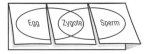

Egg Zygote Sperm

Picture This

4. Identify Circle the structure that connects the embryo to the placenta.

What happens during birth?

Birth begins with labor, when the muscles of the uterus contract. As the contractions become stronger and closer together, the opening to the uterus widens and the baby is pushed out through the vagina. Then the umbilical cord is clamped and cut. The placenta also is pushed out of the mother's body after the baby is born by the contractions in the uterus.

What are the stages after birth?

Humans go through four stages of development after birth. These stages are infancy, childhood, adolescence, and adulthood.

Infancy is the time from birth until 18 months of age. During this stage, the infant's nervous and muscular systems develop and the infant begins to interact with the world.

Childhood lasts from 18 months until around 12 years of age. The child learns many new skills during this time. The skills include control of the bladder, dressing and undressing, speaking, reading, writing, and reasoning. Children develop at different rates.

Adolescence starts around 12 to 13 years of age. During this time puberty occurs. This means that the person is maturing sexually. Puberty generally starts in girls between ages 9 and 13. It starts in boys between ages 13 and 16. During puberty, girls develop breasts and grow pubic and underarm hair. Boys develop a deeper voice, an increase in muscle size, and facial, pubic, and underarm hair.

The final stage of human development is adulthood. It starts at the end of adolescence and continues through the rest of a human's life. During this time the muscular and skeletal systems stop growing. The average human life span is about 75 years. Some people, however, live much longer. As body systems get older, they break down, and eventually the result is death. ☑

Copyright © Glencoe/McGraw-Hill, a division of The McGraw-Hill Companies, Inc.

FOLDABLES™

ⓒ Describe Make four quarter sheets, as shown below. As you read, write notes on each sheet to describe one of the four life stages after birth.

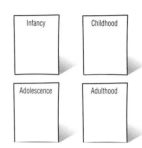

☑ Reading Check

5. **Explain** What happens to body systems during adulthood?

_____

_____

_____

● After You Read

Mini Glossary

embryo: the zygote after it attaches to the wall of the uterus

fetus: the developing embryo after the first two months of pregnancy

menstrual cycle: the monthly cycle of changes in a sexually mature female reproductive system

ovulation (ahv yuh LAY shun): the process of an egg being released from one of the ovaries

pregnancy: the period of development from fertilized egg to birth

semen (SEE mun): the mixture of fluid from the seminal vesicles and sperm

sperm: the male reproductive cells

1. Review the terms and their definitions in the Mini Glossary. Choose two or three terms and write a sentence that shows how the body develops before birth.

_____

_____

2. In the sequence chart below, list the stages of development after birth and describe one development in each stage.

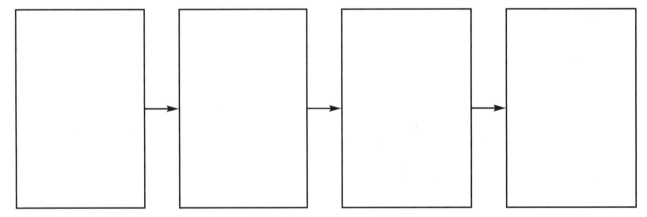

3. How did summarizing the main idea in each section help you understand the information about human reproduction?

_____

_____

End of Section

Science Online Visit **red.msscience.com** to access your textbook, interactive games, and projects to help you learn more about human reproduction.

chapter 20

The Role of Genes in Inheritance

section ➊ Continuing Life

🖜 Before You Read

Have you ever seen a potato that has sprouts growing from it? What do the sprouts look like? What would happen if the sprouts were planted?

_____

_____

_____

What You'll Learn

- how cells divide
- the importance of reproduction for living things
- the differences between sexual and asexual reproduction
- the structure and function of DNA

🖜 Read to Learn

Reproduction

Organisms produce offspring that are similar to themselves through reproduction. Frogs reproduce by laying hundreds of eggs. Tadpoles hatch from these eggs and grow into adult frogs. Humans usually produce only one offspring at a time.

Why is reproduction important?

Reproduction is important because it continues the species. For all organisms, hereditary material is passed from parent to offspring during reproduction. This material is found inside cells and is made up of the chemical deoxyribonucleic (dee AHK sih ri boh noo klay ihk) acid, called DNA. **DNA** controls how offspring will look and how they will function by controlling what proteins each cell will produce.

What is the role of DNA?

DNA is found in all cells in structures called chromosomes. DNA is like a genetic blueprint that contains all of the instructions for making an organism what it is. Your DNA controls the texture of your hair, the shape of your ears, your blood type, and even how you digest the food you had for lunch.

▸ **Mark the Text**

Locate Information Read all the headings for this section and circle any word or term you cannot define. At the end of each heading, review the circled words and underline the part of the text that helps you define the words.

FOLDABLES™

Ⓐ **Explain** Make a half book using notebook paper, as shown below. Use the Foldable to explain the role of DNA in reproduction.

DNA

Copyright © Glencoe/McGraw-Hill, a division of The McGraw-Hill Companies, Inc.

What does DNA look like?

As you can see in the figure below, DNA is shaped like a twisted ladder. The two sides of the ladder form the backbone of the DNA molecule. The sides support the rungs, or steps, of the ladder. The rungs hold all the genetic information. Each rung is made up of a pair of chemicals called bases. There are only four bases in DNA, and they form specific pairs. A DNA ladder has billions of rungs. The bases are arranged in thousands of different orders. The order of the bases along the DNA ladder forms a code. From this DNA code, the cell gets instructions about what materials to make, how to make them, and when to make them.

Picture This

1. **Identify** Add the label *Genetic information* to show the part of the DNA molecule that holds the genetic information.

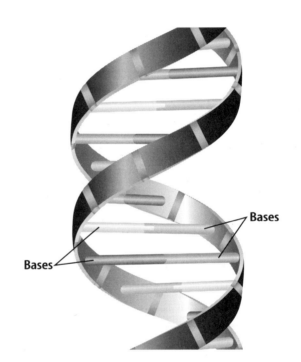

Bases

Bases

Cell Division

How did you become the size you are now? The cells of your body are formed by cell division. Cell division has two big steps. First, DNA in the nucleus is copied. Then the nucleus divides into two nuclei that are exactly the same. Each nucleus receives a copy of the DNA.

Division of the nucleus is called **mitosis** (mi TOH sus). Follow the steps in mitosis in the figure on the next page. After mitosis has taken place, the rest of the cell divides into two cells of about equal size.

Almost all plant and animal cells undergo mitosis. Cell division results in growth and the replacement of aging or injured cells.

FOLDABLES

B Describe Make a two-tab concept map book, as shown below. Use the Foldable to describe the process of mitosis.

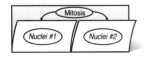

Mitosis

Nuclei #1   Nuclei #2

Steps in Mitosis

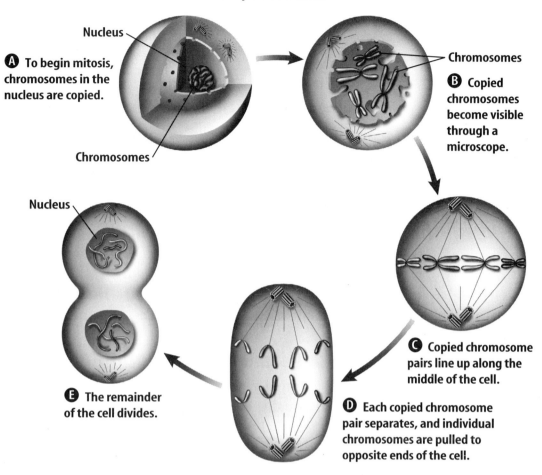

Nucleus

A To begin mitosis, chromosomes in the nucleus are copied.

Chromosomes

Chromosomes

B Copied chromosomes become visible through a microscope.

Nucleus

C Copied chromosome pairs line up along the middle of the cell.

E The remainder of the cell divides.

D Each copied chromosome pair separates, and individual chromosomes are pulled to opposite ends of the cell.

Reproduction by One Organism

In <u>asexual</u> (ay SEK shoo ul) <u>reproduction,</u> a new organism is produced from a part of another organism by cell division. All the DNA in the new organism comes from one other organism. An example is shoots growing from the eyes of potatoes. The DNA of the shoot is the same as the DNA in the rest of the potato.

Some one-celled organisms divide in half, forming two cells. First the DNA copies itself. Then the cell divides, forming two new cells that are alike. Each new organism has an exact copy of the first organism's DNA. The first organism no longer exists.

What is budding?

A new individual, or bud, grows in the asexual reproduction process known as budding. Some plants and a few animals reproduce by budding. The bud has the same shape and characteristics as the parent. In time, the bud matures and breaks away to live on its own.

Picture This

2. Identify Circle the chromosomes on diagrams C, D, and E.

FOLDABLES

C **Describe** Make a two-tab book Foldable, as shown below. Use the Foldable to describe asexual and sexual reproduction.

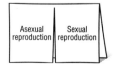

Asexual reproduction | Sexual reproduction

3. Analyze People sometimes cut a living sponge into many pieces and return the pieces to the water. New sponges will grow from the pieces. Which process of asexual reproduction is being described?

_____

_____

Reading Check

4. Explain how a new organism is produced in sexual reproduction.

_____

_____

_____

What is regeneration?

In regeneration (rih je nuh RAY shun), some organisms are able to replace body parts that have been lost. For example, a sea star can grow a new arm if one is broken off.

What is cloning?

Making copies of organisms is called **cloning**. The new organism produced is called a clone. The clone receives DNA from just one parent cell, so it has the same DNA as the parent cell. Gardeners clone plants when they take cuttings of a plant's stem, leaves, or roots. They can grow many identical plants from one plant.

Only since the 1990s has cloning large animals become possible. In 1997, an adult Finn Dorset sheep was cloned. The new sheep, named Dolly, was the first mammal to be successfully cloned. Scientists studied Dolly and learned more about how cells reproduce.

Sex Cells and Reproduction

Does a human baby look exactly like its father or its mother? Usually, a human baby has features of both its parents. The baby might have her dad's hair color and her mom's eye color. In most cases, the baby does not look exactly like either of her parents. That's because humans and many other organisms are produced through sexual (SEK shoo ul) reproduction. In **sexual reproduction**, a new organism is produced from the DNA of two cells. **Sex cells** are specialized cells that carry DNA and join in sexual reproduction. A female sex cell usually is called an egg, and a male sex cell usually is called a sperm. DNA from each sex cell contributes to the formation of a new individual and to that individual's traits. ☑

Production of Sex Cells

Remember that your body is made up of different types of cells. When a skin cell or a bone cell divides, it produces two identical cells by cell division.

Recall that DNA can be found in structures called chromosomes. A human body has 46 chromosomes arranged in 23 pairs. Each chromosome of a pair has genetic information about the same things. For example, if one chromosome has information about hair color, its mate also will have information about hair color.

Copyright © Glencoe/McGraw-Hill, a division of The McGraw-Hill Companies, Inc.

What happens during meiosis?

Sex cells are different than body cells. Instead of being formed by cell division like body cells are, sex cells are formed by **meiosis** (mi OH sus). Only certain cells in reproductive organs divide by meiosis. Before meiosis begins, DNA is copied. During meiosis, the nucleus divides twice. Four sex cells form, each with half the number of chromosomes of the original cell. Human eggs and sperm have only 23 chromosomes each—one chromosome from each pair of chromosomes.

When a human egg and a sperm join in a process called **fertilization,** a new individual forms with a full set of 46 chromosomes. The table below compares cell division and sex cell formation.

Cell Division and Sex Cell Formation in Humans		
	Cell Division	**Sex Cell Formation**
Process used	Mitosis	Meiosis
DNA duplicated?	Yes	Yes
Nucleus divides	Once	Twice
Number of cells formed	2	4
Chromosome number of beginning cell	46	46
Chromosomes in each new cell	46	23

Applying Math

5. **Use Numbers** Write a simple addition problem that shows how chromosomes join when fertilization occurs.

_____

_____

_____

Sex Cells in Plants

Plants can reproduce sexually. How this occurs is different for each plant group. But in all cases, a sperm and an egg join to create a new cell. The new cell eventually will become a plant.

Flowers may seem to be just a decoration for many plants. But flowers have the structures for reproduction. Male flower parts produce pollen, which contains sperm cells. Female flower parts produce eggs. When a sperm and an egg join, a new cell forms. In most flowers, the cell divides many times and becomes enclosed in a seed. A fruit that contains seeds soon develops. ☑

Reading Check

6. **Explain** Where are the sperm cells in a flower found?

_____

_____

● After You Read

Mini Glossary

asexual (ay SEK shoo ul) reproduction: a new organism is produced from a part of another organism by cell division

cloning: making copies of organisms

DNA: hereditary material inside cells, which controls how offspring will look and how they will function

fertilization: a process in which an egg and sperm join together

meiosis (mi OH sus): cell division by sex cells

mitosis: (mi TOH sus): division of the nucleus

sex cell: a cell involved in reproduction; carries DNA

sexual (SEK shoo ul) reproduction: a new organism is produced from the DNA of two cells

1. Review the terms and their definitions in the Mini Glossary. Write two sentences that explain the difference between asexual reproduction and sexual reproduction.

_____

_____

_____

2. Complete the Venn diagram below to help you compare cell division and sex cell formation in humans.

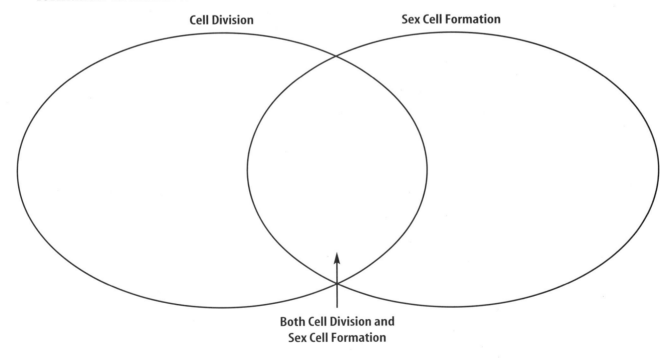

Cell Division　　　　**Sex Cell Formation**

Both Cell Division and Sex Cell Formation

End of Section

Science **Online** Visit **red.msscience.com** to access your textbook, interactive games, and projects to help you learn more about continuing life.

The Role of Genes in Inheritance

section ② Genetics—The Study of Inheritance

Before You Read

On the lines below, describe the physical characteristics you have that are similar to physical characteristics of your mother, father, or a grandparent.

_____

_____

_____

What You'll Learn

■ how traits are inherited
■ the relationship of chromosomes, genes, and DNA
■ how mutations add variation to a population

Read to Learn

Heredity

When you go to a family reunion or look through family pictures, you will notice similarities and differences among your relatives. You may notice that your mother's eyes look just like your grandmother's. One uncle is short while his brother is tall.

The similarities and differences are the result of the way traits are passed from one generation to the next. The passing of traits from parents to offspring is called **heredity** (huh REH duh tee).

Look around at the students in your classroom. What makes each person an individual? You will see many differences. The features you observe are the traits of the individuals. A trait is a physical characteristic of an organism. Eye color, hair color, skin color, and nose shape are examples of traits.

Traits are inherited from a person's parents. Every organism, including you, is made up of many traits. The study of how traits are passed from parents to offspring is called **genetics** (juh NE tihks).

▸ **Study Coach**

Two-Column Notes Fold a piece of paper in half lengthwise. In the first column, write the main ideas of each paragraph. In the second column, write the details that support the main ideas.

FOLDABLES

Ⓓ **Identify** Use quarter sheets of notebook paper, as shown below, to identify the importance of genes, chromosomes, mutations, and selective breeding to heredity.

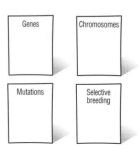

What do genes control?

You get half your genetic information from your father and half from your mother. This information was contained in the chromosomes of the sperm and egg that joined to form the cell that eventually became you.

All chromosomes contain many genes. A **gene** (JEEN), as shown in the figure to the right, is a small section of DNA on a chromosome that has information about a trait. Humans have thousands of different genes arranged on 23 pairs of chromosomes. Genes control all of the traits of organisms—even traits that can't be seen, such as your blood type. Genes provide all the information needed for growth and life.

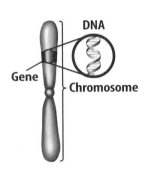

What determines traits?

In body cells, such as skin cells or muscle cells, chromosomes are in pairs. One pair of chromosomes can contain genes that control many different traits. Each gene on one chromosome of the pair has a similar gene on the other chromosome of the pair.

Each gene of a gene pair is called an allele (uh LEEL), as shown in the figure to the right. The genes that make up a gene pair might or might not contain the same information about a trait. For example, the genes for the flower color trait in pea plants might be purple or white. If a pair of chromosomes contains different alleles for a trait, that trait is called a hybrid (HI brud). When a trait has two alleles that are the same, it's called pure.

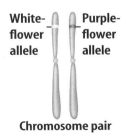

Copyright © Glencoe/McGraw-Hill, a division of The McGraw-Hill Companies, Inc.

Picture This

1. Determine The statement below is false. Write a correct statement on the lines below.

Each chromosome contains one gene.

_____

_____

_____

Picture This

2. Identify Is the chromosome pair in the figure from a pure bred or a hybrid?

_____

When are alleles dominant or recessive?

The combination of alleles in a gene pair decides how a trait will be shown, or expressed, in an organism. Dominant (DAH muh nunt) means that one allele covers over or hides another allele of the trait. For example, if a pea plant has one purple-flower allele and one white-flower allele, its flowers will be purple. This is because purple is the dominant flower color in pea plants. The dominant allele is seen when the trait is hybrid or dominant pure. White flowers, the hidden allele, are recessive. Recessive alleles are seen only when a trait is recessive pure.

Humans also have traits that are controlled by dominant and recessive alleles. To show a recessive allele, a person needs to inherit two copies of the recessive allele for that trait—one from each parent. To show a dominant allele, a person can have either one or two alleles for the trait. One dominant allele in humans is the presence of dimples, as shown in the figure above. ☑

How can the environment affect the expression of traits?

Traits are coded in the DNA. However, the environment can play a role in the way that a trait is expressed. A person may have naturally dark hair, which lightens when exposed to sunlight. A person may have light skin that darkens in sunlight. Human hair color and skin color are traits that are coded for by genes, but the environment can change the appearance of these traits. The environment can affect the ways traits are expressed in every kind of organism.

Sometimes the effect of the environment allows adaptations that aid in the survival of a species. For example, the arctic fox's fur color depends on the environment. In the winter months, the arctic fox does not produce fur coloring, and the fox's fur appears white. The fox blends in with its snow-covered surroundings. This helps the fox avoid predators. In the warmer months, the fox produces brown pigment, and the fox blends in with the land.

FOLDABLES™

E **Compare** Make a two-tab book Foldable using notebook paper, as shown below. Use the Foldable to compare the characteristics of dominant and recessive alleles.

| Dominant alleles | Recessive alleles |

✔ **Reading Check**

3. **Analyze** If a person shows a recessive trait, what do you know about the alleles that were inherited?

_____

_____

_____

💡 **Think it Over**

4. **Conclude** How does the fox benefit from the brown pigment during the warm months?

_____

_____

_____

Passing Traits to Offspring

The flower color trait in pea plants can be used as an example of how traits are passed from parents to offspring during fertilization. Suppose a hybrid purple-flowered plant (one purple-flower allele and one white-flower allele) is mated with a white-flowered pea plant (two white-flower alleles). What color flowers will the offspring have? ✔

Two alleles, one from each parent, will be passed to the offspring. The white-flowered plant will contribute a white allele. The purple-flowered plant will contribute either a purple allele or a white allele, as shown in the figure below. In this case, the offspring will have a 50 percent chance of having white flowers and a 50 percent chance of having purple flowers. Chance is involved in heredity.

✔ **Reading Check**

5. **Explain** why the purple-flowered plant is a hybrid.

_____

_____

_____

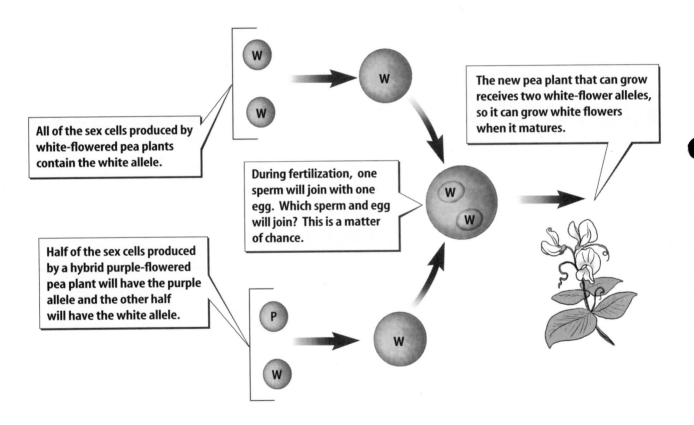

All of the sex cells produced by white-flowered pea plants contain the white allele.

During fertilization, one sperm will join with one egg. Which sperm and egg will join? This is a matter of chance.

Half of the sex cells produced by a hybrid purple-flowered pea plant will have the purple allele and the other half will have the white allele.

The new pea plant that can grow receives two white-flower alleles, so it can grow white flowers when it matures.

Picture This

6. **Infer** What flower color would the offspring have if it received a white-flower and a purple-flower allele?

_____

Differences in Organisms

Variations (vayr ee AY shuns) are the different ways that a certain trait appears, and they result from permanent changes in an organism's genes. Some gene changes produce small variations, and others produce large variations.

What happens when traits have multiple alleles and multiple genes?

Flower color in pea plants shows a simple pattern of inheritance. Flower color is determined by one allele from each parent. Sometimes the pattern of inheritance of a trait is not so simple. Many traits in organisms are controlled by more than two alleles. For example, in humans, multiple alleles A, B, and O control blood types A, B, AB, or O.

Traits also can be controlled by more than one gene pair. For humans, hair color, eye color, and skin color are traits that are controlled by several gene pairs. This type of inheritance is the reason for the differences, or variations, in a species. ☑

What are mutations?

The word *mutate* means "to change." In genetics, a **mutation** (myew TAY shun) is a change in a gene or chromosome. A four-leaf clover is the result of a mutation. Mutations can happen because of an error during meiosis or mitosis. Mutations can also occur because of something in the environment. Many mutations happen by chance.

What are the effects of mutations?

Mutations can be helpful, harmful, or have no affect on an organism. A mutation that affects the way cells grow, repair, and maintain themselves is usually harmful. A mutation, such as a four-leaf clover, has no effect. All mutations add variations to the genes of a species.

What is selective breeding?

Sometimes a mutation produces a different kind of trait that many people like. To continue this trait, selective breeding is practiced.

Nearly all breeding of animals is based on their observable traits. Breeding is controlled, instead of random, to produce desired traits. For example, dairy cattle are bred selectively for the amount of milk that they can produce. Racehorses are bred according to how fast they run. Selective breeding helps produce more offspring with the desired traits. ☑

☑ **Reading Check**

7. Explain what causes variations in a species.

_____

_____

_____

☑ **Reading Check**

8. Apply Why is breeding controlled in some animals?

_____

_____

_____

● After You Read

Mini Glossary

gene (JEEN): a small section of DNA on a chromosome that has information about a trait

genetics (juh NE tihks): the study of how traits are passed from parents to offspring

heredity (huh REH duh tee): the passing of traits from parents to offspring

mutation (myew TAY shun): a change in a gene or chromosome

variation (vayr ee AY shun): the different ways a certain trait appears that result from permanent changes in an organism's genes

1. Review the terms and their definitions in the Mini Glossary. Write a sentence that explains how heredity affects the way you look.

_____

_____

_____

2. Choose one of the question headings in the Read to Learn section. Write the question in the space below. Then write your answer to that question on the lines that follow.

Write your question here.

_____

_____

_____

3. Explain how your two-column notes help you as you learn about genetics.

_____

_____

_____

End of Section

 **Science Online** Visit **red.msscience.com** to access your textbook, interactive games, and projects to help you learn more about genetics— the study of inheritance.

322 The Role of Genes in Inheritance

Ecology

section ❶ What is an ecosystem?

● Before You Read

Think about where you live. Make a list of two living things and one nonliving thing in your neighborhood.

_____

_____

_____

● Read to Learn

Ecosystems

An **ecosystem** (EE koh sihs tum) is made up of organisms interacting with one another and with nonliving factors to form a working unit. In a stream ecosystem, a frog eating an insect is an example of organisms interacting with each other. A frog diving into a stream is an example of an organism interacting with a nonliving factor.

What is ecology?

Ecology (ih KAH luh jee) is the study of the interactions that take place among the living and nonliving parts of an ecosystem. Ecologists are scientists who study ecosystems. They spend much of their time outdoors watching, experimenting, recording, and analyzing what happens there.

What is the largest ecosystem?

Ecosystems come in all sizes. Some are small, like a pile of leaves. Others are big, like a forest or the ocean. The **biosphere** (BI uh sfihr) is the part of Earth where organisms can live. It is the largest ecosystem on Earth. The biosphere is made up of all the ecosystems on Earth combined. Ecosystems include deserts, mountains, rivers, prairies, wetlands, forests, oceans, and many more.

What You'll Learn
■ the living and nonliving factors in an ecosystem
■ how the parts of an ecosystem interact

Mark the Text

Identify Answers Review each of the question heads. As you read, highlight the text that answers the question.

FOLDABLES

Ⓐ Describe Make a two-tab Foldable using notebook paper. Use it to take notes about ecosystems and biospheres.

Copyright © Glencoe/McGraw-Hill, a division of The McGraw-Hill Companies, Inc.

Living Parts of Ecosystems

The organisms that make up the living part of an ecosystem are called **biotic** (bi AH tihk) **factors.** An organism depends on other biotic factors for food, shelter, protection, and reproduction. For example, a snake might use a rotting log for shelter. A termite might depend on the same log for food.

Nonliving Parts of Ecosystems

Abiotic (ay bi AH tihk) factors affect the type and number of organisms living in an ecosystem. **Abiotic factors** are the nonliving things found in an ecosystem. Air and soil are examples of abiotic factors. The figure below shows how biotic and abiotic factors interact in a desert ecosystem.

<u>Picture This</u>

1. **Identify** Circle two biotic factors. Highlight one abiotic factor in this desert ecosystem.

The giant Saguaro cactus stores water in its tissues. It provides food, water, and shelter for many organisms.

A hawk soars overhead hunting prey.

Creosote bushes and rocks provide some shelter from the hot sun.

A scorpion hides in underground burrows during the day, and comes out at night when the temperature is cooler.

How do soil and temperature affect an ecosystem?

Soil is an abiotic factor that affects which plants and other organisms are found in an ecosystem. Soil is made up of minerals, water, air, and organic matter. Organic matter is the decaying parts of plants and animals. Different amounts of minerals, water, air, and organic matter make different types of soil. The kind of soil a place has determines the kinds of organisms that live there. ☑

Temperature also determines which organisms live in a particular place. An organism that lives in a cool mountainous ecosystem may not survive in a hot tropical rain forest.

Why is water important to an ecosystem?

Water helps all living things carry out important life processes, such as digestion and waste removal. The bodies of most organisms are made up mostly of water. About two-thirds of the weight of the human body is water. Water also is important to an ecosystem. The amount of water in an ecosystem can determine how many organisms can live in a particular area.

Why is sunlight important in an ecosystem?

The Sun is the main source of energy for most organisms on Earth. Green plants use energy from the Sun to produce food. Humans and other animals obtain their energy by eating these plants and other organisms that have fed on the plants.

A Balanced System

An ecosystem is made up of many different biotic and abiotic factors working together. When these factors are in balance, the ecosystem is in balance too.

Many events can affect the balance of an ecosystem. One example is a drought, or a long period of time without rain. A stream in a drought area might dry up. Some organisms, like fish, could not survive in this area. Other organisms, such as frogs and insects, might have to find new homes. Organisms that live in dry areas might come to live in the dried-up stream.

☑ **Reading Check**

2. Recall What four things make up soil?

_____

_____

_____

_____

💡 **Think it Over**

3. Determine What is another example of an event that can affect the balance of an ecosystem?

_____

_____

_____

● After You Read

Mini Glossary

abiotic (ay bi AH tihk) factor: a nonliving thing found in an ecosystem

biosphere (BI uh sfihr): the part of Earth where organisms can live

biotic (bi AH tihk) factor: an organism that makes up the living part of an ecosystem

ecology (ih KAH luh jee): the study of the interactions that take place among the living organisms and nonliving parts of an ecosystem

ecosystem (EE koh sihs tum): a place where organisms interact with one another and with nonliving factors to form a working unit

1. Review the terms and their definitions in the Mini Glossary. Write one or two sentences that explain the similarities and differences between an ecosystem and the biosphere.

_____

_____

_____

2. Complete the graphic organizer below to show the four abiotic factors that are necessary to ecosystems.

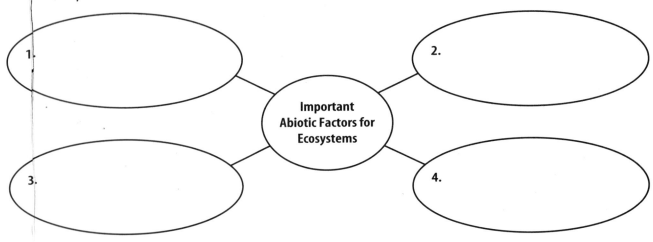

1.

2.

Important Abiotic Factors for Ecosystems

3.

4.

End of Section

Science Online Visit **red.msscience.com** to access your textbook, interactive games, and projects to help you learn more about what an ecosystem is.

 **Ecology**

section ❷ Relationships Among Living Things

● Before You Read

On the lines below, name four groups of organisms that live around your school. If you were an ecologist, how could you classify these things?

_____

_____

● Read to Learn

Organizing Ecosystems

Ecologists study the biosphere by organizing living things into small groups. Then they study how members of a group interact with each other and their environments.

How do ecologists group organisms?

A **population** is a group of the same type of organisms living in the same place at the same time. All of the populations that live in an area make up a **community** (kuh MYEW nuh tee). The members of a community depend on each other for food, shelter, and other needs. For example, a shark depends on fish populations for food. Fish populations depend on coral animals to build coral reefs that they use to hide from sharks.

Ecologists study the characteristics of populations. They study the size of the population, where its members live, and how the population is able to stay alive.

What is population density?

Population density (DEN suh tee) is the size of the population compared to its area. For example, if 100 daisies are growing in a field that is one square kilometer in size, then the population density is 100 daisies per square kilometer.

What You'll Learn
- how ecologists organize living systems
- the relationships among living things

◄ Mark the Text

Identify the Main Point
Underline the main idea of each paragraph. Review the ideas after you have read the section.

FOLDABLES™

Ⓑ Describe Make a two-tab book, as shown below. Use the Foldable to take notes about populations and communities.

Population

Community

How do ecologists study migrating populations?

Monarch butterflies travel to warm climates for the winter. They return to the same place year after year. This seasonal travel is called migration.

To study migrating monarch butterflies, an ecologist catches a butterfly and attaches a tag to one of its wings. The tag tells where the butterfly was caught. Later, someone else who catches the same butterfly can use the tag to figure out how far the butterfly has flown. The information from many butterflies is combined to build a picture of the monarch's migration pattern, like the one shown below. Tagging is used to study populations of wolves, birds, and other animals that travel long distances.

Copyright © Glencoe/McGraw-Hill, a division of The McGraw-Hill Companies, Inc.

Picture This

1. **Identify** Label the countries on the map that the monarch butterflies start in and migrate to.

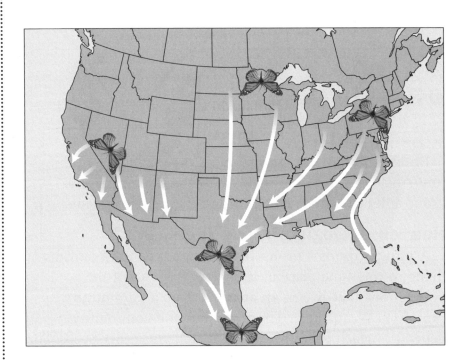

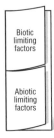

FOLDABLES™

C Create Make a two-tab book using notebook paper, as shown below. Use the Foldable to take notes about biotic and abiotic limiting factors.

Biotic limiting factors

Abiotic limiting factors

Limits to Populations

Populations cannot grow larger forever. Resources such as food, water, and living space would eventually run out. The things that limit the size of a population, such as food or amount of rainfall, are called **limiting factors**. In a stream ecosystem, an abiotic limiting factor might be a lack of rain. If the stream dries up because of lack of rain, the population of mosquitoes might not have places to breed. The mosquitoes are a biotic limiting factor. If the population of mosquitoes goes down because of lack of rain, then frogs might not have enough food. This would limit the size of the frog population.

Interactions in Communities

There are many other animals besides frogs in a stream ecosystem that eat mosquitoes. Spiders and birds also eat mosquitoes. This means that frogs, birds, and spiders all compete for the same food. The greater the size of the population in an area, the greater the competition for resources such as food. Organisms compete for any resource that is in limited supply.

One of the most common ways organisms interact in a community is by being food for another organism, as shown in the figure below.

Picture This

2. **Apply** Draw another animal that birds eat and connect the drawing to the bird with an arrow.

What is a predator?

A falcon is a predator (PRE duh tur), which means it captures and eats other animals, such as field mice. The animals the falcon catches and eats are its prey. The act of one organism feeding on another is called predation (pre DAY shun).

Why do some organisms live together?

In one type of relationship, both organisms benefit. For example, an African tickbird gets its food by eating insects off the skin of zebras. The tickbird gets food, and the zebra gets rid of harmful insects. In another type of relationship, only one organism benefits. For example, a bird builds a nest in a tree. The bird gets shelter from the tree, but the tree is not harmed. In yet another type of relationship, one organism is helped and another is harmed. For example, the insects on the zebra's skin benefit from the zebra, but the insects can harm the zebra. ☑

Reading Check

3. **Describe** two relationships among organisms.

_____

_____

_____

Where and How Organisms Live

How can a small ecosystem such as a classroom aquarium support a variety of different organisms? It's possible because each type of organism has a different role to play in the ecosystem. The role of an organism in an ecosystem is called the organism's **niche** (NICH). For example, an aquarium may contain fish, snails, algae, and bacteria. Each of these organisms has a role in the aquarium. The snails eat algae to help keep the glass clear for light to get in. The algae provide food for the snails and fish, and provide oxygen for the system through photosynthesis. The niche of the fish is to provide nutrients to the ecosystem through its waste products.

What is a habitat?

The place where an organism lives is called its **habitat** (HA buh tat). The habitat of a catfish is the muddy bottom of a lake or pond. The habitat of a penguin is the icy waters of the Antarctic.

Different species of organisms live in the same habitat, as shown in the figure below. Resources, such as food and space, are shared among all the species living in a habitat. For example, the branches of an apple tree provide a habitat for spiders, fruit flies, beetles, caterpillars, and birds. These different organisms can live in the same habitat because each organism has different ways of feeding, finding shelter, and using other resources. Spiders feed on beetles and other insects. Caterpillars eat leaves. Fruit flies feed on apples. Birds eat spiders, caterpillars, or flies. Each species has a different niche within the same habitat.

Picture This

5. Explain Why can different species live in the same habitat?

_____

_____

_____

● After You Read

Mini Glossary

community (kuh MYEW nuh tee): all the populations that live in an area

habitat (HA buh tat): the place where an organism lives

limiting factor: something that controls the size of a population

niche (NICH): the role of an organism in an ecosystem

population: a group of the same type of organisms living in the same place at the same time

1. Review the terms and their definitions in the Mini Glossary. Write two sentences that explain the relationship between a population and a community.

_____

_____

_____

2. Choose one of the question headings in the Read to Learn section. Write the question in the space below. Then write your answer to that question on the lines that follow.

Write your question here.

_____

_____

_____

3. How did underlining the main ideas help you understand what you have read?

_____

_____

_____

Science Online Visit **red.msscience.com** to access your textbook, interactive games, and projects to help you learn more about the relationships among living things.

End of Section

Ecology

chapter 21

section ❷ Energy Through the Ecosystem

What You'll Learn
- how organisms get the energy they need
- how energy flows through an ecosystem

Study Coach

Sticky-Note Discussions
As you read the section, use sticky-note paper to mark paragraphs you find interesting or that you have a question about. Share the interesting information with another student. Ask your teacher to answer your questions.

FOLDABLES

D Describe Make a three-tab book, as shown below. Use it to take notes about producers, consumers, and decomposers.

Producers

Consumers

Decomposers

● Before You Read

On the lines below, list three foods you eat. Then classify the foods as plant, animal, or a mixture of both.

_____

_____

_____

● Read to Learn

It's All About Food

Most interactions in this chapter involve food. Energy moves through an ecosystem in the form of food.

What is the role of producers and consumers?

Many different populations interact in an ecosystem. The plants in the ecosystem produce food through photosynthesis. An organism that makes its own food, like a plant, is a **producer**. An organism that eats other organisms is called a **consumer**. A grasshopper eats plants, so, like you, it is a consumer.

What is the role of decomposers?

Some organisms, such as bacteria and fungi, are small but play an important role in an ecosystem. They are called **decomposers** because they use dead organisms and the waste material of other organisms for food.

Modeling the Flow of Energy

A food chain is a model that shows how energy from food passes from one organism to another. Arrows show the flow of energy from one organism to another.

What do food webs show?

Food chains often overlap. For example, a bird may eat seeds, and then a cat eats the bird. A cat may also eat a rabbit or a mouse. One food chain cannot model all of these overlapping relationships. Instead scientists use a model called a food web. A food web is a series of overlapping food chains that shows all the possible feeding relationships in an ecosystem. An ocean food web is shown below.

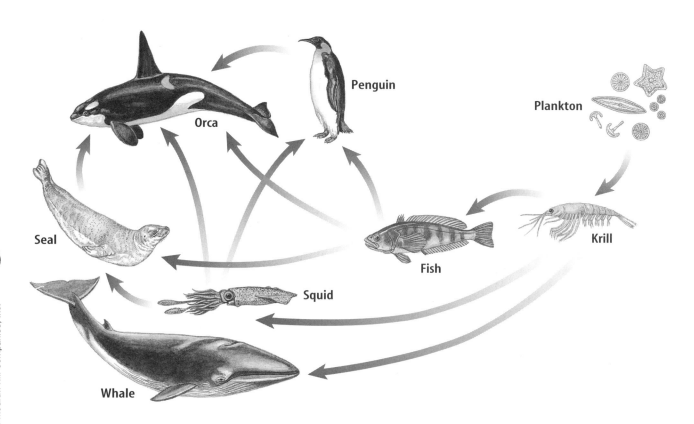

Cycling of Materials

Cycles are important to ecosystems. Materials that make up organisms get recycled in an ecosystem. The bodies of living things are made up of matter, including water, nitrogen, and carbon. To get the matter needed to build bones, muscles, and skin, you need to eat food made of the right kinds of matter. In an ecosystem, matter cycles through food chains. The amount of matter on Earth never changes. So matter used in ecosystems is recycled, or used again and again. Living organisms depend on these cycles for survival.

Picture This
1. **Identify** Highlight the organisms that are eaten by an orca.

● After You Read

Mini Glossary

consumer: an organism that eats other organisms

decomposer: organisms that use dead organisms and the waste material of other organisms for food

producer: an organism that makes its own food

---

1. Review the terms and their definitions in the Mini Glossary. Write a sentence or two that explains the difference between a producer and a consumer.

_____

_____

_____

_____

2. Complete the flow chart below to show one of the food chains from plankton to an orca. Use the simplest path in the figure on the previous page.

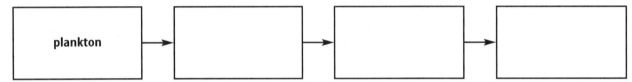

plankton	→		→		→	

3. In the space below, use words to show two food chains from the figure on the previous page that include the seal.

End of Section

Science Online Visit **red.msscience.com** to access your textbook, interactive games, and projects to help you learn more about how energy flows through the ecosystem.

chapter 22 Earth's Resources

section ❶ Natural Resource Use

◉ Before You Read

Choose two objects in your home. What materials were used to make the objects?

_____

_____

_____

What You'll Learn

- how resources are used
- how resources are classified

◉ Read to Learn

Mark the Text

Identify Main Ideas
Highlight the main idea of each paragraph. Underline details that support the main idea.

News Flash: Trouble in the Rain Forest

Recent information shows that rain forests are being destroyed at the rate of about a football field a day. Once a rain forest is cut down, it might never grow back. When rain forests are removed, wildlife is lost. Rain forests contain more than half of Earth's known plant species and one-fifth of the known bird species. Some important medicines, such as drugs to fight cancer, originally came from rain forest plants. Destroying rain forests could mean that important medicines might not be discovered. ☑

Many people who live in rain forest areas clear the forests to grow crops or to graze cattle. They sell the wood to companies that use it to make paper and other products.

How do the things you use affect the environment?

When you are shopping, notice that many products and their packaging are made of cardboard. Cardboard is a wood product. The wood may have come from a rain forest or another type of forest. A CD player is made of plastic and often comes in a package made of cardboard. Some of its parts are made of metal. Metal and plastic are not made from wood. However, they did come from natural resources.

✔ Reading Check

1. **Explain** one problem that results from rain forests being destroyed.

_____

_____

_____

Think it Over

2. Describe five resources used to create the building you are sitting in.

_____

_____

_____

Natural Resources

Natural resources are things found in nature that living organisms use. Organisms use natural resources to meet their needs. The trees and minerals that were used to make the lumber, plastic, and metal in your house are natural resources. They fill your need for housing. Natural resources are also used to make other items in our lives, such as CD players.

What goes into making a CD player?

The cardboard box that a CD player comes in was made from trees, which are a natural resource. The plastic used to make the CD player is made from crude oil. Crude oil is a thick, dark liquid found underground. Substances taken from crude oil can go to factories where they are made into things such as plastic, gasoline, and inks.

What natural resources are used to make energy?

Cutting down trees, drilling for oil, and getting natural resources to factories all require energy. The energy needed to make the natural resources into the products you use also comes from natural resources. Trucks that take natural resources to factories use diesel fuel, which is made from crude oil. The electricity that powers the machines in the factories often comes from burning coal. Coal, like crude oil, is a natural resource that forms underground.

What organisms use natural resources?

It takes many natural resources to make a CD player. Think of all the natural resources it takes to build a house. These resources include wood, metal, glass, plastic, and many more. All the people of the world need a place to live. Do you think there are enough natural resources to meet everybody's need for a place to live? Maybe. However, people also need natural resources to meet other needs, such as food and clothing. All living things on Earth use natural resources. Will we ever run out of natural resources? That may depend on the particular resource.

Availability of Resources

Things such as sunlight, water, trees, and apples are all natural resources. These kinds of resources have another thing in common. They are all renewable (ree NEW uh bul) and will likely be around for a long time.

What are renewable resources?

Resources that can be replaced by natural processes in 100 years or less are called **renewable resources**. Energy from the Sun is a renewable resource because the Sun gives off light energy every day. It will continue to do so for millions of years. Plants use the Sun's energy to make food. You and other animals eat plants for food.

Trees are renewable resources because new trees will grow back and be cut down in less than 100 years. Trees provide wood for houses and furniture. People burn wood for fuel.

Water is a renewable resource. Heat from the Sun evaporates water from lakes and oceans. The heat turns it into water vapor, which is a gas that rises into the atmosphere. Later, the water vapor changes back into liquid and falls to Earth as rain or snow. So, the same water is used over and over again. Wind also is a renewable resource. It can be used to run windmills that are used to make electricity. ☑

What are nonrenewable resources?

The figure below shows how the world's energy needs are currently being met. Resources such as coal, natural gas, and crude oil take millions of years to form inside Earth. They are nonrenewable resources. **Nonrenewable resources** are resources that cannot be replaced by natural processes within 100 years. After all the oil and coal are used up, no more will be available for millions of years. This could result in having to reduce energy use.

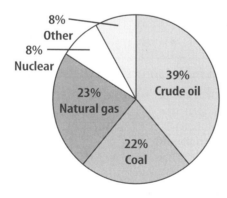

What is conservation?

Conservation is the practice of protecting and preserving natural resources so they will always be available. Renewable and nonrenewable resources need to be conserved. The quality of air, water, and land also needs to be protected.

✔ **Reading Check**

3. **Identify** two renewable resources.

_____

_____

Picture This

4. **Calculate** the percentage of the world's energy needs that are met today by crude oil, natural gas, and coal.

_____

_____

● After You Read

Mini Glossary

natural resource: things found in nature that living organisms use

nonrenewable resource: resource that cannot be replaced by natural processes within 100 years

renewable resource: resource that can be replaced by natural processes in 100 years or less

1. Review the terms and their definitions in the Mini Glossary. Write a sentence that explains the difference between renewable and nonrenewable resources.

_____

_____

_____

2. In the diagram, write examples of each type of resource.

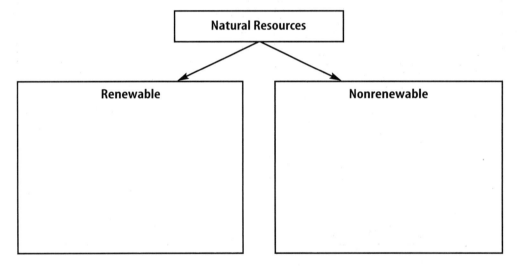

3. How did highlighting the main ideas help you remember what you read about natural resources?

_____

_____

_____

End of Section

Science Online Visit **red.msscience.com** to access your textbook, interactive games, and projects to help you learn more about natural resource use.

Earth's Resources

section ❷ People and the Environment

● Before You Read

What environmental problems does your community face?

_____

_____

_____

Copyright © Glencoe/McGraw-Hill, a division of The McGraw-Hill Companies, Inc.

● Read to Learn

Exploring Environmental Problems

When people do things such as build highways, they destroy the trees and plants that grow on the land. The animals that lived on the land depended on the trees and plants for food and shelter. Many of the animals have to find new places to live. But what if there is no other place to live? Without a place to live and resources for food, individual plants and animals may die. Eventually, the entire species might be faced with extinction. Human activities can affect the quality of land, water, and air.

Our Impact on Land

The amount of space you need to live includes more than just the land for your home. Think about where your food comes from, where your trash goes, the space taken up by your school, and other spaces you use. The food you eat requires land on which to grow the crops and raise the animals. A simple peanut butter-and-jelly sandwich requires land for the following items.

1. To grow wheat for the bread.
2. To grow peanuts for the peanut butter.
3. To grow the fruit and sugar cane for the jelly.

Study Coach

Summarize As you read, make an outline to summarize the information in the section. Use the main headings in the section as the main headings in the outline. Complete the outline with the information under each heading in the section.

FOLDABLES

Ⓑ Describe Make a layered-look book, as shown below. On each flap, describe the impact people have on the environment.

People and the Environment
Our impact on land
Our impact on water
Our impact on air

What You'll Learn
- how people affect the environment
- the different types of pollution

Why is it important to preserve habitats?

All of the things you use every day take some amount of land, or space, to make. Building a house, a mall, or a road requires land. The amount of land available for people to use is limited.

People need food, clothing, and places to live. These things take land. But preserving natural habitats also is important. Once a habitat is used to build a mall or a road, many of the organisms living there are lost.

How do laws protect the land?

Today there are laws to help protect against habitat loss and to use land wisely. Before major building can take place in an area, the land has to be studied to find out how the building will affect the habitats, organisms, the soil, and water in the area. If the area is home to endangered organisms, building may not be allowed to take place. ☑

What are landfills?

Each day, every person in the United States makes about 2.1 kg of garbage. More than half of the garbage ends up in landfills. A **landfill** is an area where garbage is deposited. Any material that can harm living things by interfering with life processes is called a **pollutant** (puh LEW tunt). Landfills are lined with plastic or clay to keep chemical pollutants from escaping. But some chemicals still seep into the environment. If these chemicals get into the food people eat or the water they drink, they can cause health problems.

Sometimes dangerous items such as batteries and paints end up in landfills. These items have harmful chemicals that could leak into the soil. Eventually they find their way into rivers and oceans. Garbage that contains dangerous chemicals or other pollutants is called hazardous waste. These kinds of wastes can be taken to special places where they are collected and gotten rid of safely.

Our Impact on Water

People need clean water for drinking and other uses. The average person in the United States uses about 397 L of water each day. Although water is a renewable resource, in some places it is being used up faster than natural processes can replace it. Only a small part of Earth's water is freshwater that people can drink. Many places on Earth are running out of usable freshwater.

Copyright © Glencoe/McGraw-Hill, a division of The McGraw-Hill Companies, Inc.

What causes water pollution?

Many everyday activities can cause water pollution. When you scrub a floor, you use a household cleaner. You pour the dirty water that contains the cleaner down the drain. The polluted water usually goes to a water-treatment plant. There it is cleaned before being used again.

If you dumped the polluted water onto your grass, it would soak into the ground where it could damage the soil. Or it might wash into a river or lake. If too many people do this, it could pollute our drinking water. Water can become polluted when rain washes pesticides and fertilizers from farmland into lakes or oceans. Rain falling on roads and parking lots washes oil and grease onto the soil and into nearby waterways. Factories and industrial plants sometimes release polluted water into rivers. Dumping garbage into rivers or lakes can also cause water pollution.

How can laws help reduce water pollution?

Countries are working together to reduce water pollution. The U.S. government has passed laws to keep water supplies clean. The Safe Drinking Water Act is a set of standards that makes sure that the drinking water in the United States is safe. Much of our drinking water comes from rivers, lakes, and underground sources, as shown in the figure. This water must be treated to remove harmful particles before it is used by people. The Clean Water Act gives money to the states to build water-treatment plants. The best way that people can protect Earth's water is by using it wisely and by controlling their water use.

Think it Over

3. Analyze What is one thing you can do to prevent water pollution?

_____

_____

_____

Picture This

4. Identify Write two things that can pollute drinking water.

_____

_____

Our Impact on Air

On some days, the air in a city looks hazy. This is caused by pollutants such as dust and gases in the air. Some natural processes can cause air pollution, such as volcanoes emitting smoke and ash into the air. Most air pollution, however, is caused by humans.

What causes air pollution?

The two biggest sources of air pollution are cars and factories. When the gasoline used to run cars burns, pollutants are released into the air. They cause more than 30 percent of all air pollution. ☑

Many factories and power plants burn coal or oil for the energy they need. The burning of fuel releases pollutants into the air. These pollutants can cause health problems. For people with lung or heart problems, air pollution can be deadly.

What is acid rain?

Organisms other than people are also harmed by air pollution. Acid rain causes a lot of damage to other organisms. **Acid rain** happens when the gases released by burning oil and coal mix with water in the air to form acidic rain or snow. When acid rain falls to the ground, it can harm trees and other plants. When acid rain falls into rivers and lakes, it can kill fish and other organisms that live in the water.

Spare the Air

The best way to solve pollution is to prevent it. Reducing the number of pollutants in the environment is easier to do than cleaning up pollution. Cars today release fewer harmful gases than they did in the past. Governments around the world are looking for ways to reduce the amount of air pollutants that factories release.

You can help protect the atmosphere by reducing the amount of energy you use at home. Conserve electricity by turning off lamps, radios, and fans when you are not using them. Keep doors and windows closed to save heat energy in the winter. To keep the environment healthy, everybody needs to think about how their actions affect the land, water, and air.

✔ **Reading Check**

5. **List** the two leading causes of air pollution.

_____

_____

💡 **Think it Over**

6. **Apply** What are some ways that you can reduce the amount of energy you use?

_____

_____

_____

● After You Read

Mini Glossary

acid rain: occurs when the gases released by burning oil and coal mix with water in the air to form acidic rain or snow

landfill: an area where garbage is deposited

pollutant: any material that can harm living things by interfering with life processes

1. Review the terms and their definitions in the Mini Glossary. Use the terms to write one sentence that describes a cause and an effect of pollution.

_____

_____

_____

2. In the ovals below, write ways that humans can make wise choices in their use of land, water, and air.

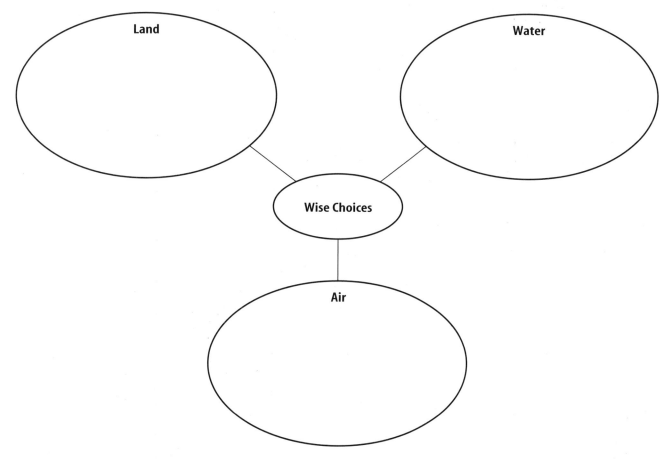

Science **Online** Visit **red.msscience.com** to access your textbook, interactive games, and projects to help you learn more about people and the environment.

End of Section

Earth's Resources

section ❸ Protecting the Environment

What You'll Learn
- the problems of solid waste
- how to reduce, reuse, and recycle resources

Study Coach

Make Flash Cards Think of a quiz question for each paragraph. Write the question on one side of the flash card and the answer on the other side. Keep quizzing yourself until you know all of the answers.

⬤ Before You Read

How can schools help reduce solid waste, such as paper, cardboard, and drink containers?

_____

_____

⬤ Read to Learn

Cutting Down on Waste

About five billion tons of solid waste is thrown away each year in the United States. **Solid waste** is whatever people throw away that is in a solid or near-solid form. The chart below shows some sources of solid waste. Most of the waste from homes, schools, and businesses is paper and cardboard products. For example, school lunch programs depend upon paper plates, straw wrappers, milk cartons, and napkins. People can reduce the amount of trash they throw away each day by reducing, reusing, and recycling.

Picture This
1. **Interpret Data** What is the largest source of solid waste?

_____

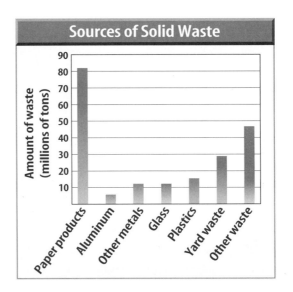

Sources of Solid Waste

Copyright © Glencoe/McGraw-Hill, a division of The McGraw-Hill Companies, Inc.

How can wastes be reduced?

A good way to help solve the problem of solid wastes is to reduce the total amount of solid waste that you throw away. You can buy things with little or no packaging. For example, if you buy a toy that has no packaging, you reduce your use of paper made from wood or plastic made from oil.

How can wastes be reused?

Suppose you put the toy in a cloth gift bag instead of wrapping it in paper. The cloth bag can be reused many times. As a result, a lot of wrapping paper will not end up in a landfill. Reuse means using an item again rather than throwing it away and replacing it. When you no longer need an item, you can give it to someone else who may want or need it. By not throwing it away, you can avoid sending the item to a landfill.

How can wastes be recycled?

When you have lunch in a cafeteria, you often have paper cups and plates, cans, or bottles to throw out. Many communities provide special bins that let you separate your garbage so that certain items can be recycled. **Recycling** (ree SI kling) means reusing materials after they have been changed into another form. For example, used paper can be processed to make recycled paper. Glass can be melted and made into new containers.

How are recycled products used?

Recycled items are used to make many different products. For example, plastic soft-drink bottles are sometimes used to make carpeting. Recycling means more than only separating your garbage. It also means buying recycled goods when you can. Recycling can save a lot of energy compared to making new materials. Reducing and reusing use even less energy, because they do not need the reprocessing of materials. ☑

Habits for a Healthier Environment

By practicing the three Rs—reducing, reusing, and recycling—you can help make a healthier environment. The best way to protect the environment is to develop habits that conserve and protect the resources we have.

FOLDABLES

C Identify Make a trifold book, as shown below. Use the Foldable to identify ways that humans can reduce, reuse, and recycle.

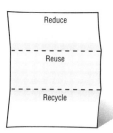

Reduce

Reuse

Recycle

✓ Reading Check

2. **Explain** Why does reusing an item use less energy than recycling it?

_____

_____

_____

● After You Read

Mini Glossary

recycling: reusing materials after they have been changed into another form

solid waste: whatever people throw away that is in a solid or near-solid form

1. Review the terms and their definitions in the Mini Glossary. Write a sentence that describes one way of limiting solid waste.

_____

_____

_____

2. In the space below, draw a poster or cartoon that encourages people to reduce, reuse, or recycle resources.

End of Section

Science nline Visit **red.msscience.com** to access your textbook, interactive games, and projects to help you learn more about protecting the environment.

PERIODIC TABLE OF THE ELEMENTS

Columns of elements are called groups. Elements in the same group have similar chemical properties.

Gas
Liquid
Solid
Synthetic

Element — Hydrogen
Atomic number — 1
Symbol — **H**
Atomic mass — 1.008

State of matter

The first three symbols tell you the state of matter of the element at room temperature. The fourth symbol identifies elements that are not present in significant amounts on Earth. Useful amounts are made synthetically.

1

Hydrogen
1
H
1.008

2

Lithium
3
Li
6.941

Beryllium
4
Be
9.012

Sodium
11
Na
22.990

Magnesium
12
Mg
24.305

3

Scandium
21
Sc
44.956

4

Titanium
22
Ti
47.867

5

Vanadium
23
V
50.942

6

Chromium
24
Cr
51.996

7

Manganese
25
Mn
54.938

8

Iron
26
Fe
55.845

9

Cobalt
27
Co
58.933

Potassium
19
K
39.098

Calcium
20
Ca
40.078

Rubidium
37
Rb
85.468

Strontium
38
Sr
87.62

Yttrium
39
Y
88.906

Zirconium
40
Zr
91.224

Niobium
41
Nb
92.906

Molybdenum
42
Mo
95.94

Technetium
43
Tc
(98)

Ruthenium
44
Ru
101.07

Rhodium
45
Rh
102.906

Cesium
55
Cs
132.905

Barium
56
Ba
137.327

Lanthanum
57
La
138.906

Hafnium
72
Hf
178.49

Tantalum
73
Ta
180.948

Tungsten
74
W
183.84

Rhenium
75
Re
186.207

Osmium
76
Os
190.23

Iridium
77
Ir
192.217

Francium
87
Fr
(223)

Radium
88
Ra
(226)

Actinium
89
Ac
(227)

Rutherfordium
104
Rf
(261)

Dubnium
105
Db
(262)

Seaborgium
106
Sg
(266)

Bohrium
107
Bh
(264)

Hassium
108
Hs
(277)

Meitnerium
109
Mt
(268)

The number in parentheses is the mass number of the longest-lived isotope for that element.

Rows of elements are called periods. Atomic number increases across a period.

The arrow shows where these elements would fit into the periodic table. They are moved to the bottom of the table to save space.

Lanthanide series

Cerium
58
Ce
140.116

Praseodymium
59
Pr
140.908

Neodymium
60
Nd
144.24

Promethium
61
Pm
(145)

Samarium
62
Sm
150.36

Actinide series

Thorium
90
Th
232.038

Protactinium
91
Pa
231.036

Uranium
92
U
238.029

Neptunium
93
Np
(237)

Plutonium
94
Pu
(244)